GRAHAM KERR'S

MINIMAX COOKBOOK

Illustrated Step-by-Step Techniques
Plus 150 All-New Minimax Recipes to Guarantee
Minimum Risk and Maximum Flavor
in Everything You Cook

DOUBLEDAY
New York   London   Toronto   Sydney   Auckland

For Kareena and Ronald
Have fun—it's still the best ingredient of all!

PUBLISHED BY DOUBLEDAY
a division of Bantam Doubleday Dell Publishing Group, Inc.
666 Fifth Avenue, New York, New York 10103

DOUBLEDAY and the portrayal of an anchor with a dolphin
are registered trademarks of Doubleday,
a division of Bantam Doubleday Dell Publishing Group, Inc.

NUTRIENT CALCULATION: Nutrient calculation was performed using the Minnesota Nutrition Data System (NDS) software developed by the Nutrition Coordinating Center, University of Minnesota, Minneapolis, Minnesota, Food Database version 4A, Nutrition Database version 19.

PHOTOGRAPHY: Recipes by Allyson Gofton and Alan Gillard, Auckland, New Zealand. Minimax Techniques by Susan Anderson, Seattle, Washington.

ILLUSTRATION: Sandy Silverthorne, Eugene, Oregon.

Library of Congress Cataloging-in-Publication Data
Kerr, Graham.
[Minimax cookbook]
Graham Kerr's minimax cookbook : illustrated step-by-step techniques plus 150 all-new minimax recipes to guarantee minimum risk and maximum flavor in everything you cook / Graham Kerr.—1st ed.
p. cm.
Includes index.
1. Cookery. I. Title. II. Title: Minimax cookbook.
TX714.K484   1992
641.5—dc20   92-5810
                                                                        CIP
ISBN 0-385-42488-4

Author's Note

*O*nce again it's time to gratefully thank all those who have helped me to author this book. The recipe creation process starts inevitably with grocery shopping, which was done by Cynthia Morse. Once in the kitchen, Cynthia and my Senior Food Assistant, Robert Prince, were constant in their concern to gather every scrap of information from my initial tests. They also generously offered helpful ideas during the lengthy development process.

Then the recipes moved on to Chris Rylko, my first line editor, under whose supervision the initial draft was produced and the first numbers emerged. After my rewrites, Judy Ewings double-checked the nutritional analysis with nutritionist Alice Dowdy, representing the American Heart Association, and our super friends at the Seattle Public Library checked our research. In the meantime I wrote the Introduction and my personal secretary, Natalie Hall, discreetly rearranged my text with her usual delicate diplomacy and skillful use of English.

It was then old enough (or bold enough?) a document to go forth to John Duff at Doubleday, the project editor, who added a whole new dimension to the creative process. He actually *cares* about both me as author and you as reader. Karen Van Westering then received the unpolished text and began the "find Waldo" search for innocent errors and omissions in her endless search for clarity. What a joy to work with her.

At the same time finished recipes were sent off to New Zealand to my dear friend and past culinary collaborator, food stylist Allyson Gofton, and photographer Alan Gillard. Didn't they do a lovely job of the recipes? The photographs of the techniques were taken at my test kitchen, using my very own hands, by Susan Anderson, who is both a delight to work with and extremely talented. Finally the corrected text went before the copy editor, Carol Catt, who acts as a kind of fine seine net to catch any wriggling commas that might have got away. When all this was done it remained for Sandy Silverthorne to decorate the pages with his whimsy.

My literary agents and joint venturers, John McEwen and John McLean (John I & II), helped oversee the administration and funding, and my beloved wife, Treena, ate dish after dish in her capacity as final judge.

My mother, Mardi, continues to cast her elegant shadow over my entire career with very direct observations about everything from my diction to suspenders.

Lastly, but never least, there's Andy, my son, who keeps Dad on the rails. Often, when there is too much to do, the reason for being here gets submerged. Then Andy makes the tide of minutiae go out.

Now the book is in your hands and its contents I hope will please you in a comforting kind of way. My prayers for good health come with it for both yourself and all those for whom you care.

Table of Contents

Minimax Explained

What is the *least* I need to eat that gives me the *most* vitality *consistent* with *good health, long life* and . . . can it possibly *taste delicious?*

That one simple question sums up the essence of our food needs. It breaks down into:

LEAST   Small amounts of food *can* lead to consumption of fewer calories, less expense and permanent weight loss.

MOST   We all need enough vitality to deal with our daily tasks with enthusiasm.

CONSISTENT   Any change in personal food habits *must* be consistent with good nourishment if it is to be linked to long-term good health.

GOOD HEALTH This is an *overall* issue, not just weight loss; it involves our whole body, from the immune, cardiac and digestive systems, to our emotional relationships both at home and in the workplace.

LONG LIFE   Better food choices often result in better circulation and movement and that means better years and a quality life less dependent on medication.

DELICIOUS   Isn't that an attractive word? It sums up so many joyful memories, not just of food, but people and places. It also emphasizes the absolutely crucial point that good taste is *essential* to food enjoyment.

THE MINIMAX METHOD

"*Minimax*" describes two very different courses of action in preparing food, both of which must take place together.

MINI stands for minimizing known health risks because you *care*.
MAX stands for maximizing eating enjoyment by adding aroma, color and texture because you want to *please*.

Minimizing risks is an objective, scientific process that some might consider unpleasant. It may sound to you like a wrist-slapping, eat-it-up-it's-good-for-you experience. Taken by itself it seems to ban such delights as cheese, cakes, cookies, pastries, hamburgers, fries and ice cream.

Maximizing enjoyment, on the other hand, is a subjective, emotional experience that feels good. We love the idea of warm aromas, bright, fresh colors and crisp, crunchy textures, as well as what I call "mouthroundfullness"—the luscious textural sense of smooth flowing richness that we *usually* associate with fat.

In my food career, I spent nineteen years concentrating only on maximizing enjoyment in my cooking. In those MAX days I wanted to please, and I wouldn't listen to a single MINI suggestion. It wasn't that I didn't care, I was simply having too much fun learning how to turn on my senses.

Since 1972 I've spent the same amount of time learning how to minimize health risks. During my first years of MINI, I made some major mistakes. I read scientific studies copiously and, as a result, developed a kind of food phobia. There seemed to be nothing left to eat that wasn't somehow contaminated. When my family objected to the loss of enjoyment at our table, I stupidly stiffened my resolve and insisted. They rebelled, and I went off into a private corner with my broccoli and brewer's yeast.

Years later my wife, Treena, suffered a stroke and a spasm heart attack in quick succession. We then discovered her blood cholesterol was over 300 and her LDL level was too high. Treena had no choice but to change her eating habits, and she knew it. I wanted to help her so I took my MINI food ideas and began to enhance them with what I had learned about aroma, color and texture during my career in hotels and restaurants and as the Galloping Gourmet.

In doing so, MINI and MAX started to overlap, and I became a *"carepleaser."* I reduced the risks because I cared and I increased enjoyment because I wanted to please. Without really understanding it at the time, I had let *objective* science blend with *subjective* feelings. The big thing was . . . it worked!

Over the years I've developed a list of ten Minimax lifestyle guidelines that I've come to see as a ten-sided frame within which a carepleasing, or Minimax, recipe is created. It is a somewhat unusual frame because most pictures have only four sides.

THE MINIMAX FRAME—A PICTURE OF HEALTH

"She is a picture of health." How often have you heard this phrase used to describe someone in full bloom, eyes sparkling and radiant?

Pictures usually come in frames, which helps to distinguish them from murals. Unrestricted, unlimited food choices are rather like a mural. When the only criterion is to please the palate, the boundaries of creativity are virtually unlimited. Recipes can go wall to wall, floor to ceiling . . . the sky is the limit and often with calories to match!

When limits are applied, a framework is literally put around creativity, and suddenly every "brushstroke"—every seasoning, every ingredient of cooking—*really* counts. Over the years I have established my Minimax food lifestyle within this ten-sided frame. Because of this boundary, my eating style is less expansive than in my "mural past," but it is much better for creating a *picture of health.*

Here then are the guidelines that form the frame that I've used as a boundary in creating every one of my Minimax recipes. Since my *specific* nutritional needs are bound to be different from yours, I've provided space for you to make your own frame, with your own guidelines, according to the advice of your health professional. This I can promise: once you establish your own frame, you will have a starting point for healthful, creative cooking. I hope you will experience a new enthusiasm for what can be a most rewarding pastime.

Of the ten guidelines, seven relate to food and beverage, and three to lifestyle. Please remember these are *not* hard-and-fast rules. You may wish to photocopy this page and use it as a worksheet for your family.

For example, in one guideline I suggest three to four eggs a week, and in another, no more than 30 percent of your daily calories from fat. Both of those recommendations are upper limits for healthy people with low health risks. If you are like Treena, at high risk, then you may need to omit egg *yolks* (use a good egg substitute) and limit your daily calories from fat to 15 percent. Only your health professional knows what your limits should be, and you owe it to yourself and your loved ones to discover the frame within which you can be creative.

Because people's needs do vary, I have given the *exact* percentage of calories from fat for each of the recipes. With that information you can quickly identify dishes that are in your range. However, the individual recipe percentages are not the whole story. The key is to keep below

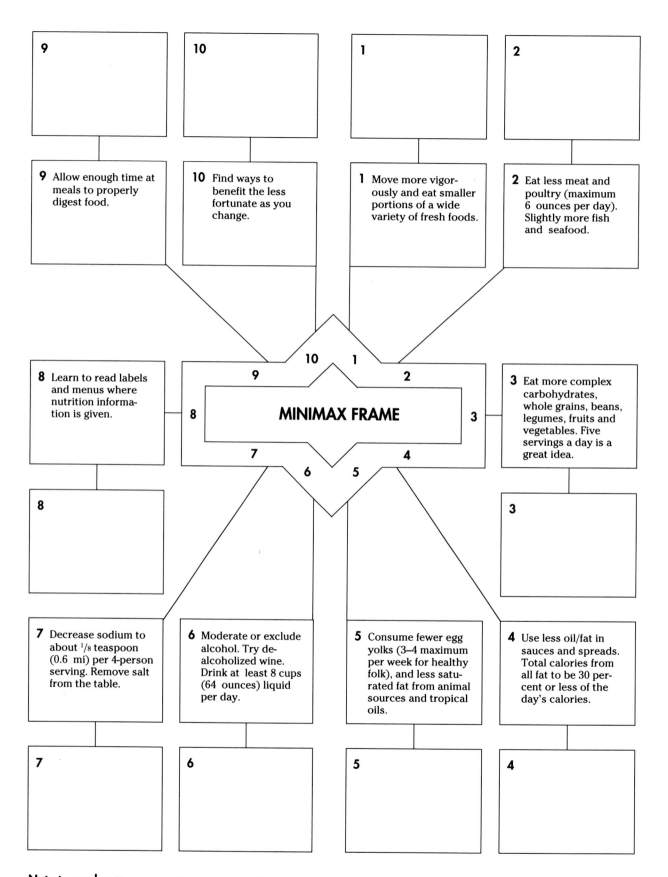

9 Allow enough time at meals to properly digest food.

10 Find ways to benefit the less fortunate as you change.

1 Move more vigorously and eat smaller portions of a wide variety of fresh foods.

2 Eat less meat and poultry (maximum 6 ounces per day). Slightly more fish and seafood.

8 Learn to read labels and menus where nutrition information is given.

MINIMAX FRAME

3 Eat more complex carbohydrates, whole grains, beans, legumes, fruits and vegetables. Five servings a day is a great idea.

7 Decrease sodium to about 1/8 teaspoon (0.6 mi) per 4-person serving. Remove salt from the table.

6 Moderate or exclude alcohol. Try de-alcoholized wine. Drink at least 8 cups (64 ounces) liquid per day.

5 Consume fewer egg yolks (3–4 maximum per week for healthy folk), and less saturated fat from animal sources and tropical oils.

4 Use less oil/fat in sauces and spreads. Total calories from all fat to be 30 percent or less of the day's calories.

Note to reader: You may wish to photocopy this page and have your health professional prescribe specific limits for each member of your family, according to their needs. You may also wish to record personal goals or commitments to change in the blank boxes.

one's ceiling in the total day's consumption. To help you do this, I've also included the total number of calories and grams of fat.

Each recipe has been subjected to both science and the senses in order to make it fit both the Minimax frame and the taste test of either my excellent creative team or the audiences that have attended and tasted the final results at the TV shows.

Every recipe has been analyzed by the Minnesota Nutritional Data System's computer program and checked by a representative of the American Heart Association, who we respectfully refer to as "our lady of the lipids." Computers are, of course, totally objective. When one of my recipes goes beyond the Minimax frame of 30 percent calories from fat, the read-out shows me exactly where the extra fat comes from and how much.

How can you figure the percentage of calories from fat in other foods you eat? You have to know the number of grams of fat and the total calories. Each gram of fat contains 9 calories. So the fat grams multiplied by 9, divided by the total number of calories, equals the percentage of total calories from fat. For example, if you know that each serving has 13 grams of fat and 415 calories:

$$13 \text{ gm (fat)} \times 9 \text{ (calories)} = 117 \text{ calories}$$

$$\frac{117}{415} \times 100 = 28\% \text{ (calories from fat)}$$

THE MINIMAX TECHNIQUES

*K*nowing that we should reduce our consumption of fat, salt and sugar is only part of the story, however. How do you actually change your use of these ingredients when faced with the task of preparing a healthful meal? That's where my Minimax techniques come in.

Within the culinary world there are literally thousands upon thousands of recipes but relatively few techniques. A recipe is basically a list of measured ingredients to be assembled in a given order, and calling for a basic method of cooking, such as roasting, poaching, frying or steaming. Techniques are specific ways of handling the food while it goes through its method of cooking. Traditionally, many of these techniques used large quantities of butter, cream, eggs, salt and sugar, all ingredients that increase our dietary health risks.

In this book you will find a full range of classic cooking techniques, all looked at from the perspective of Minimax. Each of these Minimax techniques is designed to reduce the health risk and increase eating enjoyment at the same time. They can be divided into three basic types:

- Cooking techniques that apply to many different types of dishes
- Cooking procedures that change specific classic recipes
- Methods of using special utensils to achieve Minimax results

Each Minimax technique begins with a discussion of the "reservoir of risk" inherent in the classic preparation technique. Because the classic dish presents risks doesn't make it forbidden fruit, but it does make it an intriguing opportunity for change, especially for those at risk. The Minimax technique demonstrates how the classic has been changed, using a simple recipe application and step-by-step photographs of the critical elements in each technique.

The basic recipe is then followed by two slightly more complex recipes that show the same Minimax technique used in other dishes.

I suggest you begin your Minimax journey by attempting several of the basic recipes to gain confidence using the techniques. Then try the more complex recipes given with the technique or any of the other recipes in this book or in my earlier book *Smart Cooking.* The recipes in both books make use again and again of these Minimax techniques.

When you taste the finished product, try to resist, as much as humanly possible, the temptation to compare it with the original. My father used to say, "All comparisons are odious," and they are, especially when you take a low-fat, low-sodium, low-sugar dish and compare it to one that is high in each category.

Rather, try to appreciate the food in terms of the following concepts:

Concept #1: Exceptional and Excellent: I allow that the original classic dish is "exceptional," that is, *far above the ordinary.* Then I ask myself if the more healthful alternative warrants the term "excellent," by which I mean a dish that *can be eaten day after day without risk.* I do not call high-risk classics "excellent" because I must then regard my day-to-day dishes as either "ordinary" or "diet," and the result would be a life of continual self-denial. And it is this very state of suppressed desire that causes most people to go back to the high-fat, high-salt, high-sugar "classics."

Concept #2: Creative Alternative: If the dish passes as excellent and suited to daily consumption, then it can go up against the ultimate test: *do I enjoy it just for what it is?*

The best way to explain this is to use an absolute basic as an example. I have *always* used butter on my morning toast, along with some Seville orange marmalade (bitter/sweet), but recently I've switched to using strained yogurt (see page 84). It looks different, smells different, tastes different and it doesn't compare to butter. But it is excellent because it has absolutely *no* fat and therefore can be eaten day after day without risk.

After the initial sensual conflict with fifty-seven years of buttered toast experiences, I discovered that the creamy mouthfeel and the slight tang of the yogurt, make a superb combination with the Seville marmalade. Therefore, it became a "creative alternative." The fact that I've seen this happen time and time again with these Minimax techniques makes me believe that their use can truly help create a lifestyle change over a period of months of creative experiments.

Once again, I repeat, Minimax does not mean that you must forget forever your hollandaise sauce, eggs Benedict, or high-butterfat ice cream. These still have their honored place as "exceptional" occasional treats, but they must be replaced with "excellent" daily alternatives that withstand the test of being enjoyed just for what they are.

THE MINIMAX KITCHEN

*A*s you try the recipes in this book, you will discover that some Minimax recipes have unusual ingredients that help develop aroma, color and texture, and others use pieces of special equipment that help to make this kind of cooking easier and great fun.

Many home cooks pick up a cookbook on an impulse to "have something different for dinner tonight." A brief glance at a recipe may disclose you are missing several ingredients and, rather than go out to the store for one or two herbs, the bold experimenter makes do. It is, of course, entirely possible that this improvization may result in a truly remarkable innovation, but it may also be a great disappointment and give the recipe an undeserved reputation for not working.

Over the years I have learned that every gram of fat and sugar, every miligram of sodium, that I remove from a recipe *must* be balanced by a corresponding addition of aroma, color and texture, the acronym for which, happily for everyone's memory, spells out the word "ACT." Therefore, if you decide to go without, or to replace one herb with another, you *may* have failed to compensate for the lower fat, sugar or sodium and will therefore be disappointed.

One way of avoiding this problem is to set up a Minimax pantry with a selection of ACT seasonings. My suggestions follow. Those seasonings listed in **boldface** type are recommended as a part of a *basic* supply for any kitchen. The number in parentheses beside each seasoning indicates the number of Minimax recipes in which I have used the seasoning.

The wonderful thing about having ACT seasonings on hand is that as you learn to enjoy the flavors, you can begin to use them in your own recipes as well as mine. You can also be much more spontaneous in your last-minute selection of "something different for dinner."

The Minimax Pantry

SPICES AND BRIGHT NOTES

Allspice berries (2) Pungent, spicy; use in fruit sauces
Anchovy fillets (5) Extremely salty; great for salads, pizza
Black peppercorns (50 +) Used whole in bouquet garni and freshly
ground
Capers (6) Very salty, pickled seeds
Caraway seed (4) Complements cabbage dishes
Cardamom (3) Fine astringent spice with a bite
Cayenne pepper (24) For that spice-hot zip
Chili powder (4) Hot and spicy (cayenne and cumin)
Cinnamon (12) Favorite spice from aromatic tree bark
Cloves, whole (30) Essential for bouquet garni
Cumin seed (5) The perfect spice for beans and Indian dishes
Garlic, fresh (51) Aromatic, heady, essential for Minimax
Garam masala (3) A mix of aromatic spices (see page 44)
Gingerroot, fresh (7) Keeps well wrapped in paper, enclosed in a plastic
bag and refrigerated
Juniper berries (1) Adds gamelike flavor to casseroles
Kaffir lime leaves (2) A Thai seasoning, somewhat like bay leaves
Lemon grass (4) Excellent, astringent flavor; best when fresh
Mozzarella cheese, low fat (5) Use for melted cheese toppings
Nutmeg, whole (18) Very spicy; use freshly grated on vegetables, etc.
Paprika, Hungarian sweet (4) Dusky red spice
Pimento, bottled (6) Bright red roasted sweet peppers
Saffron, powdered (4) I prefer the powder from Spice Islands
Salt, freshly ground sea salt (throughout) My salt of choice, pure and
simple
Sardines, water packed (1) Superb source of Omega-3 Fatty acids and
calcium
Sun-dried tomatoes (3) Concentrated sweet/acid flavor
Tea, Earl Grey (2) My favorite perfumed black tea; use to smoke fish and
chicken
Tomato paste, low sodium (15) Essential for dark sauces and casseroles
that depend upon the Maillard reaction (see page 17)
Turmeric (3) Lovely yellow color; the poor man's saffron, but has good
spice flavor thrown in
White peppercorns (4) Useful for seasoning white-sauced dishes

LIQUIDS, SAUCES AND SPREADS

Apple butter (2) Smooth sweet coating; side dish
Arrowroot (24 +) Thickening agent used in dark sauces or in coating
  pasta to reflect light
Chutney, mango (1) Spicy, fruity condiment for Indian dishes
Cornstarch (20) A thickening agent for light-colored sauces, especially
  those made with dairy products
Fish sauce (4) Anchovies steeped in salt and fermented; essential Asian
  flavor
Guava nectar (1) A wonderful dessert sauce
Jelly, red currant (2) The best condiment for lamb
Marmalade, Seville (2) This bittersweet conserve makes great
  puddings and is terrific on toast
Mint sauce (1) Try Crosse & Blackwell brand; use with mutton, not with
  lamb
Mustard, French Dijon (6) Good flavor base for many sauces
Olive oil, extra light (80 +) My basic choice, extra light in flavor, not in
  fat content, and with a touch of toasted sesame oil to give a nutty
  aroma
Oyster sauce (1) Dark and pungent; an important Cantonese flavoring
Sesame oil, toasted (80 +) Essential Minimax flavor; used with olive oil
Tahini (2) Sesame butter; excellent Asian/North African flavor
Tomato sauce (1) Vital for Karewai style food.
Vinegar, balsamic (4) Incredibly complex woody flavor; great for salads
  and sauces
Vinegar, cider (5) Good basic flavor for salad dressings
Vinegar, rice wine (8) Crisp, light, mild; superb for salads
Wines, (40) De-alcoholized classic varieties
    Blanc in dessert sauces
    Cabernet sauvignon in red-wine sauces and casseroles
    Chardonnay with seafood and chicken
Worcestershire sauce, regular (1) Strong, spiced dark brown vinegar
Worcestershire sauce, white wine (1) Used in white sauces for punch

BAKING

Almond extract (3) Heady flavor for desserts
Applesauce and apple butters (5) Adds moisture to baked goods
Baking powder (5) Added as leavening to batters and cakes
Baking soda (5) Added as leavening to batters and cakes
Brown sugar (15) Sweet, extra-light molasses flavor

Cocoa powder, unsweetened (4) Used in place of chocolate
Flour, all purpose (11) General use, especially batters, pastry
Flour, cake (4) Very good for added tenderness in low-fat baked goods
Gelatin, unflavored (10) Helps set no-bake cheesecakes and sorbet
Honey, fireweed (6) Superb flavor for general use
Maple syrup (5) Be sure it's 100 percent pure and natural; wonderful taste
Milk, dried nonfat (1) Very good for Papufa
Molasses (3) Important background flavor and adds color, as for bran muffins
Sugar, superfine (5) Useful for meringues and cakes
Vanilla, extract (8) Essential flavor for desserts; make sure it's pure, not imitation
Wheat germ (4) Added to plain flour for pastry

DRIED AND CANNED LEGUMES; GRAINS AND PASTAS

Barley (5) Wonderful textural grain for pilaf, etc.
Beans, black (3) Good taste, elegant texture/color garnish
Beans, butter (2) Canned; buttery color and smooth texture
Beans, fava (1) Canned; very large and "meaty"
Beans, pinto (4) One of the best Latin American beans
Bulgur (wheat) (5) Useful extender for meat dishes
Oats, rolled (3) Try the organic—there's more texture
Pasta (6) A low-fat, versatile base for innumerable sauces; choose the shape that suits your fancy
Peas, dried split (2) Hearty stuff for soups and casseroles
Rice, arborio (3) A "fat" rice grain, excellent for risotto
Rice, basmati (5) Fine, aromatic long grain white rice
Rice, wild (6) Actually a grass seed; great in pilaf

FRUITS, NUTS AND SEEDS

Almonds, flaked (4) Crunchy textural garnish
Apricots, dried (2) Mellow acidic garnish
Cashews (2) Excellent nut, full of creamy flavor
Figs, dried (4) Vital element for cheesecake crusts
Minimax Seed Mix (3) Crunchy textural variety (see page 112)
Pine nuts (5) Smooth-tasting, oily pine seeds; great texture
Plums (2) Canned fruit that makes terrific sauces
Quinoa (1) Wonderfully nutritious tiny seed used as a side dish

Raisins, flame (2) The best of all raisins (to my taste!)
Walnuts, pickled (1) Rare, but wonderful zesty flavor

PERISHABLES

Canadian bacon (15) Very lean loin, used as garnish
Cheese, goat (4) Stupendous tangy flavor in savory dishes
Cheese, hard grating (25) I prefer dry Monterey Jack or Parmesan
Egg substitute, liquid (10) Frozen; Fleischmann's Egg Beaters is my pick
Tofu (2) Soybean curd and vegetable protein, used to replace meat

In the Minimax Pantry you'll notice de-alcoholized wines. A quick reminder on this issue. Some years ago I made a decision to limit my use of alcohol when I became aware of the millions who were at risk from *any* quantity of *any* type of alcohol. I didn't want my recipes to cause them any harm.

I fully recognize that we live in a pluralistic society that strongly defends individual freedom of choice and therefore I have never, ever, proposed prohibition of any substance. However, since I do have the freedom to choose what I do, and since what I do is so public, I want you to understand the reason for my decision. This isn't in response to personal problems with alcohol, from which, contrary to outdated public opinion, I have never suffered.

If a truly interesting wine is served at a dinner where I am a guest I might sniff and sip a spoonful so that I can remain current in my appreciation of wine making as an art and to keep my judgment objective when selecting de-alcoholized wines for my own table.

MINIMAX EQUIPMENT

I have grown to enjoy the tools of my trade. In a very real way they have become extensions of my hands and valued as a result. I've listed below those that I believe help me to cook better and make it simpler to easily remove some of the dietary risks. Where a tool is almost essential to the successful completion of the recipe, I've asked my friend Sandy Silverthorne to add a simple sketch on the recipe page itself.

SOFT-FOOD SLICER: A special perforated blade that releases as it cuts. This permits very thin slices of cheese to be cut.

YOGURT STRAINER: Simple, reusable 1-cup (236 ml) strainer that comes two per pack and allows you to have a constant supply of strained yogurt on hand.

FAT-STRAINER JUG: Large, Lexan measuring jug with a spout that pours from the bottom, leaving the fat on the surface. It is in daily use in a Minimax kitchen.

SKINNY SKIMMER: A perforated ladle that skims stocks and casseroles of surface fat. Must have wide slots.

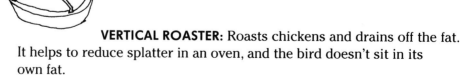

VERTICAL ROASTER: Roasts chickens and drains off the fat. It helps to reduce splatter in an oven, and the bird doesn't sit in its own fat.

CHOPPER SCRAPER: An all-purpose preparation picker-upper. I invented this simple tool in 1960 and have used it on hundreds of TV shows. It chops and crushes garlic and softer vegetables; even cores apples.

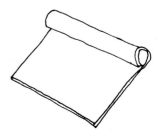

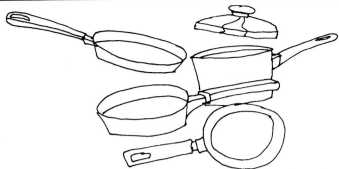

NONSTICK CAST COOKWARE: I've used Scanpan 2000+ in developing every single recipe in this book, as well as those in the "Graham Kerr" TV series and *Smart Cooking.* This is cookware designed for Minimax use and guaranteed to last for the life of the buyer.

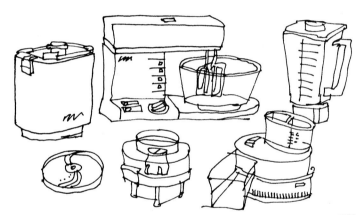

KITCHEN CENTER: A small, quiet, multipurpose electric machine built to fit into the modern kitchen. It makes consuming an enormous increase in fresh fruit and vegetables possible by reducing preparation time to seconds. A more versatile machine than the traditional food processor.

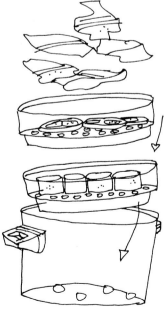

STACK AND STEAM: Multiple stainless-steel steamer units that fit standard-size skillets. With this device you can master the steaming technique and prepare perfectly cooked vegetables.

STEAMER BASKET: Stainless-steel steamer insert with long legs. I use this for the smoke technique (see page 73).

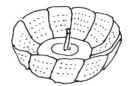

SPURTLE: A bamboo tool that scrapes, whips, turns, stirs and strains. I codesigned this in New Zealand back in 1961 and have been using it ever since.

COUNT UP AND DOWN TIMER: Very useful when starting out on new recipes. If you miss the signal when it reaches zero, it counts back up to let you know how long your mistake has been!

TURNER/SERVER: Useful when serving whole tender foods like canneloni, filled crêpes and whole fish fillets. I wanted something like this for years!

SALAD TOSSER AND STRAINER: Important for completely dressed salads with less oil. (See page 80 for Split Spun Salad ideas.)

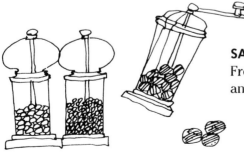

SALT, PEPPER AND NUTMEG MILLS: Freshly ground or shaved salt crystals and spices give *much* better flavor. In Minimax food every single seasoning must count . . . the fresher, the better!

LEMON TWIST SQUEEZER: Fresh lemon juice *without* pips. Lemon is the most readily available of all the "bright notes" that are added to Minimax food. This small unit keeps lemon fresh and immediately available.

STAINLESS-STEEL COLANDER AND BOWL: Essential for proper pasta cooking. I cook a great deal of pasta and, when done, tip half the water away down the drain, then pour the pasta and remaining water into a colander set over a large bowl. The water drains off and heats the bowl, which is then used to toss and serve the pasta in its sauce.

PRESSURE COOKER: Makes wonderful bean dishes in a very short time. It's also great for quick stocks, soups and casseroles. (See page 66 for specific ideas.)

STAINLESS-STEEL HAND SIEVE: Another essential tool that helps me strain yogurt and hot foods. It's also used to make great boil-and-steam rice.

careful graham, you'll strain your voice...

FLAVOR INJECTOR: This is *something* like a hypodermic syringe but clearly not able to be used for medical or illegal uses. The marinades or infusions are placed in the barrel of the unit and injected through a series of holes along the side of the solid tipped needle.

IS CHANGE POSSIBLE?

A great deal of our sense of personal and national identity comes from what we eat and even how we eat it. Helping us with our choices are millions and millions of words of good advice from hundreds of agencies and organizations. Sometimes this advice conflicts and we get confused. I'm often asked, "Isn't there a simple "silver bullet" approach that could just get us started in the right direction?" Basically I don't believe in "magic bullets," especially as an alternative to the creative discipline we all seem to need. However, there is one small, easy-to-apply idea that can get you excited about the changes you can make with Minimax . . .

> *Cut in half everything you eat that has fat in it and replace it with fresh foods that you like and are fat free.*

This simple action will get you started TODAY, at your next meal, and could easily result in much better health for yourself, your loved ones and even for future generations who may be positively influenced by your lifestyle.

I meet a great many people who tell me that they don't think their husbands, or sometimes their wives, could possibly enjoy smaller portions of meat and greatly reduced fat content. Mostly those folks have tried a few recipes for "healthful food" that are often "subsistence" beans-and-rice dishes. In my opinion this is too big a leap for the meat-and-potatoes brigade. My dad used to say "softly, softly catchee monkey." Translated, it cautions to *make haste slowly* when dealing with any kind of change.

The idea behind Minimax is quite well illustrated by the weather. If the temperature rises sharply in the north, there will be a thermal in which the hot air rises. As it lifts it causes a south wind to fill in the gap. In Minimax, the action of lifting out fats, salts, sugars and large meat portions, causes aroma, colors and textures to rush in to take their place. To attempt the MINI without the MAX is to court disaster.

It is my fondest hope that you will cook from this book and become convinced that Minimax is possible for your family and friends. But in my dreams, I most of all hope that you will "springboard," or experiment, using some of my ideas in your favorite dishes or, better still, in the development of your very own creations.

In any event, I do sincerely wish you well with the creative changes that you can make. You have everything to gain except disease and nothing to lose. Have fun. That is, after all, the best ingredient.

Minimax Techniques
THE MAILLARD REACTION

When fat is removed from classic dishes "depth" is often the missing sensation. It's hard to describe depth, so let me try to explain what it isn't. Low-fat dishes have a "thin" mouthfeel; they don't make you wonder "What's in this?" because there is often little or no aroma.

Depth manifests itself as a more complex taste, with a textural quality that you can really feel and an aromatic quality that fills the nose. A technique that provides depth in many of my Minimax dishes is based on the "Maillard reaction," which takes place when tomato paste is heated in order to caramelize its natural sugars. This singular technique provides complex taste, textural smoothness, rich glossy color and a good clean aroma.

In short, the Maillard reaction provides an easy way to replace the missing sensation when you've removed at least two thirds of the fat. I've illustrated this technique of providing depth without fat by showing you how to make a basic tomato sauce that goes very well in Italian "food of the people" dishes (spaghetti, lasagne, etc.). Then you'll discover a simple chicken breast and pasta dish that makes up in only twenty minutes and a slow-simmering hearty vegetable stew seasoned with beef.

Incidentally, "Maillard" refers to Dr. Louis-Camille Maillard, the French scientist who, in 1912, first identified the chemical reaction . . . for which millions of "Minimaxers" now extend their thanks.

USES: As a substitute in dark sauces, soups, stews and casseroles, for the classic brown roux of flour and butter.

■ Add the tomato paste when the pan is hot and let it sizzle on contact. It is now hot enough to caramelize the tomato sugars in the Maillard reaction.

■ Stir gently and slowly with a flat-ended spurtle or spatula. Continually scrape the residues back into the still-bright tomato paste. The color will deepen. Don't overdo this stage and burn the sugars. It only needs to be dark brown, not black.

■ When other ingredients are added, the overall color becomes deep and rich. With meat sauces, the result is a golden mahogany. In this case, I use chopped tomatoes, oregano, and finely snipped parsley stalks for added crunch.

BASIC TOMATO SAUCE

Yield: 2½–3 cups
INGREDIENTS

½ teaspoon extra-light olive oil, with a dash of sesame oil (2.5 ml)

2 tablespoons low-sodium tomato paste (30 ml)

1 medium onion, peeled and finely diced

2 cloves garlic, peeled, smashed and finely diced

One 28 ounce can crushed tomatoes (794 gm)

2 tablespoons fresh oregano (30 ml), one tablespoon chopped, one left whole

1 tablespoon arrowroot (15 ml), mixed with 2 tablespoons water (30 ml)

2 tablespoons fresh chopped parsley stalks (30 ml)

¼ teaspoon freshly ground black pepper (1.25 ml)

¼ cup de-alcoholized wine (59 ml) (optional)

NOW COOK

■ Over medium-high heat, brush a large skillet with the oil to coat, add the tomato paste and cook until the color darkens, stirring to prevent scorching—about 5 minutes.

■ Stir in the onion and garlic and cook 5 minutes, stirring occasionally to prevent scorching. Add the tomatoes with the tablespoon of chopped oregano, bring to a boil, reduce the heat and simmer 10 minutes. Remove from the heat, stir in the arrowroot slurry, parsley stalks, pepper and remaining oregano. A last aromatic splash of de-alcoholized wine is your choice. Serve hot on your favorite pasta or other dish.

Nutritional Profile

PER SERVING	CLASSIC	MINIMAX
Calories	178	66
Fat (gm)	14	1
Saturated fat (gm)	2	0
Calories from fat	70%	16%
Cholesterol (mg)	0	0
Sodium (mg)	851	33
Fiber (gm)	3	3

■ *Classic Compared: Italian Tomato Sauce*

BLUSHING CHICKEN FETTUCINE

Serves 4
INGREDIENTS

1 recipe Basic Tomato Sauce

Four 6-ounce boneless chicken breasts (170 gm each), with skin

1 teaspoon extra-light olive oil, with a dash of sesame oil (5 ml)

8 ounces uncooked spinach fettucine (227 gm)

¼ cup de-alcoholized white wine (59 ml)

Fresh chopped oregano leaves

FIRST PREPARE

■ Make the Basic Tomato Sauce and set aside.

NOW COOK

■ Pat the chicken breasts dry with a paper towel. Pour the oil into a large skillet over medium heat. Place the chicken breasts in the skillet, skin side down, and brown for 10 minutes, turning them every 2 minutes. Resist the temptation to turn the heat up to just cook them quickly. The hotter the pan, the more the surface moisture evaporates, and the stringier the meat. Low-heat cooking will retain maximum tenderness and juiciness. Remove chicken from the pan and set aside.

■ While the chicken browns, cook the fettucine in boiling water according to directions on the package until just tender—about 9 to 11 minutes. Drain. Pour half of the tomato sauce into a large pot, add the cooked pasta, toss well and keep warm until ready to serve.

■ Remove the skin from the cooked chicken, dipping your fingers in a bowl of ice water every few seconds to keep them cool. Using a paper towel, blot the breasts to remove residual fat.

■ Blot the chicken-browning skillet with a paper towel to remove excess fat. Pour in the remaining tomato sauce and the wine, add the browned breasts, cover and let them heat through.

■ To Serve: Divide the pasta onto individual dinner plates. Spoon a small pool of the sauce on the side and lay a chicken breast on top of it, coating with another spoonful of sauce. Garnish the pasta with the remaining sauce and a sprinkle of fresh oregano leaves.

NOTE ON CHICKEN BREASTS: To get boneless chicken breasts with skin, you can buy whole or split fryer breasts and debone them. However, from an economic point of view, you will experience greater financial savings over the long run by purchasing a whole chicken, and freezing the other parts for later use. An added benefit for Minimax cooks is that you will also be able to use the bones for chicken stock (see page 34).

Nutritional Profile

PER SERVING	CLASSIC	MINIMAX
Calories	614	465
Fat (gm)	31	11
Saturated fat (gm)	17	3
Calories from fat	45%	20%
Cholesterol (mg)	174	141
Sodium (mg)	1244	498
Fiber (gm)	4	6

■ *Classic Compared: Chicken Casserole*

HEARTY VEGETABLE STEW SEASONED WITH BEEF

One-sided browning of the meat leaves the other sides "open" to absorb the flavors of this delicious stew.

Serves 4
INGREDIENTS

8 ounces beef bottom round (227 gm), all visible fat removed, cut into 4 equal pieces

1 teaspoon extra-light olive oil, with a dash of sesame oil (5 ml)

2 medium onions, peeled and thickly sliced

6 ounces low-sodium tomato paste (170 gm)

3 cups enhanced canned beef stock (708 ml) (see page 35), reduced to 1½ cups (354 ml)

4 tablespoons de-alcoholized red wine (60 ml)

16 ounces carrots (227 gm), peeled and cut in 1-inch pieces

12 small red new potatoes

12 medium-sized whole fresh mushrooms

1 tablespoon arrowroot (15 ml), mixed with 2 tablespoons de-alcoholized red wine (30 ml)

2 cups frozen green peas (472 ml), thawed

2 tablespoons fresh chopped parsley (30 ml)

¼ teaspoon freshly ground black pepper (1.25 ml)

⅛ teaspoon freshly ground salt (0.6 ml) (optional)

NOW COOK

■ Pat the meat dry with a paper towel to maximize browning. Pour the oil into a large saucepan over medium high heat, add the meat and let it brown on one side—about 3 minutes. Remove and set aside.

■ Into the same hot pan, stir in the onions and tomato paste, scraping the brown meat residue into the mixture, and cook for 5 minutes. This step accomplishes three important Minimax functions at one time: the onions release their aromatic volatile oils; the tomato paste caramelizes; and a flavor-filled glaze builds on the pan. Return meat to pan, add the stock and wine, bring to a boil, reduce the heat and simmer, covered, over very low heat for 30 minutes.

■ Then add the vegetables to the pan in the following order: carrots first; 5 minutes later, add the potatoes and mushrooms. Another 15 minutes of simmering, and all is perfection!

■ Remove from the heat and add the peas. Stir in the arrowroot slurry, return to the heat and stir until thickened. Add the parsley, pepper and a very little freshly ground sea salt if necessary. Serve in bowls.

Nutritional Profile

PER SERVING	CLASSIC	MINIMAX
Calories	834	616
Fat (gm)	32	6
Saturated fat (gm)	10	1
Calories from fat	35%	8%
Cholesterol (mg)	172	48
Sodium (mg)	1366	306
Fiber (gm)	9	17

■ *Classic Compared: Old-Fashioned Beef Stew*

BASIC BROWN ONION SAUCE

ℋere is an important new sauce: it delivers a delicious, sweet taste, has a dark glossy finish and has less than 1 gram of fat in each serving. If you like French onion soup, you'll love this.

I've used a readily available yellow onion in my tests, but if you can rustle up a sweet local variety, like the West Coast's Walla Walla or the East Coast's Vidalia onion, the sauce will be even sweeter and a little darker.

What delivers the sweet taste without additional sugar? It's another example of the Maillard Reaction (see page 17). Cooking the onions over high heat releases their sugars, which caramelize, turning the onions a glossy brown. Make sure that all the brown residue on the pan is scraped up into the liquid, because this is where the concentration of color and flavor has taken place.

The Turkey Mountain recipe combines this sauce with mashed potatoes and leftover meats. It appears to pack a few calories, but please note that there are only 3 grams of fat, which is only 6 percent of total calories from fat. That's very good news for comfort-food lovers on really cold days.

The Turkey and Brown Onion Chutney Salad recipe is unique in its use of this sauce, chilled, in a salad. This idea came from my food associate Robert Prince's fertile mind and fits into what he calls a "composed" salad: it's not tossed, but the ingredients are artfully placed on serving plates. By adding a few pine nuts for texture, we have actually turned this sauce into an onion chutney that (in my humble opinion) comes very close to rivaling Crosse & Blackwell's Branston pickle at only a fraction of the price.

USES: With the lighter meats, like pork or veal, and with chicken. Best served as a side sauce to a pan sauté or broiled dish, or as a chutney served hot or cold with sliced luncheon meats.

■ The idea here is to get the onions to caramelize at frying temperature. Leave them alone, without stirring, to brown fully. After 5 minutes, the color should look like this picture. I'm holding up a spoonful of raw onion to show the radical color change.

■ This is where you get depth of flavor and color for the final sauce. The liquid comes from a combination of beef or chicken stock and de-alcoholized dry red wine.

■ When you stir in the arrowroot slurry, the sauce thickens immediately and reflects the light beautifully, resulting in a rich appearance much like that imparted by fat gloss.

BASIC BROWN ONION SAUCE

Yield 2 cups (472 ml)
INGREDIENTS

¼ teaspoon extra-light olive oil, with a dash of sesame oil (1.25 ml)
2 large onions, peeled and thinly sliced
1 teaspoon dill seed (5 ml)
1 teaspoon caraway seed (5 ml)
1 cup beef stock (236 ml) (see page 35)
1 cup de-alcoholized dry red wine (236 ml)
1 tablespoon arrowroot (15 ml), mixed with 2 tablespoons de-alcoholized dry red wine (30 ml)

NOW COOK

■ Pour the oil into a large skillet over medium-high heat, add the onions, dill and caraway and cook, uncovered, 5 minutes, without stirring. Stir once, then cover and cook 5 minutes. Add the stock and wine and quickly scrape up all the pan residues into the liquid until the bottom of the pan is perfectly clean; simmer 5 minutes. Remove the pan from the heat, stir in the arrowroot slurry, return to the heat and stir until thickened. Use on your favorite steak or chop, or on chicken or turkey.

Nutritional Profile

PER SERVING	CLASSIC	MINIMAX
Calories	180	84
Fat (gm)	13	1
Saturated fat (gm)	5	0
Calories from fat	65%	10%
Cholesterol (mg)	12	0
Sodium (mg)	389	20
Fiber (gm)	1	12

■ *Classic Compared: Brown Onion Sauce*

TURKEY MOUNTAIN

Serves 4
INGREDIENTS

Eight 8-ounce russet potatoes (227 gm each), peeled, cut into chunks
2 cups Basic Brown Onion Sauce (472 ml)
½ cup skim buttermilk (118 ml), room temperature
1 teaspoon freshly grated nutmeg (5 ml)
¼ teaspoon freshly ground white pepper (1.25 ml)
¼ teaspoon freshly ground salt (1.25 ml)
4 slices leftover ham, thinly sliced
4 slices leftover turkey breast, thinly sliced
4 tablespoons parsley (60 ml)

FIRST PREPARE

■ Boil the potatoes for 30 minutes, drain and return to the same pot over low heat. Put a kitchen towel over the top of the pot and let them dry out. This will prevent a watery consistency in your final product.

■ Make the Basic Brown Onion Sauce and keep warm.

NOW COOK

■ In a medium-sized bowl, mash together the boiled potatoes, buttermilk and seasonings.

■ To give your leftovers an elegant presentation, create an informal mold: rub the ham around the inside of a medium-sized cereal or soup bowl to lubricate the surface. Layer the ham and turkey to cover the inside of the bowl. Spoon in the hot potatoes, completely covering the meat to about ¼ inch (0.75 cm) from the top of the rim, and smooth out the top. Invert the bowl over the middle of a large serving plate, grasp the edges firmly and give it a couple of sharp shakes. The potatoes should unmold in a graceful, meat-covered mound. If you don't feel up to this procedure, you can always mound the potatoes on the plate and lay the meats decoratively on top. Whichever way, it tastes wonderful!

■ To Serve: Make a depression in the center of each serving, pour on the onion sauce and sprinkle with the parsley. Surround with a wreath of vegetable leftovers and your meal is complete.

Nutritional Profile

PER SERVING	CLASSIC	MINIMAX
Calories	893	422
Fat (gm)	22	3
Saturated fat (gm)	11	1
Calories from fat	22%	6%
Cholesterol (mg)	131	8
Sodium (mg)	926	333
Fiber (gm)	8	7

■ *Classic Compared: Hot Turkey Sandwich with Mashed Potatoes*

TURKEY AND BROWN ONION CHUTNEY SALAD

Serves 4
INGREDIENTS

2 cups Basic Brown Onion Sauce (472 ml)

2 tablespoons pine nuts (30 ml)

1 teaspoon arrowroot (5 ml), mixed with 2 teaspoons de-alcoholized red wine (10 ml)
4 tablespoons strained yogurt (60 ml) (see page 85)

2 teaspoons balsamic vinegar (10 ml)

8 leaves Bibb leaf lettuce

4 leaves red lettuce

8 slices turkey breast

8 red new potatoes, about 2 inches (5 cm) in diameter, steamed until tender and cut in half

1 teaspoon fresh chopped dill (5 ml)

FIRST PREPARE

■ Prepare the Basic Brown Onion Sauce. Simmer the sauce until it reduces to a glaze—about 15 minutes. Remove from the heat and stir in the pine nuts and arrowroot slurry. Transfer to a small bowl and refrigerate until cool.

NOW COOK

■ Make a Dressing: In a small bowl, stir the yogurt and vinegar until the mixture turns tawny brown.

■ In a large bowl, toss the lettuces with the dressing until well coated.

■ To Compose the Salad: On one half of a dinner plate, lay out 2 leaves of the dressed Bibb lettuce and 1 leaf of the dressed red lettuce. On the other half of the plate, artfully arrange 2 pieces of turkey, next to a small mound of the onion sauce and a quarter of the potatoes. Sprinkle with dill and it's ready to be un-composed (eaten, that is)!

Nutritional Profile

PER SERVING	CLASSIC	MINIMAX
Calories	1128	388
Fat (gm)	74	5
Saturated fat (gm)	11	1
Calories from fat	59%	12%
Cholesterol (mg)	213	24
Sodium (mg)	672	277
Fiber (gm)	5	7

■ *Classic Compared: Warm Lemon Chicken Salad*

STARCH-THICKENED SAUCES

Throughout most of my recipes, I use pure starches, rather than flour, as thickeners. With dark hot sauces, gravies and casseroles, I use arrowroot because of its clarity and its lack of taste to mask the food flavor. I also like it for a pasta glaze when I want the look of oil—lots of sparkle—without the fat.

There is a drawback, however, because when arrowroot cools, especially in contact with dairy products and crisp cooked vegetables, it develops an unusually slippery texture. For this reason I prefer to use cornstarch in such recipes. Cornstarch causes a slightly misty film that dulls the light reflection, but since this also takes place in dairy sauces as well as lighter colored casseroles that include beans for example, it isn't a real loss.

Cornstarch does need thirty seconds at the boil to remove its starchy taste. Arrowroot, however, clears in very hot liquid without the need to boil.

My principal reason for the use of pure starches is to thicken without the need for the classic roux (a combination of equal parts flour and butter that holds up to six times its own weight in liquid). The classic roux sauce does have one significant advantage: it holds up longer than pure starch sauces, which tend to thin rapidly if held before serving. So the moral is, use the slurry (combined liquid and starch) at the last moment, and you will have the best of both worlds.

USES: Wherever you need to thicken a seasoned liquid.

■ To thicken each cup (236 ml) of liquid, make a slurry with 1 tablespoon (15 ml) of arrowroot or cornstarch and double the amount—in this case 2 tablespoons (30 ml)—of your base liquid or of wine. Stir until perfectly smooth—no lumps.

■ *Always* pull the pan from the heat before adding the slurry. Rapidly stir in the slurry throughout the dish and return pan to the heat. Arrowroot will thicken very quickly and does not need to come to a boil; cornstarch must return to a boil for at least 30 seconds, in order for the starch flavor to disappear.

■ When there is a full pan, tilt it to one side and allow the juices to pool together. Add the slurry to this liquid and mix well to dissolve before incorporating the juices back into the rest of the ingredients.

SCALLOPS STIR-FRY

Serves 4
INGREDIENTS

2 teaspoons extra-light olive oil, with a dash of sesame oil (10 ml)

1 clove garlic, peeled, smashed and finely chopped

8 "dime-size" paper-thin slices fresh peeled gingerroot, cut into thin matchsticks

8 ounces snow peas (227 gm)

8 ounces sweet red bell pepper (227 gm), cut into thick matchsticks

¼ teaspoon toasted sesame oil (1.25 ml)

12 ounces sea scallops (340 gm)

2 tablespoons fresh minced cilantro (30 ml)

1 cup vegetable stock (236 ml) (see page 36)

1 cup de-alcoholized white wine (236 ml)

2 tablespoons cornstarch (30 ml), mixed with 4 tablespoons de-alcoholized white wine (60 ml)

¼ teaspoon freshly ground black pepper (1.25 ml)

4 cups cooked hot white rice (944 ml)

NOW COOK

■ Put half the olive oil in a large wok or skillet and sauté the garlic and ginger over medium heat, just to release their fragrance—about 1 minute. Bao Syang! (See page 47). Turn up the heat to medium high, add the vegetables and toss vigorously until just crisp-tender—about 4 minutes. Transfer to a bowl and set aside.

■ Add the remaining olive oil and the toasted sesame oil to the same wok and cook the scallops over medium-high heat for 2 minutes. Transfer to a bowl, sprinkle with the cilantro, cover and set aside.

■ Return the vegetables to the hot wok. Pour in the stock and wine and heat through. Remove from heat, add the cornstarch slurry, return to heat, bring to a boil and stir until thickened—about 30 seconds. Remove from the heat, stir in the scallops and sprinkle with the pepper.

■ To Serve: Spoon the scallops and vegetables over the rice on dinner plates.

Nutritional Profile

PER SERVING	CLASSIC	MINIMAX
Calories	581	493
Fat (gm)	31	5
Saturated fat (gm)	18	1
Calories from fat	49%	9%
Cholesterol (mg)	191	27
Sodium (mg)	859	250
Fiber (gm)	3	4

■ *Classic Compared: Scallops Parisienne*

BISTRO VEGETABLES WITH ROSEMARY

Serves 4
INGREDIENTS

1 teaspoon extra-light olive oil, with a dash of sesame oil (5 ml)

8 small onions, peeled and quartered

20 small carrots, cut in half lengthwise

6 small red new potatoes, quartered

2 cups vegetable stock (472 ml) (see page 36)

One 4-inch branch of fresh rosemary (10 cm)

⅛ teaspoon freshly ground salt (0.6 ml)

8 ounces fresh mushrooms (227 gm), halved

One 15-ounce can butter beans (425 gm), rinsed

1 tablespoon arrowroot (15 ml), mixed with 2 tablespoons vegetable stock (30 ml)

1 teaspoon fresh chopped thyme (5 ml)

1 tablespoon fresh chopped parsley (15 ml)

NOW COOK

■ Put the oil in a large skillet, add the onions and cook over medium heat until they're brown— about 5 minutes. Add the carrots, potatoes, vegetable stock, rosemary branch (making sure the rosemary is submerged in the liquid) and salt, cover and simmer 10 minutes; add the mushrooms and simmer an additional 10 minutes.

■ Remove from the heat, and take out the rosemary branch; stir in the butter beans and arrowroot slurry. Return to the heat and stir until thickened. Sprinkle with the thyme and parsley.

NOTE: May be served either as a complete vegetable entree for 4, or for 6 as a vegetable side dish.

Nutritional Profile

PER SERVING	CLASSIC	MINIMAX
Calories	412	481
Fat (gm)	24	3
Saturated fat (gm)	15	1
Calories from fat	53%	6%
Cholesterol (mg)	68	0
Sodium (mg)	224	533
Fiber (gm)	12	22

■ *Classic Compared: Beans and Vegetables au Gratin*

TROPICAL RICE PUDDING

*C*ultures comingling in comfort—no, not the United States, but a dessert that combines the delights of a creamy Italian risotto with sweet English rice pudding and the fruits of the tropics:

Serves 6
INGREDIENTS

2 cups 2% fat milk (472 ml)
2 cups water (472 ml)
¼ cup brown sugar (59 ml)
1⅓ cups uncooked short grain white rice (314 ml)
¾ teaspoon nutmeg (3.75 ml)
1 cup de-alcoholized white wine (236 ml)
⅛ teaspoon ground cloves (0.6 ml)
1 mango, peeled and coarsely chopped
1 papaya, peeled and coarsely chopped
½ pineapple, peeled, cored and coarsely chopped
2 tablespoons cornstarch (30 ml), mixed with
4 tablespoons de-alcoholized white wine (60 ml)

NOW COOK

■ Pour the milk, water and sugar into a small saucepan and stir until the sugar is dissolved. Put over very low heat, just to keep warm.

■ Put the rice in a large saucepan and, over medium heat, add one quarter of the milk mixture, stirring occasionally, until the liquid is absorbed. Repeat the process, adding a small portion of the milk mixture each time and cooking until all the milk is absorbed and the rice is tender. The entire process takes about 30 minutes. Remove from the heat and stir in ½ teaspoon (2.5 ml) of the nutmeg.

■ Pour the wine into a medium-sized skillet and bring to a boil. Add the remaining nutmeg, the cloves and fruit and return to a boil for 4 minutes. Remove from the heat, stir in the cornstarch slurry, return to the heat, bring to a boil and stir until thickened—about 30 seconds. Remove from the heat.

■ To Serve: For an elegant presentation, put the rice in a small mold and turn out onto a serving plate. Spoon the fruit in a bright golden circle around and on top of the molded rice.

Nutritional Profile

PER SERVING	CLASSIC	MINIMAX
Calories	506	496
Fat (gm)	29	3
Saturated fat (gm)	18	2
Calories from fat	52%	6%
Cholesterol (mg)	102	9
Sodium (mg)	208	74
Fiber (gm)	0	4

■ *Classic Compared: Baked Rice Pudding*

ROAST GRAVIES

*H*ere is yet another major fat collection point in traditional cooking: gravies made from fat and the juice of meat, drippings released during long, slow roasting.

The classic method for making gravy is to stir flour into the pan and to cook the resulting roux on a stovetop burner for four minutes, then add either a good stock or the water from freshly cooked vegetables and simmer for at least 20 minutes to cook out the raw flour taste. This method will give you several ounces of saturated fat held in suspension in a thick floury gravy—so much for tradition!

You needn't give up gravy for Minimax roasts with this new technique. For liquid, I use either an appropriate stock (chicken for chicken), fresh vegetable cooking water, de-alcoholized wine or mixed fruit juices. This liquid is added to the pan, fat and all; ¼ cup liquid per serving (59 ml) is about right. I pour this through a fat-strainer jug into a small pot and thicken with arrowroot or cornstarch.

The whole process takes two minutes or less, there is very little fat, no floury taste and it takes one tenth the time. It's really up to you to decide whether Minimax is progress!

USES: Whenever you roast any meat or poultry. A gravy is such a welcome "slosh" of nostalgia.

■ Stock, vegetable water or fruit juices are added to roasting pan fats and everything is poured through a sieve into a fat strainer.

■ Here you can see how much fat has floated to the surface and how the meat juices pour from *below* the fat. Wine can be added to gravy at this stage.

■ A skinless roast breast of chicken gets its fat-free gravy thickened slightly with arrowroot. (See page 23.) The vegetables are bistro style. (See page 24.)

ROAST CHICKEN AND VEGETABLES

Serves 4

INGREDIENTS

One 3-pound whole chicken (1.4 kg)

4 large russet potatoes, scrubbed

8 ounces Brussels sprouts (227 gm)

8 ounces carrots (227 gm), peeled and cut in 1-inch pieces

1 cup chicken stock (236 ml) (see page 34)

1 tablespoon arrowroot (15 ml), mixed with 2 tablespoons white wine (30 ml)

1 tablespoon fresh chopped parsley (15 ml)

NOW COOK

■ Preheat oven to 350°F. (180°C). Put the chicken on a rack in a roasting pan and roast until the internal temperature reaches 165°F. (75°C)—about 90 minutes. Put the potatoes in the oven to bake while the chicken is roasting.

■ When the chicken is cooked and taken from the oven, put 1 inch (2.5 cm) of water in a steamer and steam the Brussels sprouts and carrots until tender —about 10 minutes. They should be perfectly cooked when the chicken is ready to serve.

■ To Make the Gravy: Pour as much of the fat as you can out of the pan and reserve for the potatoes. Put the roasting pan on a stovetop burner, pour in the chicken stock, scrape up the pan residues completely and pour through a sieve into a fat strainer. The fat strainer allows the remaining fat to rise to the top, and you are able to utilize only the relatively nonfat juices on the bottom. Pour the juices into a medium-sized saucepan, stopping when you get to the fat layer. Heat juices to a boil.

■ Take the saucepan off of the heat, add the arrowroot slurry, return to the heat and stir until the gravy thickens. You can use fruit juices or vegetable water instead of the wine in the arrowroot slurry, but our signature is the wine splash. Strain out any meat scraps and pour into a serving bowl or gravy boat.

■ Just before serving, slice the potatoes in half lengthwise, put on a baking sheet and brush the exposed surface of each potato with 1 teaspoon (5 ml) of the reserved chicken roasting fat drippings and pop under the broiler until just golden brown —about 4 minutes.

■ To Serve: Put the chicken on a flat surface, remove the skin and separate the chicken into pieces. Trim the leg ends with poultry scissors. Divide the meat, potatoes and vegetables among the 4 plates and spoon on the gravy. Don't forget to sprinkle with the parsley; it distracts attention from the skinless meat.

NOTE: If there are insufficient darkened meat juices in the roasting pan—less than ¼ cup (59 ml)—you can drain off 1 teaspoon (5 ml) of the roasting juices into the skillet. Over high heat, add a sliced onion and cook until it caramelizes and you see brown pan residues—about 10 minutes. Add to the chicken stock, bring to a boil for 1 minute, then strain to clear the gravy of onion pieces.

Nutritional Profile

PER SERVING	CLASSIC	MINIMAX
Calories	507	409
Fat (gm)	18	9
Saturated fat (gm)	8	3
Calories from fat	32%	21%
Cholesterol (mg)	134	103
Sodium (mg)	462	160
Fiber (gm)	6	6

■ *Classic Compared: Chicken with Creamy Gravy*

SOUL FOOD PORK ROAST WITH GLAZED VEGETABLES

What to do when you're not serving a gravy: try a glaze!

Serves 4

INGREDIENTS

1 quart ham hock stock (944 ml) (see page 35)
1 cup dried black-eyed peas (236 ml)
1 teaspoon extra-light olive oil, with a dash of sesame oil (5 ml)
¼ teaspoon freshly ground black pepper (1.25 ml)
Four 4-ounce center-cut pork chops (113 gm each) without bone
One 16-ounce bunch collard greens (454 gm), 8 ounces leaves after trimming (227 gm)
2 cups frozen corn (472 ml)
1 tablespoon freshly squeezed lemon juice (15 ml)
¼ teaspoon cayenne pepper (1.25 ml)
2 tablespoons arrowroot (30 ml), mixed with 4 tablespoons water (60 ml)
Freshly ground black pepper to taste

FIRST PREPARE

■ Make the ham hock stock using 2½ quarts (2.4 l) water instead of 2 quarts (1.9 l). You will need 1½ quarts (1.4 l) when the stock is cooked. Coarsely chop the hock meat and set aside—you should have ½ cup (118 ml).

■ In a large saucepan, pour 3 cups (708 ml) of the stock, add the peas, bring to a boil, reduce the heat and simmer until tender—about 25 minutes.

NOW COOK

■ Preheat the oven to 350°F. (180°C) On a dinner-size plate, pour the oil. Sprinkle on the fresh cracked black pepper. Place an 11-inch (28-cm) ovenproof pan over medium-high heat. Take each pork chop and dredge both sides through the oil and pepper. Place the pork chops in the heated pan, and brown on one side—about 2 minutes. Turn the chops over, put the pan into the preheated oven and cook the chops for 15 minutes. Remove chops from the pan and keep warm.

■ To Make the Glaze: Pour the remaining 3 cups (708 ml) of the ham hock stock into the pan with the roasting juices. Cook on the stovetop over high heat and scrape up the pan residues; pour into a fat strainer.

■ In a large saucepan, heat the pan juices from the fat strainer jug, add the collard greens and the reserved ham hock meat and cook over medium heat for 4 minutes. Add the corn, cooked peas, lemon juice and cayenne pepper. Remove from the heat and add the arrowroot slurry. Stir gently until thickened. Cover and just heat through. Don't stir too roughly or you'll break the peas.

■ To Serve: On dinner plates make a mound of the vegetables and set a chop in the center. Scatter a spoonful of glazed vegetables over each chop and sprinkle with freshly ground black pepper.

Nutritional Profile

PER SERVING	CLASSIC	MINIMAX
Calories	317	440
Fat (gm)	21	11
Saturated fat (gm)	10	3
Calories from fat	61%	22%
Cholesterol (mg)	79	79
Sodium (mg)	482	395
Fiber (gm)	3	16

■ *Classic Compared: Creamed Pork and Peas*

ROAST LAMB WITH APPLE AND ORANGE GRAVY

Serves 6
INGREDIENTS

⅔ cup unsweetened apple juice (156 ml)

⅔ cup unsweetened orange juice (156 ml)

One 3½-pound leg of lamb (1.6 kg)

1 tablespoon all-purpose flour (15 ml)

2 tablespoons arrowroot (30 ml), mixed with
4 tablespoons water (30 ml)

SIDE DISHES: Mashed Yams and Steamed Lemon
Swiss Chard

6 medium yams, scrubbed

Two 16-ounce bunches Swiss chard (454 gm each)

1 tablespoon freshly squeezed lemon juice (15 ml)

FIRST PREPARE

■ Pour half the apple juice and half the orange juice into a medium-sized saucepan, bring to a vigorous boil and reduce to ¼ cup (59 ml)—about 17 minutes. Remove from the heat and let cool.

NOW COOK

■ Preheat the oven to 325°F. (165°C). Pour the reduced juice into a flavor injector (see page 15). Put the lamb on a flat surface and inject all over with small amounts of the juice. Dust lamb with the flour, put on a rack in a roasting pan and roast for 80 minutes. During the roasting time, add ½ cup (118 ml) of water to the roasting pan to keep the pan drippings from burning.

■ While the lamb is cooking prepare the yams and the chard. After the lamb has been cooking for 30 minutes, place the yams in the oven and bake for 40 minutes. Remove from the oven and remove the flesh from the skins and mash. Keep warm until ready to serve. Just before you make the gravy, place the chard in a steamer and steam for 5 minutes; sprinkle with the lemon juice.

■ Remove the lamb from the roasting pan when done and set aside. Put the pan full of cooking juices on the stovetop over medium heat, pour in the remaining apple and orange juices and completely scrape up all the residues. Strain and pour into a fat-strainer jug.

■ Pour the juices from the strainer into a medium-sized saucepan, stopping when you get to the fat, and heat through. Remove from the heat, stir in the arrowroot slurry, return to the heat and stir until thickened. Remove from the heat and set aside.

■ To Serve: Carve the lamb into thin slices, put 3 slices on each plate and cover with the gravy. Spoon a mound of yams and one of chard on the side.

Nutritional Profile

PER SERVING	CLASSIC	MINIMAX
Calories	1431	718
Fat (gm)	91	25
Saturated fat (gm)	40	9
Calories from fat	57%	31%
Cholesterol (mg)	403	243
Sodium (mg)	298	427
Fiber (gm)	3	7

■ *Classic Compared: Roast Lamb with Potatoes and Vegetables*

WHITE SAUCE

Whenever I'm asked to name my favorite dish, my mind turns to creamy white-sauced anything! I don't mean sauces that mask or obscure the taste of the star attraction. What I really admire is the combination of a dairy product, concentrated stocks, fresh herbs and a splash of wine. These supersauces, in their classic constructions, include butter and flour (roux) and whole milk, half-and-half, heavy cream or egg yolks. No wonder the mouthroundfullness is attractive—there's all that fat to carry the flavor.

I looked for a "white dairy" appearance and velvet texture without the fat and experimented with a number of alternatives until I found smooth tasting, nonfat, strained yogurt (see page 84). The straining process makes yogurt into a dense, white, almost cream cheese-like, dairy product. I kept the classic reduced stock base with herbal enhancement and thickened it with cornstarch and added a splash of de-alcoholized wine.

There are some important points to note in following the recipe for Basic White Sauce that relate to temperature, seasoning and holding time, but one run-through should make you an expert.

The recipes that follow show you how to adapt the basic sauce for use with creamy pastas and a comfort-food alternative to the classic chicken à la king.

USES: Literally can be used almost anywhere in a menu. It is an excellent alternative to creamy white sauces, both sweet and savory. Try it with fettucine, in place of Alfredo sauce, or as a coating sauce on chicken breast or poached fish. Always season the sauce well with fresh herbs and garnish it for color and texture—such as with capers and sweet red peppers. If you enjoy using this sauce, you've made a major dent in your old fat habits.

■ You may vary the kind of stock to boost the flavor of the main ingredient, i.e., fish stock for seafood. When you have added the cornstarch slurry, bring the sauce back to a boil for 30 seconds to clear the raw starch taste. It is *very* thick.

■ Add your favorite seasoning garnish—fresh herbs, peppers, capers, etc. Cool the sauce quickly with a couple of ice cubes to not more than 105°F. (40°C). If you don't have a thermometer, just plunge your finger in—it's ready if you don't yell "ow"! Make sure it's cool—too much heat and the yogurt will break into tiny pieces.

■ Now you can add the strained yogurt. Fold it in gently —too much heating will reduce the mouthfeel. Cornstarch can lose its consistency after prolonged heating. It's best to make this sauce just before it's needed or keep cool and gently reheat without boiling.

BASIC WHITE SAUCE

Yield: 2½ cups (590 ml)

INGREDIENTS

3 cups chicken stock (708 ml) (see page 34)

3 tablespoons cornstarch (45 ml), mixed with 6 tablespoons de-alcoholized white wine (90 ml)

1 cup strained yogurt (236 ml), at room temperature (see page 85)

1 tablespoon fresh finely chopped parsley (15 ml)

⅛ teaspoon freshly grated nutmeg (0.6 ml)

⅛ teaspoon freshly ground salt (0.6 ml)

⅛ teaspoon freshly ground white pepper (0.6 ml)

NOW COOK

■ Pour the chicken stock into a medium-sized saucepan, bring to a boil and reduce by half—about 10 minutes. Remove from the heat; whisk in the cornstarch slurry, return to the heat and boil for 30 seconds until clear and thick, stirring constantly. Remove from the heat and let the sauce cool.

■ Put the yogurt in a small bowl and stir gently until all the lumps are gone. Stir the yogurt into the cooled sauce. Reheat the sauce slowly over low heat and add the parsley, nutmeg, salt and white pepper. Serve with your favorite fish or white meat.

Nutritional Profile

PER SERVING	CLASSIC	MINIMAX
Calories	179	89
Fat (gm)	14	1
Saturated fat (gm)	9	0
Calories from fat	70%	8%
Cholesterol (mg)	39	1
Sodium (mg)	566	157
Fiber	0	0

■ *Classic Compared: Béchamel Sauce*

"I REMEMBER" CHICKEN WITH NOODLES

After tasting this dish, my senior food assistant assures me that it's a taste he remembers from his childhood: the kind of dish he craved after a hard soccer practice. This Minimax version is the real thing folks: heartwarming sauce, comforting chicken, colorful peas and carrots.

Serves 4

INGREDIENTS

One 3½-pound whole chicken (1.6 kg)

1 bouquet garni (see page 36)

1 recipe Basic White Sauce with an additional ⅛ teaspoon salt (0.6 ml)

8 ounces diced carrots (227 gm), diced the same size as the peas

8 ounces frozen peas (227 gm)

2 tablespoons fresh chopped parsley (30 ml)

6 cups hot cooked white rice (1.4 l)

FIRST PREPARE

■ The Stock: Here is a simple, easy way to make a light stock and cook your chicken at the same time: rinse the chicken, put it in a large saucepan and cover with cold water. Add the bouquet garni, bring to a boil, reduce the heat and simmer gently for 1 hour and 15 minutes, occasionally skimming the surface. Drain, reserving both the stock and the chicken. For this recipe, pour 3 cups (708 ml) into a fat-strainer jug (see special equipment, page 12) and freeze the rest for later use.

■ The Chicken: To serve 4 ounces (113 gm) of chicken per person, remove the meat from the bone, discarding the fat, skin and bones. The thigh meat will fall naturally into the muscles of which it's comprised. Take the breast meat and break it into roughly 2-inch (5-cm) pieces.

NOW COOK

■ Make the Basic White Sauce, using the reserved chicken stock in the fat strainer.

■ Steam the carrots for 6 minutes, add the frozen peas and steam for an additional 2 minutes. The carrots should be cooked, but crunchy.

- Pour the Basic White Sauce into a large saucepan and stir in the chicken meat, steamed vegetables and the parsley and heat slowly over low heat.

- To Serve: Divide the rice among individual dinner plates and spoon on the sauced chicken and vegetables.

Nutritional Profile

PER SERVING	CLASSIC	MINIMAX
Calories	839	683
Fat (gm)	29	7
Saturated fat (gm)	15	2
Calories from fat	31%	9%
Cholesterol (mg)	159	63
Sodium (mg)	502	369
Fiber (gm)	5	6

- *Classic Compared: Creamed Chicken with Peas*

CREAMY PASTA PRIMAVERA

Serves 4
INGREDIENTS

8 ounces penne pasta (227 gm)
8 ounces cauliflower florets (227 gm)
8 ounces diagonally sliced carrots (227 gm)
8 ounces broccoli florets (227 gm)
4 ounces diagonally sliced zucchini (113 gm)
1 recipe Basic White Sauce
¼ cup fresh chopped basil (59 ml)
¼ cup freshly grated Parmesan cheese (59 ml)

GARNISH

4 tablespoons freshly grated Parmesan cheese (60 ml)
Freshly ground black pepper to taste

NOW COOK

- Cook the penne according to the package directions, drain and set aside. Keep warm.

- Steam the vegetables in the following order: Start with the cauliflower and carrots and steam for 5 minutes; add the broccoli and zucchini to the same steamer and steam for an additional 5 minutes. Remove from the heat and set aside (but not for long).

- Just before serving, in a medium-sized saucepan, make the Basic White Sauce and stir in the basil and the cheese. Remove 1 cup (236 ml) and set aside.

- To Serve: Put the penne in a large hot bowl, pour in the sauce from the saucepan and toss the penne until well coated. (This is not globs and globs of sauce; each piece of penne is perfectly coated and glistens.) Divide the sauced pasta among individual dinner plates and surround with a colorful crescent of vegetables. Drizzle with the reserved sauce and dust with the Parmesan cheese. A little coarsely ground black pepper adds visual interest and a zesty bite to each forkful.

NOTE: If you take basil leaves and put them into a ½ cup (118 ml) measure, loosely packed, you'll get exactly ¼ cup (59 ml) when chopped.

Nutritional Profile

PER SERVING	CLASSIC	MINIMAX
Calories	1723	419
Fat (gm)	130	5
Saturated fat (gm)	80	2
Calories from fat	68%	11%
Cholesterol (mg)	435	9
Sodium (mg)	2144	408
Fiber (gm)	7	9

- *Classic Compared: Noodles Alfredo*

STOCKS

I am absolutely convinced than any savory Minimax recipe that calls for stock, regardless of its kind, means exactly what it says. You can, of course, add water instead; that is your privilege. You can claim that stock takes too long to make, and millions will agree. But over the years, as I've replaced flavor-carrying fat in my recipes, I have found that water just doesn't make the grade. Therefore, if you are going to follow any part of this book, this is the essential *section.*

I have done everything possible to simplify the process of making stocks and to keep the seasonings standard. But you should feel free to add your own seasoning twists . . . after *you have tried mine, please!*

Important points to remember:

■ Never use scraps to make stock. *The stockpot is not a stopover spot en route to the garbage. The best stock comes from the best and freshest ingredients.*

■ Use fresh herbs whenever possible. *Bay leaves are the exception. At the end of this section I've given you a variety of bouquets garnis (bunches of herbs) for different dishes.*

■ Simmer, don't boil. *No more than twenty-five minutes for fish bones; not less than sixty minutes for chicken or two hours for beef (unless pressure cooked). These times are to create poaching liquids or soup stock that will later be reduced for sauces.*

■ Sauce stocks need longer simmering. *Chicken from two to four hours; beef from four to eight hours, depending upon your commitment and the level of appreciation you get from your guests!*

■ Skim as you go. *Keep skimming the surface for coagulated protein foam. I use a special skimmer and a fat-strainer jug so that I can use the liquid with the least amount of fat. Skimming helps to reduce the time it takes to make stock since it eliminates the need for a cooling period to let the fat rise to the surface and solidify to the point at which it can be easily removed.*

■ When it's ready, strain it! *Don't let it hang around full of useless vegetables and soured bones. Strain the stock and cool it, or freeze for later use.*

■ Try making twice the amount. *Freeze the leftover stock in ice cube trays and store the cubes in plastic bags. Stock will keep up to a week in the refrigerator and six months in the freezer. Remember to label each bag with the type and date.*

USES: Whenever you are tempted to add water to poach fish or poultry, please use stock. Also, many vegetarian dishes are greatly enhanced by using a good vegetable stock. With this Minimax tool at your side you can cheerfully cut fat by up to 50 percent without losing flavor.

■ If you buy a whole chicken, it is easy to cut off the legs and thighs and (with a *little* practice) to remove the breasts. The bonus you get, apart from at least 7 to 8 cents a pound savings, is a free carcass that will make at least 4 cups (944 ml) of *great* stock.

■ After boiling, surface protein coagulates as a foam on the surface. This should be skimmed off occasionally throughout the simmering process. I skim into a fat strainer, so I can return the extra juice to the pot.

■ Some dishes have obscured (not clear) sauces, and straining the clear stock through the cheesecloth is not essential. I do it as a matter of *habit* because I want the best possible flavors and absolutely no odd bits of overcooked debris *anywhere!*

BASIC CHICKEN OR TURKEY STOCK

Makes 4 cups (944 ml)
INGREDIENTS

1 teaspoon extra-light olive oil, with a dash of sesame oil (5 ml)
1 onion, peeled and chopped
½ cup coarsely chopped celery tops (118 ml)
1 cup coarsely chopped carrots (236 ml)
Carcass from a whole chicken or turkey
1 bay leaf
2 sprigs fresh thyme
4 sprigs fresh parsley
6 black peppercorns
2 whole cloves

NOW COOK

■ Pour the oil into a large stockpot over medium heat, add the onion, celery and carrots and fry to release their volatile oils—about 5 minutes. Add the chicken bones and seasonings, cover with 8 cups (1.9 l) water, bring to a boil, reduce the heat and simmer for 2 to 4 hours, adding water if needed. Skim off any foam that rises to the surface. After 1 hour, add 1 cup (236 ml) of cold water— this will force fat in the liquid to rise to the surface so you can remove it.

■ Strain; use with relative abandon.

BASIC BEEF, LAMB OR VEAL STOCK

Makes 4 cups (944 ml)
INGREDIENTS

1 pound beef, lamb or veal bones (454 gm), fat trimmed off

1 teaspoon extra-light olive oil, with a dash of sesame oil (5 ml)

1 onion, peeled and coarsely chopped

½ cup coarsely chopped celery tops (118 ml)

1 cup coarsely chopped carrots (236 ml)

1 bay leaf

2 sprigs fresh thyme

6 black peppercorns

2 whole cloves

NOW COOK

■ Preheat the oven to 375°F. (190°C). Place the beef, lamb or veal bones in a roasting pan and cook until nicely browned—about 25 minutes. The browning produces a richer flavor and deeper color in the final stock.

■ Pour the oil into a large stockpot and fry the vegetables, releasing their volatile oils, for 5 minutes. Add the bones and the seasonings, cover with 8 cups (1.9 l) water, bring to a boil, reduce the heat and simmer 4 to 8 hours, adding more water if necessary. Skim off any foam that rises to the surface.

■ Strain and you've got a marvelous Minimax tool.

QUICK BEEF STOCK IN A PRESSURE COOKER

Makes 4 cups (944 ml)
SAME INGREDIENTS AS FOR BASIC BEEF STOCK (minus the carrots)

NOW COOK

■ Brown the bones in the oven as for Basic Beef Stock.

■ Pour the oil into a pressure cooker over medium heat and fry the onion and celery tops for 5 minutes. Add the browned bones and the seasonings, cover with 6 cups (1.4 l) of water, fasten the lid, bring to steam, lower the heat and cook for 40 minutes from when the cooker starts hissing.

■ Remove from the heat, leave the lid on and let cool naturally—about 30 minutes. Strain—you will have about 4 cups (944 ml) of stock.

NOTE: Whenever you're using a pressure cooker, check your manufacturer's instruction book for maximum levels of liquids, etc.

BASIC HAM HOCK STOCK

Makes 6 cups (1.4 l)
INGREDIENTS

One 1 pound ham hock (454 gm)

1 bay leaf

3 whole cloves

NOW COOK

■ In a pressure cooker, cover the ham hock with 2 quarts (1.9 l) of cold water, bring to a boil, remove from the heat and drain, discarding the water. Put the ham hock back in the pressure cooker, add the bay leaf and cloves, pour in 2 quarts (1.9 l) of water, fasten the lid and put over high heat. When the cooker starts hissing, turn the heat down to medium low and let simmer 30 minutes. Strain and have at it.

BASIC FISH
OR SHRIMP STOCK

Makes 4 cups (944 ml)
INGREDIENTS

1 teaspoon extra-light olive oil, with a dash of sesame oil (5 ml)

1 onion, peeled and coarsely chopped

½ cup coarsely chopped celery tops (118 ml)

2 sprigs fresh thyme

1 bay leaf

1 pound fish bones (no heads) or shrimp shells (454 gm)

6 black peppercorns

2 whole cloves

NOW COOK

■ Pour the oil into a large saucepan and sauté the onion, celery tops, thyme and bay leaf until the onion is translucent—about 5 minutes. To ensure a light-colored stock, be careful not to brown.

■ Add the fish bones or shrimp shells, peppercorns and cloves, cover with 5 cups (1.2 l) water, bring to a boil, reduce the heat and simmer for 25 minutes. Strain through a fine-mesh sieve and cheesecloth.

BASIC VEGETABLE STOCK

Makes 4 cups (944 ml)
INGREDIENTS

1 teaspoon extra-light olive oil, with a dash of sesame oil (5 ml)

½ cup coarsely chopped onion (118 ml)

2 cloves garlic, peeled and smashed

½ teaspoon freshly grated gingerroot (2.5 ml)

½ cup coarsely chopped carrot (118 ml)

1 cup coarsely chopped celery (236 ml)

1 cup coarsely chopped turnip (236 ml)

¼ cup coarsely chopped leeks (59 ml), white and light green parts only

3 sprigs fresh parsley

½ teaspoon black peppercorns (2.5 ml)

NOW COOK

■ Pour the oil into a large stockpot over medium heat, add the onion and garlic and fry for 5 minutes. Add the rest of the ingredients, cover with 5 cups (1.2 l) water, bring to a boil, reduce the heat and simmer for 30 minutes. Strain, and great flavor is at your fingertips.

EASY QUICK ENHANCED
CANNED STOCKS

INGREDIENTS

Canned stock
Bouquet garni

NOW COOK

■ Pour the canned stock into a saucepan, add the appropriate bouquet garni, bring to a boil, reduce the heat and simmer 30 minutes. Strain and move forward, enhanced, of course.

Basic Bouquet Garni: For ease of operation, I suggest you use our basic "bunch of herbs": 1 bay leaf, 2 sprigs fresh thyme (1 teaspoon dried), 6 black peppercorns, 2 whole cloves, 3 sprigs parsley.

■ For Poultry: Add a 4-inch branch (10 cm) of tarragon (2 teaspoons dried) or 6 sage leaves (1 teaspoon dried).

■ For Fish; Use either a few small branches of fennel or of dill, incorporated into the basic bunch of herbs.

■ For Beef: Use a few branches of marjoram or rosemary incorporated into the basic bunch of herbs.

I let my herb bunches go around twice when I use them to flavor a canned broth. In this case, I simply simmer for up to 20 minutes and then put it into a sealable plastic bag and keep it deep-frozen until its next appearance. Do be sure to label it: frozen herb bags could be a disappointing late-night microwave snack for twenty-first-century teenagers!

REDUCTIONS

A great deal of attention has been given to "reductions" over the past ten years, by professional chefs, working in commercial kitchens where they have a ready availability of well-made stocks. By simply boiling the stock until it reduces in volume, they get reductions: dense, flavor-packed liquids that are used instead of fats to carry flavor.

In the home kitchen we seem less and less inclined to use stocks and therefore the reduction technique is seldom used. What a pity—it's a great idea, and it works so well.

The first recipe here uses reduced chicken stock to cook an unusually delicious collection of vegetables garnished with some previously cooked chicken. Using the same idea but with less reduction, you get a pasta dish studded with parsnip, ham hock and parsley and, last but never least, there's a bold experiment that pits a saffron sauce made with reduced fish stock (fumet) against the classic butter sauce used over a fillet of sole.

You'll be more likely to use reductions if you make extra stock on each occasion by doubling the recipe. The extra can then be put in sealable plastic bags and frozen. Don't forget to mark them with a freezer pencil, as all stocks tend to look alike.

USES: Whenever you might add butter or extra oil to a pan to get food "glistening" you can add a stock reduction instead. It is also useful to add to skillets to lift off the glaze that is left behind after pan broiling or "light" sautéing (shallow frying with little fat).

■ We're taking it down beyond 50 percent reduction in order to concentrate the flavor and to establish the viscosity. If you were to take a little of the final liquid and brush it on your lips, they'd stick together. It's this viscosity that allows it to take the place of oil—a *super reduction!*

■ After you have panfried any small veal slice, pork tenderloin, chicken breast, etc., remove the meat from the pan and blot away the extra fat. Then add the reduction to *clean* the pan and pick up the extra flavor from the residue.

■ Add the vegetables, and simmer them quickly in the reduced stock. Eventually they are glossed with a small amount of arrowroot-thickened sauce and served over the meat.

CHICKEN STIR-BOIL

Serves 4
INGREDIENTS

2 cups chicken stock (472 ml) (see page 34)

¼ teaspoon extra-light olive oil, with a dash of sesame oil (1.25 ml)

Four 6-ounce chicken breasts (170 gm each), with skin, boneless

¼ cup water (59 ml)

8 ounces fresh mushrooms (227 gm), quartered

8 ounces frozen lima beans (227 gm)

One 8-ounce can whole water chestnuts (227 gm), drained

1 tablespoon fresh chopped dill (15 ml)

1 tablespoon freshly squeezed lemon juice (15 ml)

¼ teaspoon freshly ground salt (1.25 ml)

¼ teaspoon freshly ground black pepper (1.25 ml)

¼ teaspoon cayenne pepper (1.25 ml)

2 teaspoons arrowroot (10 ml), mixed with 1 teaspoon water (15 ml)

NOW COOK

■ Pour the chicken stock into a large skillet and boil until reduced to ½ cup (118 ml)—about 15 minutes.

■ While the stock is reducing, brush a large skillet over medium-high heat with the oil and place the chicken breasts skin side down in the skillet to brown, turning them every 2 minutes, for a total of 10 minutes. In cooking the chicken with the skin on, less moisture is lost, resulting in a plumper, juicier chicken breast. Remove from the heat, transfer chicken to a plate, and pull off the skin and discard. Slice the chicken into 2-inch x ½-inch (5-cm x 1.5-cm) strips. If you see a little pink color, don't worry, the chicken will cook a bit more in the next step. Blot the skillet with a paper towel to absorb the excess fat.

■ Pour the water into the skillet and deglaze over high heat, scraping all the residues up into the liquid, then pour in the reduced chicken broth. The moment it comes to a boil, add the mushrooms, lima beans and water chestnuts and "stir-boil" until just tender—about 5 minutes. Stir in the cooked chicken and just heat through. Sprinkle with the dill, lemon juice, salt, black pepper and cayenne pepper and stir well.

■ Remove from the heat and tip the pan so that the juices collect in a clear space, add the arrowroot slurry, return to the heat and stir until thickened. Serve in bowls and don't miss a single drop!

Nutritional Profile

PER SERVING	CLASSIC	MINIMAX
Calories	851	305
Fat (gm)	39	6
Saturated fat (gm)	18	2
Calories from fat	42%	16%
Cholesterol (mg)	193	86
Sodium (mg)	1568	282
Fiber (gm)	4	5

■ *Classic Compared: Chicken Tetrazzini*

SWEET STUFF PASTA

Serves 4
INGREDIENTS

20 ounces parsnips (567 gm), trimmed, peeled and finely chopped

1 quart ham hock stock (944 ml) (see page 35)

8 ounces ham hock meat (227 gm) (from the stock recipe), diced the same size as the parsnips

8 ounces dried angel hair pasta (227 gm)

2 tablespoons arrowroot (30 ml), mixed with 4 tablespoons water (60 ml)

2 tablespoons fresh chopped parsley (30 ml)

GARNISH:

Freshly ground black pepper

4 tablespoons freshly grated dry cheese, (optional) (60 ml)

NOW COOK

■ Put the parsnips in a large saucepan, cover with 1 quart (955 ml) water, bring to a boil, reduce the heat and simmer 15 minutes. Drain and set aside, reserving both the liquid and the parsnips.

■ Pour the ham hock stock into a saucepan, bring to a boil, and reduce by half to 2 cups (472 ml)—about 15 minutes. Add the ham hock meat and parsnips, stir until completely incorporated, then simmer for 4 minutes.

■ At the same time that you add the parsnips and ham to the stock, bring the reserved parsnip water to a boil, add the pasta and cook until just tender —4 minutes. Stir it well so it doesn't stick to the bottom of the pan. Drain through a colander into a large serving bowl. (You can warm it this way.) Pour out the water in the warmed serving bowl and put the cooked pasta into the heated bowl.

■ Remove ham hock-parsnip mixture from the heat, add the arrowroot slurry, return to the heat and stir until thickened. Stir in the parsley.

■ To Serve: Pour the sauce into the pasta, toss and eat with reckless abandon. Garnish with pepper and a whisper of cheese. (Depends upon whether you are hard of hearing or not . . . a whisper for me is 1 level tablespoon [15 ml]. A whisper will increase your fat by 1.5 grams per serving. If you leave it out, the calories from fat are reduced to 12 percent.)

Nutritional Profile

PER SERVING	CLASSIC	MINIMAX
Calories	1054	503
Fat (gm)	67	11
Saturated fat (gm)	38	4
Calories from fat	57%	19%
Cholesterol (mg)	320	27
Sodium (mg)	1542	1003
Fiber (gm)	8	9

■ *Classic Compared: Pasta with Prosciutto and Peas*

SIMPLY "SQUISITO" SOLE

It's important to know that squisito is Italian for "exquisite"—a word that I hope you'll use often, after sampling dishes from this book . . .

Serves 4
INGREDIENTS

½ teaspoon extra-light olive oil, with a dash of sesame oil (2.5 ml)
Four 6-ounce fresh sole fillets (170 gm each)
¼ teaspoon freshly ground salt (1.25 ml)
¼ teaspoon freshly ground black pepper (1.25 ml)

2 cups very clear fish stock (see page 36)
8 small red new potatoes, steamed until tender
8 ounces green beans (227 gm)
1/16 teaspoon powdered saffron (0.3 ml)
1 teaspoon fresh chopped dill weed, (5 ml) (not the stalks)
1 tablespoon arrowroot (15 ml), mixed with 2 tablespoons reserved fish stock (30 ml)
½ teaspoon freshly squeezed lemon juice (2.5 ml)

FIRST PREPARE

■ Brush a 9 x 13-inch (23 x 33-cm) baking sheet with the oil. Lay the sole fillets on it and sprinkle with half of the salt and half of the pepper. Brush the fillets with a little fish stock.

NOW COOK

■ Pour a small amount of water in the bottom of a steamer pot (see page 62) and bring to a boil. Put the potatoes in the first rack, insert in the pot, cover and steam 10 minutes. Now add the beans to the second rack and steam both 5 minutes more until done.

■ Preheat broiler. Pour the fish stock into a medium-sized skillet, bring to a boil and reduce by half to 1 cup (236 ml)—about 5 minutes. Remove from the heat.

■ While the stock is reducing, pop the fish under the broiler to cook until tender—about 5 minutes.

■ Add the saffron, dill and the arrowroot slurry, return to medium heat and stir until thickened. Stir in the lemon juice and the remaining salt and pepper. A golden, "buttery" sauce!

■ To Serve: Divide the fish and steamed vegetables among 4 dinner plates and coat liberally with the sauce. Serve *very hot,* please!

Nutritional Profile

PER SERVING	CLASSIC	MINIMAX
Calories	557	371
Fat (gm)	25	3
Saturated fat (gm)	15	1
Calories from fat	41%	7%
Cholesterol (mg)	142	80
Sodium (mg)	300	295
Fiber (gm)	6	6

■ *Classic Compared: Sole with Dill Butter*

DE-ALCOHOLIZED WINES

S*ince 1974, I've been trying to find ways to convert "habits that hurt" into "provisions that heal." These experiments have obviously involved curtailing the excessive use of fat, salt (sodium), sugars and alcohol.*

I've included alcohol because its consumption can provoke serious reactions that are indeed harmful both physically and often socially to at least thirty-five million alcohol-sensitive people in North America alone. It was simply not consistent for me to deal with salt, fat and sugars and not with alcohol.

It is true that moderate alcoholic intake (no more than two glasses of wine or beer or one single measure of spirits a day) can be beneficial to some people who are not alcohol sensitive, and so, it must be your choice whether you include alcohol in your diet or not.

In place of alcoholic wine, I use a wine initially made the traditional way, with an alcohol content. It is then processed by reverse osmosis to remove the alcohol. At the time of writing, I have found that some de-alcoholized wines made by boiling off the alcohol are truly dreadful, and since I don't want you to ruin your food with them, I strongly suggest you use Ariel brand wines, from the Napa Valley in California. Their eleven classic and blended wines are a standard for this new industry. This means that you have a full range of wines that you can add to food, or drink with food, without concern.

USES: In the following recipes, I've used de-alcoholized wines in three different cooking methods to maximize flavor: first, in a deglazing method; second, as a braise liquid; and last, as a "splash" used in making a sauce thickener. As you'll see, it's truly amazing how aromatic and delicious dishes are when enhanced with wine— truly a perfume of the palate.

I also see offering a good de-alcoholized wine at the table as a mark of gracious hospitality toward those who, for one reason or another, place their hand over their glass in the international gesture for "I pass."

■ The key to deglazing lies in the residues left in the pan by meat after browning. Blot up excess fat from the pan with a paper towel, then, over high heat, pour in the wine and stock, scraping all the residue possible into the liquid. The resulting "broth" packs maximum flavor with minimum fat.

■ Braising meats does not mean "drowning" them in wine and stock. A good rule is to have the liquid reach halfway up the meat in the *smallest* pan possible that will hold all the ingredients.

■ This is my favorite way of bringing the fragrance of wine to the table—a last minute splash. Just before serving, I thicken the cooking liquid with a wine-starch slurry to create an aromatic, thick sauce.

QUICK BRAISED PORK LOIN

Serves 4
INGREDIENTS

Four 4-ounce pork chops (113 gm each), center loin

1 teaspoon extra-light olive oil, with a dash of sesame oil (5 ml)

1 cup de-alcoholized dry white wine (236 ml)

1 cup chicken stock (236 ml) (see page 34)

8 ounces carrots (227 gm), cut into matchsticks

8 medium fresh mushrooms, cut into quarters

2 teaspoons fresh chopped thyme (10 ml)

¼ teaspoon freshly ground black pepper (1.25 ml)

⅛ teaspoon freshly ground salt (0.6 ml)

2 teaspoons shredded orange zest (10 ml)

4 ounces penne pasta (113 gm)

8 ounces green beans (227 gm)

1 tablespoon arrowroot (15 ml), mixed with 2 tablespoons de-alcoholized dry white wine (30 ml)

GARNISH:

Minced fresh thyme

NOW COOK

■ Preheat the oven to 400°F. (205°C). Dab the meat with a paper towel to remove the surface moisture. Brush the oil evenly over the bottom of a large skillet over medium-high heat, brown the chops for 2 minutes on each side, then transfer to a plate.

■ There should be a dark brown residue on the bottom of the pan. Blot with a paper towel to remove excess fat, then deglaze pan with the wine and chicken stock, stirring until all the residue has been scraped up into the liquid. Return the pork to the liquid (the liquid should come about halfway up the pork chops), add the carrots and mushrooms, trying as much as possible to

submerge them in the liquid. Sprinkle with the thyme, pepper, salt and orange zest, bring to a boil, cover, pop in the preheated oven and bake 10 minutes.

■ Cook the penne according to the package directions, drain and set aside.

■ After the pork's been baking 5 minutes, start steaming the green beans on the stovetop—they will be ready at the same time.

■ Remove the pork from the oven and remove the green beans from the heat. The handle on the skillet is now 400°F. (205°C), so drape a towel over it to remind yourself! Transfer the pork to a plate and cover to keep warm.

■ To make a great sauce, return the skillet with the liquid and carrots and mushrooms to the stovetop, bring to a boil, remove from the heat and stir in the arrowroot slurry made with the de-alcoholized wine splash. Return to the heat, stirring until thickened. Stir in the pork, green beans and pasta and just heat through.

■ To Serve: Divide the pork, pasta and vegetables among 4 dinner plates. Cover with any sauce remaining in the pan and sprinkle with a whisper of minced thyme.

Nutritional Profile

PER SERVING	CLASSIC	MINIMAX
Calories	712	398
Fat (gm)	45	11
Saturated fat (gm)	21	3
Calories from fat	57%	25%
Cholesterol (mg)	135	79
Sodium (mg)	521	177
Fiber (gm)	5	5

■ *Classic Compared: Gruyère Glazed Pork Chops*

COQ AU VIN

A recipe that can be prepared ahead of time and easily reheated for your guests. A special aspect of this Coq au Vin is that you strip the hens of their fatty skins and small bones. It takes fifteen minutes for four portions and reduces the fat content significantly. Since you win from both presentation and fat viewpoints, I call this a "double benefit" and, therefore, well worth the time.

Serves 4
INGREDIENTS

1½ teaspoons extra-light olive oil, with a dash of sesame oil (7.5 ml)

4 medium Cornish game hens, necks removed

4 small yellow onions, peeled and beards trimmed as close to the end of the onion as possible

2 cups ham hock stock (472 ml), plus meat from cooked ham hock (see page 35)

2 cups de-alcoholized red wine (472 ml)

8 ounces whole red new potatoes (227 gm)

8 ounces turnips (227 gm), peeled

8 medium fresh mushrooms

3 tablespoons arrowroot (45 ml), mixed with 6 tablespoons de-alcoholized red wine (90 ml)

GARNISH:

Fresh chopped parsley

¼ teaspoon freshly ground salt (1.25 ml)

¼ teaspoon freshly ground black pepper (1.25 ml)

NOW COOK

■ Heat ½ teaspoon (2.5 ml) of the oil in a small skillet over medium heat and brown the hens, breast side down, 1 or 2 at a time (whatever fits in your skillet)—about 5 minutes. Remove and set aside. Don't wash the skillet, yet!

■ Pour the remaining teaspoon (5 ml) of the oil into a large Dutch oven over medium-high heat, add the onions and cook to release the volatile oils —about 5 minutes. Remove and set aside. Add the browned hens, stock, ham, wine, potatoes, turnips, onions and mushrooms, cover and cook over medium heat until tender—about 45 minutes. The vegetables will actually steam bake on top of the birds.

■ Using a slotted spoon, transfer the cooked vegetables and ham into a bowl. Don't worry about the red color—that's just the blush from the red wine and traditional with all coq au vin. Transfer the hens to a plate.

■ Strain the cooking liquid into a fat-strainer jug— you should have 6 cups (1.4 l). Rinse the Dutch oven and return to the heat. Pour in the cooking liquid, (but not the fat) bring to a boil and reduce by half to 3 cups (708 ml)—about 15 minutes.

■ While the cooking liquid is reducing, get a bowl of ice water ready to keep your fingers cool while removing the skin from the hens. Basically, you want to remove the skin and unsightly bones from the legs, wings and breast meat.

Start by putting the hens on a flat surface and breaking off the thighs. Now remove the skin, dipping your fingers in the water when they feel too warm. If you have a pair of poultry scissors, you might want to clip the ends of the legs. When the breasts are cool enough to handle, run a fine-bladed knife on either side of the breast bone and sever the wing from the wishbone. Use your thumb to peel back the 2 plump breasts from the rib cage and detach them from the wing end—you'll have 2 perfectly formed pieces of breast.

Since these hens reheat beautifully, this chore can easily be done ahead of time.

■ Remove the reduced cooking liquid from the heat, stir in the arrowroot slurry, return to the heat and stir until thickened. Add the prepared hen pieces and the vegetables and ham to the sauce, stir gently and heat through.

■ To Serve: Spoon the Coq au Vin onto dinner plates, coat with additional sauce and dust with the parsley, salt and pepper.

Nutritional Profile

PER SERVING	CLASSIC	MINIMAX
Calories	885	775
Fat (gm)	42	24
Saturated fat (gm)	18	7
Calories from fat	42%	28%
Cholesterol (mg)	289	228
Sodium (mg)	998	694
Fiber (gm)	3	5

■ *Classic Compared: Coq au Vin*

GLAZED HALIBUT FILLETS

Serves 4
INGREDIENTS

4 small sprigs fresh dill
1 bay leaf
4 small sprigs fresh thyme
3 whole cloves
Four 6-ounce halibut fillets (170 gm each)
Zest of ½ lemon, cut into small pieces
2 crookneck squash, coarsely chopped
2 sweet red bell peppers, seeded and coarsely chopped
1 zucchini, coarsely chopped
2 cups hot cooked white rice

GLAZE:

½ cup de-alcoholized white wine (118 ml)
2 teaspoons cornstarch (10 ml), mixed with 1 tablespoon de-alcoholized white wine (15 ml)
1 tablespoon fresh chopped dill (15 ml)

GARNISH:

Fresh chopped dill
Freshly ground black pepper

NOW COOK

■ Pour about ½ inch (1.5 cm) of water into a large steamer pot, add the dill, bay leaf, thyme and cloves and bring to a vigorous boil for 2 minutes.

■ Arrange the halibut on a steamer tray, evenly distribute the lemon zest on top of the fillets and insert tray in the pot. Put the vegetables on a second steamer tray, making sure the crookneck squash is on the bottom, skin side down, then layer the zucchini and red peppers. Place the vegetable tray on top of the fish tray, cover and steam for 8 minutes.

■ Remove the cooked fish and vegetables in their steamer trays, cover and set aside for 2 minutes to cook through. This is important because the fish isn't completely done when you take it out of the steamer pot.

■ The Glaze: Strain the liquid from the steamer into a bowl. Rinse the same pot and return it to the heat. Pour in ½ cup (118 ml) of the steaming liquid and the wine, bring to a boil and reduce to about ½ cup (118 ml)—about 5 minutes.

■ Remove from the heat, stir in the cornstarch slurry and the dill, return to the heat and stir until thickened—about 30 seconds.

■ To Serve: Arrange the halibut, vegetables and rice on dinner plates. Brush the fish and vegetables with the glaze and sprinkle with dill and pepper to taste.

Nutritional Profile

PER SERVING	CLASSIC	MINIMAX
Calories	780	380
Fat (gm)	27	3
Saturated fat (gm)	15	1
Calories from fat	31%	8%
Cholesterol (mg)	142	95
Sodium (mg)	295	159
Fiber (gm)	0	5

■ *Classic Compared: Glazed Cod with Dill Butter*

POP (PERFUMES OF THE PALATE)

This method of using herbs and spices comes from garam masala, the mixture of pulverized warming spices of India that is added to a dish just before serving. The uprush of aromats is tantalizing!

But it seems strange to use an Indian term for a seasoning over apples and custard, or even more so when in a Louisiana gumbo! So can I get away with the acronym "POP," standing for "Perfumes of the Palate?" We talk about colors popping out in a photograph; why not aromas popping out of a dish?

In this method, I use a small electric coffee mill to grind the seasonings and keep it for this designated use only. After each unique POP spice mixture has been blended, I put a few bread crusts in the mill and give it a whiz, making it fresh and clean for the next experiment and making wonderful bread crumbs!

USES: Once you've used the basic POP ideas suggested here you could become a POP star in your own right. Imagine fresh, heady, aromatic thermals rising from your own creations. The applications are literally without limit. Remember the spices are warm, not hot; their role is to provoke like perfume, not to grab you by the throat and make your eyes water.

■ Here are just a few of the myriad number of aromats, both herbs and spices, that can be used for POP. In general it helps to keep them as dry as possible so that sprinkling can take place, i.e., powdered ginger is better than fresh. Nutmeg is best when freshly grated or shaved.

■ Even with fresh herbs added, you can still get a light, easy-to-sprinkle mix. I whiz it long enough to completely break up the hard pieces of dried spice— about 60 seconds, usually. You can store POP in very small quantities for later use.

■ As an added precaution against the possible presence of little bits of fine twig, from say a thyme stalk, I always use a small strainer as final insurance. A fine dusting by you (as cook) is great. Then place the sieved powder in a small dish on the table for your guests to add more or less, at will!

POACHED APPLE CUSTARD

I can imagine this dish with an infinitely varied (and infinitely pleasing) variety of fruits and spices —mangoes with a gingery POP, for instance. A springboarding dream.

Serves 4

INGREDIENTS

POP:

One ½-inch piece of cinnamon stick (1.5 cm)
3 whole cloves
¼ teaspoon freshly grated nutmeg (1.25 ml)

APPLE CUSTARD:

2 large Granny Smith apples, peeled, cored and sliced into thick rings
2 cups unsweetened apple juice (472 ml)
1 cup water (236 ml)
16 canned or fresh black cherries
1½ cups 2% fat milk (354 ml)
1 teaspoon vanilla (5 ml)
2 tablespoons cornstarch (30 ml), mixed with ¼ cup 2% fat milk (59 ml)
1 cup liquid egg substitute (236 ml)
½ cup brown sugar (118 ml)

FIRST PREPARE THE POP

■ Put the cinnamon, cloves and nutmeg in a small coffee mill or blender and grind to a fine powder.

NOW COOK

■ Place the apple rings in a medium-sized saucepan, pour in the apple juice and water and cover. Bring to a boil, reduce the heat and simmer until apples are tender—about 5 minutes. A knife inserted into an apple ring should go in and come out easily. Transfer the apple rings to a small bowl, reserving the poaching liquid in the pan over very

low heat. Add the cherries and let them heat through. Remove from heat, drain and set aside.

■ Pour the milk into another medium-sized saucepan and bring to a point just before the boil. Check frequently, stirring to prevent scorching. Just before the milk boils, remove from the heat and stir in the vanilla and the cornstarch slurry, return to the heat and boil until thickened, stirring constantly—about 30 seconds. Remove from the heat and set aside.

■ Pour about 1 inch (2.5 cm) of water into a medium-sized saucepan, cover and bring to a point where the water is hot, but not at a breaking boil. There should be literally hundreds of little bubbles on the bottom of the pan. Pour the egg substitute and sugar into a medium-sized copper bowl, set the bowl over the nearly boiling water and whisk the egg substitute until thick and frothy—about 5 minutes. If the liquid should begin to boil, just pull the pan off the heat until it settles down, otherwise the egg will curdle.

■ Pour the milk mixture in a thin stream into the frothy egg mixture and whisk until well incorporated—it should increase in volume dramatically.

■ To Serve: Place 2 apple rings on a dessert plate, cover with the thickened custard and garnish with 4 artfully placed cherries. Put a small amount of the POP in a small, fine-mesh sieve and push gently through, covering the custard with an even dusting.

Nutritional Profile

PER SERVING	CLASSIC	MINIMAX
Calories	378	335
Fat (gm)	34	3
Saturated fat (gm)	21	1
Calories from fat	80%	8%
Cholesterol (mg)	120	8
Sodium (mg)	46	194
Fiber (gm)	2	3

■ *Classic Compared: Apple Custard*

MULLIGATAWNY SOUP

The thigh meat for this recipe is cooked gently in the chicken stock.

Serves 4
INGREDIENTS

POP:

1 teaspoon coriander (5 ml)
½ teaspoon cumin seed (2.5 ml)
½ teaspoon ground ginger (2.5 ml)
⅛ teaspoon cinnamon (0.6 ml)
½ teaspoon turmeric (2.5 ml)

SOUP:

4 cups chicken stock (944 ml) (see page 34)
4 chicken thighs, about 4 oz each, (113 gm), trimmed of all visible fat and skin
1 teaspoon extra-light olive oil, with a dash of sesame oil (5 ml)
1 large yellow onion, peeled and thinly sliced
2 cloves garlic, peeled, smashed and finely chopped
4 teaspoons curry powder (20 ml)
½ cup dried lentils (118 ml)
1 bay leaf
1 cup cooked white rice (236 ml)
1 teaspoon coconut essence (5 ml)
½ cup strained yogurt (118 ml) (see page 85)
Juice of 1 lemon
¼ teaspoon salt (1.25 ml)

GARNISH:

¼ cup strained yogurt (59 ml) (see page 85), mixed with ¼ teaspoon coconut essence (1.25 ml)

FIRST PREPARE

■ The POP: Spoon the coriander, cumin seed, ginger, cinnamon and turmeric into a small coffee mill and grind to a fine powder.

■ The Chicken: Bring the chicken stock to a slow boil, cook the chicken in the stock for 25 minutes or until the internal temperature of the chicken reads 165°F. (75°C) on a kitchen thermometer. Remove the chicken, let it cool enough to handle;

then pull the meat away from the bone. Separate the chunks of meat into smaller pieces and set aside. Strain and reserve the chicken stock.

NOW COOK

■ Pour the oil into a large stockpot over medium heat, add the onion and garlic and cook 2 minutes. Stir in the curry powder, until the onion and garlic are well coated and the curry powder is warmed. Add the lentils, bay leaf and reserved chicken stock, bring to a boil, reduce the heat and simmer 30 minutes.

■ Remove the bay leaf, add the chicken meat and rice and warm through. Push 1 teaspoon of the POP through a fine sieve into the soup, add the coconut essence and mix well.

■ Just before serving, remove the soup from the heat and stir in the yogurt until well incorporated. The soup cannot be too hot for this step or the yogurt will curdle. Add the lemon juice, to taste, and the salt and mix well.

■ To Serve: Ladle the soup into individual serving bowls and garnish with a dollop of the yogurt-coconut mixture. Push ¼ teaspoon (1.25 ml) of the POP mixture through a small sieve over the top of each serving.

NOTE: I've used a coconut essence to replace the classic coconut cream, which is high in saturated fat. This is a new departure for me, but it does seem to deliver the aroma, and the strained yogurt helps to bring in some of the mouthfeel. Good supermarkets and specialty foods stores stock the essence in the herb and spice section, alongside vanilla.

Nutritional Profile

PER SERVING	CLASSIC	MINIMAX
Calories	277	323
Fat (gm)	16	7
Saturated fat (gm)	9	2
Calories from fat	53%	19%
Cholesterol (mg)	62	39
Sodium (mg)	957	281
Fiber (gm)	2	6

■ *Classic Compared: Mulligatawny Soup*

BAO SYANG

The term bao syang *in Chinese cooking means "an explosion of fragrance." Among the classic ingredients most commonly used are fresh gingerroot, garlic and green onions.*

I've used these "three musketeers" of aroma to set off a chain reaction in a variety of Minimax dishes. They are a wonderful example of ACT, aroma, color, and texture: the warmth and heady promise of enjoyment that lifts off the plate into what I call the aroma zone.

One of the essential changes I've made in bao syang from the classic Chinese cooking style is not *to let it explode in very hot oil. I'm more interested in a* full *aroma extraction, letting the ingredients cook three to four minutes over medium heat, using sesame and olive oils to release the fragrance, then letting the bao syang simmer in wine or stock for another 5 minutes.*

Part of the bao syang is the oil used, and this is as good an opportunity as any to explain my signature oil— a good monounsaturated oil, either extra-light olive oil or canola oil, mixed with toasted sesame oil. I use one part sesame oil to fifteen parts olive or canola. For years I used clarified butter because of its essential nuttiness combined with its high burning point of about 450°F. (230°C). I now achieve similar benefits but without the saturated fat in butter. I use this same oil mix in recipes throughout the book.

The final flavor base can be used in sauces or soups as another "perfume of the palate"—a truly excellent idea. If used as the base for a classic stir-fry, you can use the same ingredients but without the liquid extraction. Cooking must be done over high heat, taking care not to scorch the garlic. You then remove the ginger, garlic and green onions and add the stir-fry ingredients to this fragrant base of flavor.

USES: Any Asian soup or broth used for stir-frying will derive great benefit from this idea. What is less obvious but true is that any basic stock gains from a more complex, aromatic character. I believe the more complex the aroma, the less likely the consumer is to notice the lack of fats, salt and sugars.

■ Here are the basic three musketeers that combine to release the most wonderful aroma. Notice how each is cut in very fine slices to help in the fragrance extraction. If used in a stir-fry, please slice each piece into tiny strips.

■ For stir-fry dishes the pan must be very hot. I prefer to make a slower extraction over medium heat for sauce and soup enhancement, so that nothing scorches.

■ For sauces and soups, please *always* extract as much of the bao syang flavor base as possible. If you like your food hot, you can add ¼ teaspoon (1.25 ml) of red pepper flakes at the initial frying stage and extract their "heat" along with the fragrance of the basic three.

THAI SHRIMP SOUP

Serves 4

INGREDIENTS

FLAVOR BASE:

¼ teaspoon extra-light olive oil, with a dash of sesame oil (1.25 ml)

¼ teaspoon toasted sesame oil (1.25 ml)

1 clove garlic, peeled, smashed and chopped

8 "quarter-size" slices of fresh peeled gingerroot

4 green onions, white and green parts separated, finely chopped

1 cup chicken stock (236 ml) (see page 34)

SOUP:

¼ teaspoon toasted sesame oil (1.25 ml)

12 ounces shrimp (41 to 50 count per pound) (340 gm), peeled and deveined

8 ounces fresh mushrooms (227 gm), quartered

1 tablespoon fish sauce (15 ml)

4 cups chicken stock (944 ml) (see page 34)

NOW COOK

■ The Flavor Base: Pour the oils into a large skillet over medium heat, add the garlic, ginger and the white parts of the green onions and cook 3 minutes. Reserve the dark green parts. Pour in the chicken stock, bring to a boil for 3 minutes. Strain into a small bowl, pressing firmly on the solids until they squeeze through the sieve in the form of a flavor-packed pulp. Set aside.

■ The Soup: Pour the sesame oil into a large wok over medium heat, add the shrimp all at once and cook until they turn pink, stirring constantly—about 30 seconds. Stir in the mushrooms and cook 1 minute. Add the fish sauce and ¼ cup (59 ml) of the reserved Flavor Base and cook for 3 minutes, stirring frequently.

■ Pour in the chicken stock and the remaining Flavor Base and bring *just* to a boil—if it gets to a rolling-boil stage, the shrimp will become very tough. Remove from the heat and skim the foam that rises to the surface.

■ To Serve: Ladle into bowls and sprinkle each with a tablespoon (15 ml) of the dark green parts of the chopped green onions.

Nutritional Profile

PER SERVING	CLASSIC	MINIMAX
Calories	279	99
Fat (gm)	15	3
Saturated fat (gm)	2	1
Calories from fat	49%	24%
Cholesterol (mg)	161	80
Sodium (mg)	1047	315
Fiber (gm)	5	2

■ *Classic Compared: Shrimp Gumbo*

CATFISH WITH ORANGE SAUCE

Serves 4

INGREDIENTS

ORANGE SAUCE:

¼ teaspoon extra-light olive oil, with a dash of sesame oil (1.25 ml)

¼ teaspoon toasted sesame oil (1.25 ml)

4 green onions, separated into white parts, finely chopped; dark green parts, minced, reserved for garnish

8 "quarter-size" slices of fresh peeled gingerroot

1 clove garlic, peeled, smashed and chopped

1½ cups freshly squeezed orange juice (354 ml)

2 teaspoons cornstarch (10 ml), mixed with 4 teaspoons orange juice (20 ml)

1 orange, peeled, zest reserved for garnish, pith removed and the segments separated (if you do this over a small bowl, you can use the excess juice to make the cornstarch slurry)

CATFISH:

Four 4-ounce catfish fillets (113 gm each)

½ teaspoon sesame oil (2.5 ml)

¼ cup orange juice (59 ml)

⅛ teaspoon salt (0.6 ml)

⅛ teaspoon black pepper (0.6 ml)

SIDE DISHES: RED POTATOES, CARROTS AND BROCCOLI

12 red new potatoes

8 ounces carrots (227 gm), chopped large

8 ounces broccoli florets (227 gm)

FIRST PREPARE

■ The Orange Sauce: Pour the oils into a small saucepan over medium heat, add the white parts of the chopped green onions and cook for 1 minute. Add the ginger and garlic and cook 2 minutes. Pour in the orange juice, bring to a boil, reduce the heat and simmer 8 minutes. Remove from the heat and set aside.

NOW COOK

■ Pour ½ inch (1.5 cm) of water into the bottom of a roasting pan. Lay the catfish on a rack in the roasting pan, brush with the sesame oil and orange juice, sprinkle with the salt and pepper and pop under the broiler for 8 minutes (the rack should be 4 inches (10 cm) from the heat source).

■ While the catfish is broiling, start the potatoes steaming. After 4 minutes, add the carrots; 3 minutes later, add the broccoli and cook 5 minutes —total steaming time, 12 minutes.

■ Just before serving, strain the orange sauce into a small bowl, pressing firmly on the solids to extract the pulp from the bao syang vegetables. Return to the same saucepan, pour in a little of the cornstarch slurry, bring to a boil and stir until thickened, adding more cornstarch slurry until the sauce coats the back of a spoon—about 30 seconds. Remove from the heat, stir in the orange segments and set aside.

■ To Serve: Divide the fish, potatoes and vegetables among 4 dinner plates. Spoon the sauce over the fish and sprinkle with the minced dark green onion tops and the orange zest slivers.

Nutritional Profile

PER SERVING	CLASSIC	MINIMAX
Calories	702	553
Fat (gm)	30	6
Saturated fat (gm)	16	1
Calories from fat	38%	9%
Cholesterol (mg)	129	67
Sodium (mg)	253	171
Fiber (gm)	10	11

■ *Classic Compared: Catfish with Orange Sauce*

CHICKEN ANNA SKYE

Serves 4

INGREDIENTS

GINGER-GARLIC MARINADE:

¼ teaspoon extra-light olive oil, with a dash of sesame oil (1.25 ml)

¼ teaspoon toasted sesame oil (1.25 ml)

4 green onions, separated into white and green parts, finely chopped

10 "quarter-size" slices of fresh peeled gingerroot

1 clove garlic, peeled, smashed and chopped

1 cup de-alcoholized white wine (236 ml)

CHICKEN:

Four 4-ounce boneless chicken breasts (113 gm each), with skin

1 teaspoon extra-light olive oil, with a dash of sesame oil (5 ml)

20 ounces bok choy (567 gm)

½ cup de-alcoholized white wine (118 ml)

1 teaspoon arrowroot (5 ml), mixed with 2 teaspoons de-alcoholized white wine (10 ml)

4 cups hot cooked white rice

¼ teaspoon freshly ground salt (1.25 ml)

¼ teaspoon freshly ground black pepper (1.25 ml)

FIRST PREPARE

■ The Marinade: Pour the oils into a medium-sized saucepan over medium heat, add the white parts of the green onions, the ginger and garlic and cook for 3 minutes. Pour in the wine, bring to a boil, reduce the heat, cover and simmer 5 minutes. Strain into a small bowl, pressing very lightly on the solids to extract their juices—you should have ¼ cup (59 ml).

■ Put the flavor injector needle (see page 15)

into the juices and draw up into the barrel. Place the chicken breasts on a large plate and inject small amounts of the juice throughout the meat.

NOW COOK

■ Pour the oil into a large skillet over medium heat, add the chicken breasts skin side down, along with any excess juices that have accumulated on the plate, and fry for 10 minutes, turning every 2 minutes.

■ Put the bok choy in a steamer and cook for 5 minutes.

■ Transfer the cooked chicken to a plate and remove the skin. To make an easy sauce, blot the skillet with a paper towel to remove excess fat, then deglaze the pan with the wine, scraping up all the pan residues. Strain into a small bowl, stir in the arrowroot slurry, return to the skillet, bring to a boil and reduce to a glaze.

■ Return the chicken to the glaze and turn until well coated. Cook until just heated through.

■ To Serve: Put the rice in a large bowl, sprinkle with the salt and pepper and stir in the chopped dark green parts of the green onions. Divide the chicken breasts, bok choy and rice among 4 dinner plates and spoon the excess sauce over the meat.

Nutritional Profile

PER SERVING	CLASSIC	MINIMAX
Calories	762	483
Fat (gm)	38	6
Saturated fat (gm)	22	1
Calories from fat	45%	10%
Cholesterol (mg)	188	58
Sodium (mg)	1445	239
Fiber (gm)	3	4

■ *Classic Compared: Supremes of Chicken in Wine and Cream Sauce*

MEAT IN THE MINOR KEY

I think it's important to realize that the recommendation that no more than 30 percent of daily calories come from fat indicates a ceiling for healthy people without a family history of heart problems. For people in this category a serving of meat (chicken, beef, pork or lamb) needs to be about 3½ ounces (99 gm) in weight, the size of a deck of playing cards, to stay under the 30 percent ceiling. Because fish has less saturated fat, a portion can be as large as 6 ounces (170 gm).

However, if you or someone for whom you lovingly cook has a health risk factor, like my wife, Treena, who endured a heart attack and has a high blood cholesterol level, then most authorities think that the absolute limit should be somewhere between 15 and 25 percent of daily calories from fat.

To stay within this more severe fat limitation, portion size will inevitably mean "meat in the minor key." Portions go down to 2 ounces (57 gm) (edible portion), even 1 ounce (28 gm) in certain dishes. Of course, when a serving is that small, it begins to impact our visual sense of what is a satisfying amount.

The secret to presenting meat in the minor key is to think of it as a garnish, with vegetables and whole grains filling the remaining plate space. In the photographs below, I've set out three different meat presentations.

One more secret to making the meat portion appear larger: change the dinner plate size from the standard 11-inch (28 cm) diameter to 9½ inches (23 cm). This simple change helps to give the appearance of a full plate with about 20 percent less food. The key issue here is to be aware of how the plate presentation impacts our visual satisfaction from a meal.

I also suggest that if you need to severely restrict your fat intake, you consider alternating days with and without meat. With the meat portion decision made and understood, you will be well on your way to controlling your percentage of daily calories from fat.

■ This is a 2-ounce (57-gm) meat portion! I recommend that you cut very small steaks from a *beef tenderloin.* And consider your nutritional benefit: 2 ounces (57 gm) of tenderloin has 5 grams of fat while an 8-ounce (227-gm) tenderloin could overwhelm you with 21 grams of fat.

■ Here I've used a broiled flank steak cut in very thin diagonal slices to give more width. The space it covers is about the same as a serving of classic prime rib, yet this 2-ounce (57 gm) portion of flank steak has only 3 grams of fat, compared to 68 grams of fat in the 8-ounce (227-gm) prime rib portion.

■ This picture shows you stewed meat in large 2½-ounce (71-gm) pieces that shrink to 2 ounces (57 gm) after cooking, and your fat savings when substituting 2 ounces (57 gm) of beef bottom round for the classic 8 ounces (227 gm) of chuck roast is: 3 grams of fat compared to 37 grams of fat.

WHOLE GRAINS AS "EXTENDERS"

$\mathcal{P}$art of my Minimax philosophy involves moving meat and poultry proteins to one side and looking for satisfaction from the grain foods that kept mankind healthy for multiple generations before the cow came to roost, so to speak. The idea is not to put cows, et al, into a zoo, but to use smaller and smaller amounts of meat, while, at the same time, keeping the portion volume and weight up by adding an appropriate grain. "Appropriate" means from a textural, visual and taste point of view.

Two excellent grains that I use in recipes are bulgur wheat and quinoa (pronounced ki nō a). Both are extremely easy to use, provide interesting texture and taste great.

Bulgur is usually made from hard red winter wheat. It comes precooked in boxes found close to the beans and rice section of the supermarket. The wheat kernals are boiled, dried and then cracked into small bits. The process removes bran, but bulgur is still a good source of protein and B complex vitamins.

Quinoa can currently be found in some supermarkets and most health food stores, but it should become a mainstream favorite by the mid-1990s. It is the seed of a large herb that has its origin in the high mountains of South America. The best news is that quinoa is a cereal superstar in nutrition, with 16 to 20 percent protein that is more "available" than in other cereals. It also packs good amounts of iron, calcium and phosphorus and has some B complex and vitamin E.

As a side dish it couldn't be easier to fix. To serve 4, just rinse, drain and then briefly simmer ½ cup (118 ml) quinoa to 1 cup (236 ml) water or stock. It has a light, fresh taste that goes very well with chicken, seafood and beef—well worth a try.

Of course, the potential for springboarding with the grain of your choice is almost endless. Any grains and legumes can be used with any and all of your favorite meats and poultry. May I suggest that you try each of the following simple ideas and then branch out on your own.

USES: Grains provide satisfaction when used to partly replace substantial reductions in meats and poultry but they don't provide the micronutrients that good fresh vegetables do. The moral is: extend satisfaction with grains (complex carbohydrates) and enhance micronutrients with vegetables. This works everywhere in the menu.

■ In this photograph, we show rice with chicken, quinoa with beef, and bulgur with lamb. Please take up the challenge and let your old friends mix with some healthy new arrivals.

■ In this example, the baked rice pilaf is ready. All that needs to be done is to add the 2 ounces (57 gm) of chicken per person and the texture-boosting mushrooms.

■ When you garnish with meat, it's a very good idea to spend some extra thought and time on presentation. See how this white-on-white dish benefits from a wreath of red or green chard?

CHICKEN PILAF

Serves 4

INGREDIENTS

1 teaspoon extra-light olive oil, with a dash of sesame oil (5 ml)

8 ounces chicken meat (227 gm), a breast and whole leg, all visible fat trimmed, cut into very small pieces

½ large yellow onion, peeled and finely chopped

2 cups uncooked white rice (472 ml)

4 cups chicken stock (944 ml) (see page 34)

1 bay leaf

1 branch tarragon with 12 fresh leaves

¼ teaspoon freshly ground salt (1.25 ml)

½ teaspoon freshly ground black pepper (2.5 ml)

8 ounces mushroom caps (227 gm), quartered

¼ cup minced green onions (59 ml)

1 teaspoon finely chopped fresh tarragon leaves (5 ml)

1 bunch red chard, very finely sliced

GARNISH:

Balsamic vinegar or freshly squeezed lemon juice to taste (optional)

NOW COOK

■ Preheat the oven to 450°F. (230°C). Pour the oil into a large casserole over medium heat and brush it around to cover the bottom. Add the chicken, stirring to cook all sides, for 7 minutes. Transfer chicken to a bowl and set aside.

■ Add the onion and rice to the same casserole, stirring to coat with the oil and chicken residue. Pour in the stock, stir in the bay leaf, tarragon branch, salt and pepper. Bake in the preheated oven, uncovered, for 20 minutes.

■ Take casserole from the oven, remove the tarragon and bay leaf and stir in the cooked chicken, the mushrooms and green onions, burying them in the rice. Smooth out the top and return to the oven for 5 minutes to just heat through. Remove and stir in the finely chopped tarragon.

■ While the pilaf is heating through, pour about 1 inch (2.5 cm) of water into a large pot, bring to a boil. Spread the chard on a steamer rack and steam for 1 minute. Remove from the heat and set aside.

■ To Serve: Spoon a mound of pilaf onto the center of each dinner plate and encircle in a dark red wreath of the chard. The chard taste is brightened by a sprinkle of balsamic vinegar or fresh lemon juice.

Nutritional Profile

PER SERVING	CLASSIC	MINIMAX
Calories	828	506
Fat (gm)	28	5
Saturated fat (gm)	14	1
Calories from fat	30%	10%
Cholesterol (mg)	203	31
Sodium (mg)	356	347
Fiber (gm)	5	5

■ *Classic Compared: Chicken Fricassée*

LAMB IN A PITA

"The thing is redolent with garlic and laughing with yogurt."—Graham Kerr

Serves 4
INGREDIENTS

1 cup uncooked bulgur wheat (236 ml)

1 cup boiling water (236 ml)

½ teaspoon extra-light olive oil, with a dash of sesame oil (2.5 ml)

1 yellow onion, peeled and finely chopped

3 cloves garlic, peeled, smashed and finely chopped

8 ounces ground leg of lamb (227 gm)

1 cup lamb or beef stock (see page 35)

1 teaspoon fresh finely chopped oregano leaves (5 ml)

4 teaspoons mango chutney (20 ml) (Major Grey's is preferable)

2 teaspoons cumin seed (10 ml)

¼ teaspoon cayenne pepper (1.25 ml)

½ teaspoon dried rosemary (2.5 ml)

⅛ teaspoon freshly ground salt (0.6 ml)

1 teaspoon cornstarch (5 ml), mixed with 2 teaspoons water (10 ml)

2 tablespoons fresh finely chopped parsley (30 ml)

½ cup strained yogurt (118 ml) (see page 85)

4 whole wheat pita breads, cut in half

8 Chinese cabbage leaves

NOW COOK

■ Place the bulgur in a small bowl, pour the water on top and let steep for 10 minutes.

■ Pour the oil into a large hot skillet and cook the onion and garlic until the onion browns—about 4 minutes. Add the lamb, cooking and stirring until completely browned—about 4 minutes. Stir in 1 cup (236 ml) of the cooked bulgur, the stock, oregano, chutney, cumin seed, cayenne pepper, rosemary and salt, bring to a boil, reduce the heat and simmer 9 minutes. Remove from the heat, stir in the cornstarch slurry, bring to a boil and stir until thickened—about 30 seconds. Transfer to a plate, sprinkle with the parsley and spread the mixture out to cool quickly before stirring in half of the yogurt.

■ To Serve: Spoon the lamb mixture into the pita halves; spread each with a tablespoon (15 ml) of the remaining yogurt and top with a cabbage leaf. Each guest gets 2 halves.

Nutritional Profile

PER SERVING	CLASSIC	MINIMAX
Calories	509	483
Fat (gm)	32	11
Saturated fat (gm)	15	4
Calories from fat	56%	20%
Cholesterol (mg)	107	37
Sodium (mg)	1609	420
Fiber (gm)	3	15

■ *Classic Compared: Savory Lamb Burgers*

QUINOA AND BEEF CONQUISTADOR

"It pops in your mouth."—Graham Kerr

Serves 4
INGREDIENTS

GREEN MASHED POTATOES:

4 large potatoes, peeled

½ cup buttermilk (118 ml)

¼ teaspoon freshly ground white pepper (1.25 ml)

⅛ teaspoon freshly ground salt (0.6 ml)

¼ fresh finely chopped cilantro leaves (59 ml), mixed with ⅛ cup fresh finely chopped parsley leaves (59 ml)

2 cups water (472 ml)

1 cup raw quinoa (236 ml)

½ teaspoon extra-light olive oil, with a dash of sesame oil (2.5 ml)

1 small yellow onion, peeled and finely chopped

3 cloves garlic, peeled, smashed and chopped

8 ounces beef bottom round (227 gm), ground (see page 51)

1 tablespoon low-sodium tomato paste (15 ml)

2 tablespoons low-sodium soy sauce (30 ml)

1 cup beef stock (236 ml) (see page 35)

1 red bell pepper, seeded and finely chopped

1 cup frozen corn (236 ml), thawed

2 tablespoons fresh chopped parsley (30 ml)

2 tablespoons fresh chopped cilantro (30 ml)

½ teaspoon cayenne pepper (2.5 ml)

¼ teaspoon ground cumin (1.25 ml)

1 tablespoon arrowroot (15 ml), mixed with 2 tablespoons water (30 ml)

FIRST PREPARE

■ Make the Green Mashed Potatoes according to the method described in the Turkey Mountain recipe (see page 21). Stir in the cilantro-parsley mixture until well incorporated. Set aside and keep warm.

■ In a medium-sized saucepan, bring the water to a boil, add the quinoa, bring back to the boil, reduce the heat and simmer 10 minutes. Remove from the heat and set aside.

NOW COOK

■ Pour the oil into a large casserole over medium heat and cook the onion and garlic until the onion is translucent—about 4 minutes. Add the beef and cook until fully browned, stirring often—about 3 minutes. Turn the heat to high and stir in the tomato paste until completely incorporated and deepened in color—about 2 minutes. Stir in the cooked quinoa, the soy sauce, stock, red pepper, corn, parsley, cilantro, cayenne pepper, and cumin and mix well. Remove from the heat, stir in the arrowroot slurry, return to the heat and stir until thickened. Remove from the heat and set aside.

■ To Serve: For an elegant presentation, spoon the potatoes into a pastry bag and pipe a wreath on each dinner plate. Otherwise, spoon a mound onto each plate and make a hollow in the middle. Ladle the beef filling into the center.

Nutritional Profile

PER SERVING	CLASSIC	MINIMAX
Calories	407	406
Fat (gm)	30	5
Saturated fat (gm)	14	1
Calories from fat	66%	11%
Cholesterol (mg)	202	49
Sodium (mg)	293	470
Fiber (gm)	2	6

■ *Classic Compared: Beef Lindstrom*

POULTRY—SKIN ON

Recently the near mania for both health and speed has resulted in what I call NBS (Naked Breast Syndrome). This is not a reference to National Geographic specials or, for that matter, the sensibilities of otherwise deeply committed missionaries. Rather, NBS refers to the way that both chicken and turkey breasts are being sold without their skin—and it's not good news for the quality of the finished dish.

No, I'm not advocating eating the skin, just keeping it on to the point of serving. I always keep the skin on for all dry-heat methods of cooking (pan sautéing, broiling, roasting), where evaporation can take place, and remove the skin when using moist-heat methods, such as in casseroles and all-in-one-pot stews, where the melting fat would be difficult to remove. A third way of handling tender chicken used for stews is to cook the meat separately from the vegetables as in Chicken Fantengo.

In the photographs that follow, I've compared two chicken breasts cooked in an almost dry pan, one with its skin and one without. You'll see that the skin helps to retain moisture, provides a perfect frying medium and saves the tender flesh from losing its surface juices to evaporation, which produces stringiness.

If you keep the skin on while the chicken cooks, you'll need to know a few tricks. Always blot the chicken flesh (and the pan) with paper towels. Keep the towels in a resealable plastic bag in the freezer. If you make a habit of doing this, you'll save enough to make a great firelighter for at least one aromatic fire!

USES: Poultry, especially chicken and turkey breast, has been discovered to be low in fat when the skin is removed before eating; but if the skin is removed before cooking, flavor and moisture are lost. It follows that any poultry breast recipe can benefit from this technique of cooking it with the skin on.

■ By way of an experiment, I cooked two matching breasts (same bird), one with skin removed, the other with skin on, each for the same 10 minutes.

■ After cooking, I removed the skin from the other and blotted the surface with paper towel. This is the standard technique I use for chicken breast cooked by a dry-heat method.

■ Here you can see the unretouched photographic result. There is less moisture in the skin-off-from-the-start breast. It has shrunk and the outer flesh is stringy in comparison to the skin-on breast . . . Since a picture is worth a thousand words, I'll leave it right there.

POULTRY BREAST—SKIN ON

Serves 2
INGREDIENTS

2 medium-sized boneless chicken breasts, skin on

1 teaspoon extra-light olive oil, with a dash of sesame oil (5 ml)

Freshly ground black peppercorns

Freshly ground salt

NOW COOK

■ Dab the chicken with a paper towel until dry. Brush the oil over the surface of a large skillet and place the chicken in it, skin side down. Brown over medium-high heat, turning every 2 minutes, for a total of 10 minutes.

■ Remove from the heat and remove skin, blotting surface of chicken with paper towel. Season with pepper and salt to taste and set aside. Use with your favorite vegetable and starch food.

Nutritional Profile

PER SERVING	CLASSIC	MINIMAX
Calories	228	164
Fat (gm)	12	6
Saturated fat (gm)	3	1
Calories from fat	47%	32%
Cholesterol (mg)	78	66
Sodium (mg)	201	194
Fiber (gm)	0	0

■ *Classic Compared: Fried Chicken Breast*

FRIENDLY TURKEY AND CREAMY VEGETABLES

Serves 6
INGREDIENTS

1 teaspoon extra-light olive oil, with a dash of sesame oil (5 ml)

3 yellow onions, peeled and quartered

4 parsnips, peeled and coarsely chopped

12 medium red new potatoes, halved and sliced ½ inch thick (1.5 cm)

Two 4-inch branches fresh rosemary (10 cm)

1 teaspoon fresh thyme leaves (5 ml)

One 14-ounce can low-sodium chicken stock (397 gm)

¼ teaspoon freshly ground salt (1.25 ml)

¼ teaspoon freshly ground black pepper (1.25 ml)

½ whole turkey breast (1½ pounds or 680 gm), skin removed and trimmed of all visible fat and reserved

3 pounds (1.4 kg) Swiss chard, cleaned and trimmed

2 tablespoons arrowroot (30 ml), mixed with 4 tablespoons water (60 ml)

1 tablespoon fresh finely chopped parsley (15 ml)

NOW COOK

■ Preheat the oven to 350°F. (180°C). Pour the oil into a medium flameproof casserole and cook the onions over medium-high heat until just brown—about 5 minutes. Add the parsnips and potatoes, then the rosemary and thyme. Pour in the chicken stock and add salt and pepper.

■ Place the turkey breast on top and lay the reserved skin over the meat. Cover and bake for 50 minutes. The amount of fat that drains into the vegetables is very slight providing you have done a good job of removing the visible fat.

■ Just before the turkey is done, steam the chard until tender.

■ Transfer the cooked turkey to a cutting board. Peel off the skin; you'll see how moist that skin protection has kept the flesh.

■ To make a glossy sauce, discard the rosemary branches. Remove the vegetables and set aside, leaving the juices in the casserole. Remove from the heat, add the arrowroot slurry, return to the heat and stir until thickened. Return the vegetables to the casserole, add the parsley and stir until well coated and glistening.

■ To Serve: Slice the turkey thinly and put 3 slices on each plate. Spoon the vegetables with sauce over the turkey and put the chard on the side and sprinkle with the parsley.

Nutritional Profile

PER SERVING	CLASSIC	MINIMAX
Calories	422	443
Fat (gm)	30	4
Saturated fat (gm)	16	1
Calories from fat	65%	9%
Cholesterol (mg)	127	53
Sodium (mg)	743	517
Fiber (gm)	1	13

■ *Classic Compared: Creamed Turkey*

CHICKEN FANTENGO

Please note the way I've made this casserole: the skin-on technique becomes a nutritional problem in a casserole. If you remove the skin and stew the meat, it loses succulence. You've got to keep the meat whole and with the skin on to retain its juiciness. But if you do that, the fat drains out into the casserole and you can't remove it. My way of dealing with this issue is to cook the meat and vegetables separately. In this Minimax method, you'll see how to make a major reduction in saturated fat by removing the risk AND you'll improve the texture and taste by removing the risk at the right time.

Serves 5
INGREDIENTS

Four 8-ounce whole chicken legs
1 teaspoon extra-light olive oil, with a dash of sesame oil (5 ml)
2 yellow onions, peeled and thinly sliced
2 cloves garlic, peeled, smashed and chopped
One 6-ounce can low-sodium tomato paste (170 gm)
2 cups chicken stock (472 ml) (see page 34)
12 ounces Jerusalem artichokes (340 gm), peeled and coarsely chopped
1¼ cups de-alcoholized white wine (295 ml)
1 tablespoon (15 ml) + 1 teaspoon (5 ml) fresh minced oregano leaves (20 ml)
½ teaspoon freshly ground black pepper (2.5 ml)
¼ teaspoon freshly ground salt (1.25 ml)
4 ounces spiral pasta (113 gm)
1 cup black olives (236 ml)
1 tablespoon fresh chopped parsley (15 ml)

NOW COOK

■ Preheat the oven to 425°F. (220°C). Put the chicken pieces on a rack in a roasting pan and bake for 50 minutes.

■ Pour the oil into a large saucepan over medium-high heat and fry the onions and garlic until translucent—about 4 minutes. Stir in the tomato paste until completely incorporated, turn up the heat a notch, allowing the natural sugars in the tomato paste to go light brown and caramelize (see page 17)—about 10 minutes. Pour in the stock, artichokes, 1 cup (236 ml) of the wine, 1 tablespoon (15 ml) of the oregano, half of the black pepper and the salt, cover and simmer 8 minutes.

■ While everything else is cooking, cook the pasta according to package directions until just tender—about 9 minutes.

■ Add the cooked pasta and olives to the sauce and heat through.

■ Remove the chicken from the oven and transfer to a flat surface. Pour off the excess fat from the pan, put pan on the stovetop, add the remaining wine and scrape up the residues. Pour into a fat-strainer jug. Allow the fat to rise to the top and pour the rest of the liquid into the sauce.

■ Remove the skin from the cooked chicken, using a bowl of ice water to cool down your fingers. It's about 3 seconds between dips for normal, 4 seconds for macho and 5 seconds for super-macho. I must say that tongs don't do a good job: get in and let your fingers do the working. Separate into major meat pieces according to muscle lines and add to the sauce. Stir in the remaining oregano and pepper.

■ To Serve: Spoon into individual bowls and garnish with the parsley.

Nutritional Profile

PER SERVING	CLASSIC	MINIMAX
Calories	558	520
Fat (gm)	28	15
Saturated fat (gm)	7	3
Calories from fat	45%	26%
Cholesterol (mg)	156	85
Sodium (mg)	852	599
Fiber (gm)	4	7

■ *Classic Compared: Chicken Marengo*

EGG SUBSTITUTES

Frankly, my attitude toward egg substitutes hasn't always been that friendly. I couldn't see how pasteurized egg whites with a little coloring and some mystical seaweed thickener could replace the egg! I felt this confirmed when I tried to use a well-known brand to make an omelet. "ENOUGH!" I cried. "It's eggs or nothing!" And so in our case, with Treena's high risk of heart disease, it became nothing.

But I'm happy to report that eventually I learned how to handle egg substitute and have now (literally) stirred it into our weekly menus, so that we consume the equivalent of two dozen whole eggs with no cholesterol and no saturated fat!

If you are like me and deeply devoted to the whole egg, please *give my ideas a go and try to forget how you have been cooking eggs. Egg substitutes can work, but they need lower temperatures and great garnishes to help you over the always present hurdle of mouthfeel change. We use them for scrambling and omelets and very, very occasionally have a nostalgic indulgence . . . a whole egg boiled for four minutes in its shell and dipped with crusty toast "soldiers," as we used to call the toast fingers of our past.*

USES: In place of scrambled eggs, for omelets and for custards. If you don't overcook them, you will find that egg substitutes do a creditable job of replacing the egg in everyday consumption, and this must *be done for those of us at risk from high-fat eating habits.*

■ The fat is heated until it begins to color very slightly at the edges. It is *very* important to work with a *medium-low* heat.

■ Add the entire contents of a shaken carton all at once, and then comes the big trick: LEAVE IT THERE for about 60 seconds to warm through and begin to set.

■ This is the most important part. With a flat-ended spurtle or spatula, simply push the coagulated egg into a heap in the center. Note that the surface is still very moist—*it must remain so.* The stored heat will complete the cooking on the way to the table. If you try to cook the egg substitute through in the pan it will be dry and unattractive by the time it is served.

MC KERR MUFFINS

Serves 2

INGREDIENTS

½ teaspoon extra-light olive oil, with a dash of sesame oil (2.5 ml)

2 jumbo mushroom caps (as big as your English muffin would be perfect)

1 teaspoon freshly squeezed lemon juice (5 ml)

1/16 teaspoon cayenne pepper (0.3 ml)

1 teaspoon margarine (5 ml)

1 cup liquid egg substitute (236 ml)

1 English muffin, cut in half and toasted

Two 1-ounce slices of Canadian bacon (28 gm each)

Four 1-ounce slices part-skim mozzarella cheese (28 gm each)

½ teaspoon chopped green onion or fresh parsley (2.5 ml)

NOW COOK

■ Brush the oil over the bottom of a small skillet, add the mushroom caps, round side down, drizzle the lemon juice and cayenne pepper into the space left by removing the stem and cook over medium heat until the lemon juice begins to steam—about 6 minutes. Turn them over—the heat inside kind of explodes and cooks the mushrooms through in less than 1 minute. Remove from the heat and set aside.

■ Melt the margarine in a medium-sized skillet over *medium-low* heat. Pour in the egg substitute and, when it starts to set firm, push gently, moving it into a mound in the center of the pan. It should keep a moist glossy sheen to assure proper texture in the final product. This is vitally important, because overcooking ruins the texture. When all the egg is cooked and scraped into the central mound, transfer to a plate and set aside.

■ Preheat broiler. Place the toasted muffin halves on a baking sheet. Cover each with a bacon slice and 2 ice cream scoops of the scrambled eggs, spreading the eggs completely over the muffin halves. Top each with a cooked mushroom cap, 2 slices of the cheese and a scattering of the chopped green onion. Pop under the broiler until the cheese melts—about 4 minutes.

■ Serve for brunch with sliced fresh fruit. You can see how this can work easily for a crowd. At least a dozen muffins can be put on one baking sheet under the average oven broiler.

Nutritional Profile

PER SERVING	CLASSIC	MINIMAX
Calories	471	355
Fat (gm)	38	15
Saturated fat (gm)	20	7
Calories from fat	73	39
Cholesterol (mg)	507	44
Sodium (mg)	847	1042
Fiber (gm)	0	1

■ *Classic Compared: Eggs Benedict*

EGG FOO YUNG SCRAMBLE

Serves 2

INGREDIENTS

1 teaspoon extra-light olive oil, with a dash of sesame oil (5 ml)

1 clove garlic, peeled, smashed and finely chopped

10 "dime-size" slivers of fresh peeled gingerroot, finely chopped

2 green onions, separated into the white and green parts, cut into ⅛-inch (0.5-cm) pieces

1 cup frozen corn (236 ml)

2 ounces finely chopped pimento (57 gm)

2 ounces sweet red bell pepper (57 gm), finely diced

2 ounces extra-firm tofu (57 gm), finely diced

Two 1-ounce slices of Canadian bacon (28 gm), finely diced

1 cup liquid egg substitute (236 ml)

2 cups hot cooked white rice (472 ml)

NOW COOK

■ Brush half of the oil over the bottom of a small skillet over medium heat and cook the garlic, ginger and the white parts of the green onions, stirring, until their fragrance is released—about 30 seconds. Add the remaining oil, the corn, pimento, red pepper, tofu, Canadian bacon and dark green onion tops and stir-fry for 1 minute. Transfer the vegetables to a bowl.

■ Pour the egg substitute into the same skillet and cook until firm—about 3 minutes. Keep the eggs pushed into the center of the pan. When they're almost completely set, spoon the vegetables on top and very gently lift and turn together, until completely combined.

■ To Serve: Spoon the eggs into bowls and serve with the steamed rice in separate bowls.

Nutritional Profile

PER SERVING	CLASSIC	MINIMAX
Calories	291	245
Fat (gm)	20	3
Saturated fat (gm)	6	1
Calories from fat	63%	12%
Cholesterol (mg)	338	7
Sodium (mg)	495	314
Fiber (gm)	1	3

■ *Classic Compared: Egg Foo Yung*

STACK AND STEAM

Of all the pieces of equipment that work overtime for Minimax, the steamer, especially a multilevel one, must take first place.

Stack steaming refers to several levels, trays or racks in one steamer, each one devoted to foods that reach perfection at a different time and therefore need their own space. I had a set of stainless-steel racks made. They nest and have perforated removeable bottoms. They do the trick brilliantly, perhaps soon they will be manufactured. Until then you could use the multilevel bamboo steamers that are quite readily available and reasonably priced.

I enjoy seasoning the steaming water with herbs and lemon according to the food being steamed. I get aromatic steam this way, and it condenses on the food with delicious results. I also sprinkle each piece of vegetable or meat with a small quantity of fresh chopped herbs or some freshly ground pepper or nutmeg, before putting it in the steamer.

A steamer is used in many recipes throughout the book, but here are three delicious examples to try: a platter of fresh vegetables to which you can add a small piece of fish or chicken as a garnish; a truly fantastic first course of potatoes and leeks in a creamy sauce with goat cheese; and my personal favorite fish dish, steamed halibut with slices of lemon and black pepper.

Once you've got the steamer bug, the doors of your kitchen will swing open to an avalanche of aroma, color and texture. It's Minimax heaven . . . well . . . perhaps paradise?

USES: Throughout my books I continually urge you to use fresh vegetables in season . . . as the center point rather than the garnish. The best way I know to cook several different vegetables to perfection at one time is to stack and steam. This means that you can now greatly increase the number of vegetables you serve and this will do wonders for your overall health and quality of life.

■ I use a set of stainless-steel steamers that are quite large and stack snugly. If you don't have the special steamer insert you can use the readily available bamboo steamers, which must be discarded after a while and are not as large. Put marbles in the bottom of your steamer pot with the water. They make a lot of noise when your water level is low.

■ The stacking technique is especially helpful when you're trying to steam several different vegetables of different densities and get them ready at the same time.

■ If you're going to serve the vegetables solo as a main course, double the amount of the spinach and dust with an extra tablespoon of freshly grated cheese.

STEAMED VEGETABLE MEDLEY

Serves 4 as a side dish
INGREDIENTS

2 yams, cut into ½ inch (1.5 cm) slices
2 tablespoons fresh chopped thyme (30 ml)
¼ teaspoon freshly ground pepper (1.25 ml)
2 tomatoes, halved and cored
6 ounces spinach (170 gm), well rinsed and stems trimmed
4 tablespoons freshly grated Parmesan cheese (60 ml)

NOW COOK

■ Put a small amount of water in your steamer pot and bring to a boil. Put the yams on a steamer tray, sprinkle with a bit of the thyme and pepper, put the tray in the steamer pot, cover, glance at your watch and start steaming.

■ After 16 minutes, put the tomatoes in another steamer tray, sprinkle with thyme and pepper, stack on top of the yams, cover and continue steaming for 3 minutes.

■ Now put the spinach in a third steamer tray, sprinkle with thyme and pepper, stack on top of the tomatoes, cover and steam 3 more minutes. At 22 minutes total, voilà—perfectly steamed vegetables ready for your meal.

■ To Serve: Arrange the vegetables on a serving platter: bright orange yams, scarlet tomatoes and deep green spinach. Sprinkle with the remaining thyme and pepper and the Parmesan cheese.

Nutritional Profile

PER SERVING	CLASSIC	MINIMAX
Calories	204	106
Fat (gm)	10	2
Saturated fat (gm)	6	1
Calories from fat	44%	16%
Cholesterol (mg)	30	4
Sodium (mg)	227	131
Fiber (gm)	4	3

■ *Classic Compared: Vegetables with Cheese Sauce*

STEAMED LEEKS AND POTATOES

Classic European style at its finest—a great winter weather first course! Do use the freshly grated nutmeg.

Serves 4 as a first course
INGREDIENTS

4 leeks, roots trimmed, dark green tops cut off and reserved, split open and washed well
8 red new potatoes, 2 inches (5 cm) in diameter
1 teaspoon fresh chopped thyme (5 ml)

2 teaspoons goat cheese (10 ml)

SAUCE:
1 cup vegetable stock (236 ml) (see page 36)
2 tablespoons cornstarch (30 ml), mixed with 4 tablespoons water (60 ml)
½ cup strained yogurt (118 ml) (see page 85)
⅛ teaspoon freshly ground salt (0.6 ml)
⅛ teaspoon freshly ground white pepper (0.6 ml)
¼ teaspoon freshly grated nutmeg (1.25 ml)

GARNISH:
Freshly ground black pepper
Fresh finely chopped parsley
Paprika
1 lemon

NOW COOK

■ Pour about 1½ inches (4 cm) of water into a large pot, add the leek trimmings and dark green tops and bring to a vigorous boil. Put the potatoes and leeks into a steamer tray, sprinkle with the thyme, place over the pot, cover and cook until tender—about 15 minutes. Remove the steamer tray and set aside.

■ The Sauce: In a medium-sized saucepan over medium heat, heat the stock through. Pour a small bit of hot stock into the cornstarch slurry, mix well and pour back into the saucepan. Bring to a boil, stirring constantly until thickened—about 30 seconds. Remove from the heat, drop in a couple of ice cubes to cool the sauce quickly and set aside.

■ In a medium-sized bowl, stir the strained yogurt gently until smooth. When the sauce is cool, add it to the yogurt, stirring gently until well incorporated—don't overbeat! Fold in the salt, pepper, and nutmeg.

■

■ To Serve: Coarsely chop the leeks and potatoes and mix together. Make a small mound on each plate and sprinkle evenly with the goat cheese. Cover with the sauce, sprinkle with the pepper, parsley, paprika, and a squeeze of lemon juice and enjoy.

Nutritional Profile

PER SERVING	CLASSIC	MINIMAX
Calories	307	280
Fat (gm)	15	1
Saturated fat (gm)	9	1
Calories from fat	44%	4%
Cholesterol (mg)	37	2
Sodium (mg)	620	136
Fiber (gm)	4	8

■ *Classic Compared: Leeks au Gratin*

HALIBUT DINNER IN ONE POT

Moist, flaky halibut coated with lemon essence, crisp-tender vegetables and steamy potatoes—all in one pot so cleanup's a breeze! Does life hold more?

Serves 2
INGREDIENTS

4 large fresh sage leaves

1 bay leaf

½ large lemon, skin sliced off and reserved, fruit sliced paper thin

Two 6-ounce halibut fillets (170 gm each), skin on

1 medium squash—crookneck, zucchini, etc., your choice—sliced lengthwise into quarters

4 ounces "pencil" (thin-stemmed) asparagus (113 gm)

4 red new potatoes, 2 inches (5 cm) in diameter, steamed until tender (about 15 minutes)

⅛ teaspoon freshly ground black pepper (0.6 ml)

⅛ teaspoon freshly ground salt (0.6 ml)

GARNISH:

1 tablespoon fresh chopped parsley (15 ml)

Fresh cracked black pepper

NOW COOK

■ Pour about 1 inch (2.5 cm) of water in the bottom of a large steamer pot. Add the sage, bay leaf and lemon zest (be careful to cut away the bitter white pith) and simmer until you smell a distinct heady fragrance—about 4 minutes.

■ Put the first steamer tray in the pot, cover and bring to a strong steam. Put the halibut on a plate that is almost exactly the diameter of the steamer; you need about a ¼-inch (0.75-cm) gap between the plate and the sides of the steamer. Layer the lemon slices on top. When the steam is strong, remove the cover and, after the steam dissipates, place the plate carefully into the first steamer tray.

■ Lay the squash, asparagus and potatoes in a second steamer tray, sprinkle with pepper and salt, stack on top of the fish in the steamer pot and cook until done—about 13 minutes. Remove the vegetable tray and use tongs to remove the plate of fish.

■ To Serve: Arrange 1 fish fillet and half the vegetables and potatoes on each dinner plate. Sprinkle with the parsley and cracked black pepper, making sure to get a little black pepper on the pure white fish—a marvelous Minimax moment.

Nutritional Profile

PER SERVING	CLASSIC	MINIMAX
Calories	877	363
Fat (gm)	51	2
Saturated fat (gm)	27	1
Calories from fat	52%	6%
Cholesterol (mg)	190	74
Sodium (mg)	810	273
Fiber (gm)	6	7

■ *Classic Compared: Fish with Parsley Sauce*

BEANS . . . UNDER THE RIGHT KIND OF PRESSURE

It's something that everyone is saying—North, South, East, West—regardless of culture or other opinion . . . the beans have it. Unfortunately, beans come complete with three mythical strikes against them. They are regarded as "poor-people's food"; they are known "gas" producers; they seem to take forever to cook.

While I'll agree to their low cost, I cannot agree to their exclusive use by impoverished people. I've eaten my way around the world at least thirty times, and there are dozens of elegant dishes using beans served in the finest restaurants. Add to this the fact that they deliver excellent nutrition, are low in fat and high in fiber, and the "poverty food" myth should surely go right out of the window.

Gas production is a reality until you treat beans to a precook "boil up." For regular (non-pressure) cooking, I place the beans in cold water and slowly bring them to a boil (about eight to ten minutes), let them sit off the heat for an hour, covered, then dump the water and proceed with the recipe. This treatment greatly reduces the gas problem, which, when coupled with your digestive system's own natural ability to adapt, should easily keep you from floating to the ceiling.

If you use the same gas-less preboil and then tip the beans into a pressure cooker, a radical time change takes place. Instead of the twenty-five minutes that pinto beans take to cook, now, "under pressure," they take only seven minutes . . . and less gas. Surely that's good enough to merit calling such a technique—positive feedback? I was so encouraged by the speed of cooking beans and grains with a modern pressure cooker that I've given some suggestions for using the pressure cooker on a staggered time system for various grains and legumes that go well together but have radically different cooking times.

USES: I'm totally convinced that eating more peas, beans, lentils and whole grains will make a tremendous difference to our health; especially when used to replace meats and fried foods, high in saturated fat.

■ This is an excellent example of how two "long-duration" foods can be cooked in the same pressure cooker with perfect results. The beans are given a 10 minute head start—the result is perfection. The cooking order is reversed if you adopt the gas-less approach, and the rice gets an 8 minute start on the beans.

■ It is vitally important to allow just enough liquid to cook *both* beans and rice . . . A cup of beans cooked with a cup of rice needs a total of 5 cups (1.2 l) liquid to achieve moisture without scorch! In the gas-less version, the beans need only 7 minutes to cook and 1 cup (236 ml) less liquid.

■ This is your picture-perfect result in about 35 minutes— nothing could be faster or more delicious. When you've mastered this method you've made a giant step forward toward healthier eating . . . and lower food costs.

GOLD MEDAL BEANS AND RICE

Serves 4
INGREDIENTS

6 cups ham hock stock (1.4 l) (see page 35), finely
chopped meat reserved

1 cup dried pinto beans (236 ml)

1 cup raw brown rice (236 ml)

2 tablespoons freshly squeezed lemon juice (30 ml)

One 16-ounce bunch of collard greens (454 gm),
stems trimmed, and very finely sliced

¼ teaspoon freshly ground black pepper (1.25 ml)

¼ teaspoon freshly ground salt (1.25 ml)

½ teaspoon cumin seed (2.5 ml)

¼ teaspoon cayenne pepper (1.25 ml)

2 whole cloves

¼ teaspoon dried thyme (1.25 ml)

NOW COOK

■ Pour 5 cups (1.2 l) of the ham hock stock into a
pressure cooker and bring to a boil. Add the beans,
fasten the lid, let the pressure build up inside.
When the cooker starts to hiss, turn the heat down
to medium low—the cooker should be just hissing
—and cook 10 minutes.

■ Remove from the heat and release the steam.
Unfasten the lid, add the rice, refasten the lid and
bring the liquid to a boil. When the cooker starts to
hiss, turn the heat down to medium low and
simmer 15 more minutes. Remove from the heat,

release the steam and spoon the cooked beans and
rice into a large serving dish and keep warm.

■ Put the remaining 1 cup (236 ml) of the ham
hock stock into the pressure cooker, add the lemon
juice and bring to a boil. Add the ham hock meat
and reduce the liquid by half—about 2 minutes.
Drop in the collard greens, season with the black
pepper and salt, stir well and simmer 2 minutes.

■ Make a hollow in the middle of the rice and
beans and spoon in the cooked collards and ham,
pouring in any excess juices.

■ Place the cumin seed, cayenne, cloves and
thyme into a small coffee mill and puree to a fine
powder. Sprinkle 1 teaspoon (5 ml) of the spice
mixture over the finished beans and rice.

■ Bring to the table and serve your guests.

Nutritional Profile

PER SERVING	CLASSIC	MINIMAX
Calories	745	403
Fat (gm)	40	11
Saturated fat (gm)	15	4
Calories from fat	48%	24%
Cholesterol (mg)	113	25
Sodium (mg)	1593	1351
Fiber (gm)	15	7

■ *Classic Compared: Beans and Rice*

POT OF GOLD,
SPOON OF COMFORT

$\mathcal{K}$eep this in the refrigerator and use it whenever you want a delicious, low-fat method of thickening soups, pasta sauces, etc. It will keep well for two weeks.

Makes 2 cups (472 ml)
About 16 servings, 2 tablespoons each (30 ml)
INGREDIENTS

1 teaspoon extra-light olive oil, with a dash of sesame oil (5 ml)

¼ teaspoon toasted sesame oil (1.25 ml)

½ yellow onion, peeled and finely chopped

One 1-inch (2.5 cm) cube fresh gingerroot, peeled and finely chopped

1 clove garlic, peeled, smashed and minced

8 ounces dried red lentils (227 gm)

4 fresh sage leaves, finely sliced

1 teaspoon fresh thyme leaves (5 ml)

2 cups water (472 ml)

NOW COOK

■ Pour the oils into a hot pressure cooker, add the onion, ginger and garlic and fry for 30 seconds. Add the lentils, herbs and water, stirring to make sure nothing is sticking to the bottom of the pan and every lentil is scraped from the sides. Fasten the lid and bring to a boil. When the cooker starts to hiss, turn the heat down and let lentils simmer for 15 minutes. Remove from the heat, release the steam and unfasten the lid.

■ Spoon the lentils into a bowl, cover and keep on hand in the refrigerator, adding about 2 tablespoons (30 ml) to bowls of stew or soup or whenever you feel you need a "golden spoonful of comfort."

Nutritional Profile

PER SERVING	CLASSIC	MINIMAX
Calories	320	142
Fat (gm)	10	1
Saturated fat (gm)	1	0
Calories from fat	28%	9%
Cholesterol (mg)	0	0
Sodium (mg)	364	3
Fiber (gm)	11	6

■ *Classic Compared: Spiced Lentils*

SUGAR 'N' SPICE BEANS 'N' RICE

Serves 6
INGREDIENTS

1 teaspoon extra-light olive oil, with a dash of sesame oil (5 ml)

½ yellow onion, peeled and finely chopped

1½ teaspoons cumin seed (7.5 ml)

1 tablespoon brown sugar (15 ml)

5 cups water (1.2 l)

2 bay leaves

1 cup dried great northern beans (236 ml)

1 cup raw brown rice (236 ml)

Zest of 1 orange, finely chopped

8 green onions, white and pale green part, finely chopped

Juice of 1 orange

½ teaspoon freshly ground salt (2.5 ml)

¼ teaspoon cayenne pepper (1.25 ml)

NOW COOK

■ Pour the oil into a pressure cooker over medium-high heat, add the onion, 1 teaspoon (5 ml) of the cumin seed and the sugar and cook until the onion is translucent—about 5 minutes. Add the water and bay leaves and bring to a boil. Stir in the beans, making sure none are sticking to the bottom of the pan. Fasten the lid, wait until the cooker starts to hiss, reduce the heat and simmer 10 minutes.

■ Remove from the heat, release the steam and remove the lid. Remove the bay leaves, add the rice, refasten the lid, return to the heat and bring to a boil. When the cooker starts to hiss, reduce the heat and simmer 20 minutes. Remove from the heat, release the steam and unfasten the lid. Stir in the orange zest and green onions. Season with the remaining cumin, the orange juice, salt and cayenne.

■ To Serve: I look upon this dish as a complete meal in itself. There is sufficient for 6 servings when accompanied by ample servings of freshly steamed carrots and a dark green leafy vegetable such as Swiss chard, or collard or mustard greens.

Nutritional Profile

PER SERVING	CLASSIC	MINIMAX
Calories	556	246
Fat (gm)	16	2
Saturated fat (gm)	5	0
Calories from fat	25%	8%
Cholesterol (mg)	15	0
Sodium (mg)	1340	190
Fiber (gm)	21	6

■ *Classic Compared: Boston Baked Beans*

MINIMAX METHOD—ULTRABURGERS

With the arrival of the food processor and reasonably priced Kitchen Centers, a brave new world has emerged for the old-fashioned minced beef "hamburger." The high speed blades literally melt the meat and the seasonings to form an incredibly attractive dish.

What I have learned to do is to use fairly small portions and pulse the motor rather than run it flat out. What happens is that you retain control over the texture to a fine degree and this is vitally important if you want the best product.

Although it may seem like an inconvenient step I really do recommend that you combine the vegetable seasonings separately from the meat and then hand-mix the two . . . the overall texture balance is far superior.

As you'll see from the recipes, this is wide open for creative experimentation. Chicken, seafood, or vegetables and grains . . . All are possible, delicious, and just look at the fat comparison figures.

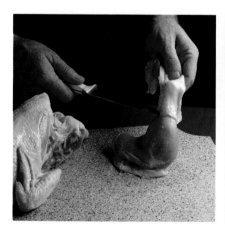

■ I'm completely convinced that any ground beef, fish or fowl *must* be ground at home. It only takes seconds and the quality and freshness of the meat is assured, as well as your being able to see and remove excess fat.

■ Miniprocessors like this one do a great job of chopping finely. In this case, the leg and thigh meat will be completely "melted" together. Be sure to cut the meat in small pieces before adding.

■ This is how it looks when the onion and rice are added. It isn't smooth; rather, the goal is to keep an interesting texture.

GARDEN BURGERS

This can be served together with the Chicken Ultraburgers as companion vegetable portions, coated with the same sauce, or as a hearty sandwich on its own.

Serves 2
INGREDIENTS

½ medium onion, peeled
2 teaspoons extra-light olive oil, with a dash of sesame oil (10 ml)
1 tablespoon curry powder (15 ml)
One 14½-ounce can red kidney beans (412 gm)
4 tablespoons dark raisins (60 ml)
1 tablespoon fresh chopped parsley leaves (15 ml)
1 tablespoon freshly squeezed lemon juice (15 ml)
1 cup cooked long grain brown rice (236 ml)
¼ teaspoon freshly ground salt (1.25 ml)

2 whole wheat buns
4 lettuce leaves
2 thick tomato slices

NOW COOK

■ Process the onion, using the fast pulse, until it's in small but still discernible pieces.

■ Heat half of the oil in a medium-sized skillet over high heat and cook the onion and curry powder for 3 minutes. Add the beans, raisins, parsley, lemon juice and cooked onion to the processor and fast pulse 12 times. Transfer to a bowl, add the cooked rice and the salt and mix well. Form into 2 patties.

■ Pour the remaining oil into a medium-sized skillet over high heat and brown the patties on each side for 3 minutes.

■ To Serve: Place a patty on each bun, top with the lettuce and tomato.

Nutritional Profile

PER SERVING	CLASSIC	MINIMAX
Calories	709	310
Fat (gm)	43	4
Saturated fat (gm)	14	1
Calories from fat	54%	12%
Cholesterol (mg)	110	1
Sodium (mg)	1184	484
Fiber (gm)	2	10

■ *Classic Compared: Fast-Food Burger*

CHICKEN ULTRABURGER

As you'll see below, this delicious burger is topped with an equally delectable sauce that has two names. If you're serving a certified burger lover, call the sauce Minimax Burger Mayonnaise. However, if you're trying to impress an elegant friend, serve the burger without the bun, drizzled with what is now called Horseradish-Wine Sauce. Either way, you're bound to make a good impression.

Serves 4
INGREDIENTS

One (3½-pound whole roasting chicken (1.6 kg)
1 onion, peeled and quartered
4 tablespoons fresh parsley leaves (60 ml)
4 tablespoons fresh parsley stalks (60 ml)
2 tablespoons Dijon mustard (30 ml)
¼ teaspoon freshly ground salt (1.25 ml)
¼ teaspoon freshly ground black pepper (1.25 ml)
1 cup cooked long grain brown rice (236 ml)
1 tablespoon extra-light olive oil, with a dash of sesame oil (15 ml)

4 whole wheat hamburger buns
8 lettuce leaves
4 thick tomato slices

MINIMAX BURGER MAYONNAISE OR
HORSERADISH-WINE SAUCE
½ cup de-alcoholized white wine (118 ml)
¼ cup strained yogurt (59 ml) (see page 85)
2 teaspoons horseradish (10 ml)

FIRST PREPARE

■ The Chicken: Remove all the skin and trim off all visible fat. Cut off the meat—you should have approximately 16 ounces (454 gm). Chop meat into small pieces and divide it into two piles, each with half of the breast meat and half of the leg and thigh meat.

■ Place the onion, parsley leaves, parsley stalks, mustard, salt and pepper into the food processor and pulse until the onion is minced but not pureed. Transfer to a large bowl and set aside.

■ Process the meat in the processor (one half at a time, if necessary); 20 fast pulses. Transfer to the bowl with the onion mixture, add the rice and stir until well mixed. Form into 4 patties of equal size. (This step is easier if you chill the chicken-rice mixture in the refrigerator for an hour.)

NOW COOK

■ Heat the oil in a large skillet over medium heat. Add the chickenburgers and cook 4 minutes on each side.

■ The Minimax Burger Mayonnaise (Horseradish-Wine Sauce): Deglaze the skillet with the wine, scraping to loosen up the bits of pan residue into the liquid. Strain into a small bowl. Stir in the yogurt and horseradish and set aside.

■ To Serve: Place a chickenburger on each bun, top with Minimax Burger Mayonnaise, passed through the same sieve used to strain the deglazing liquid. Top with the tomato slices and lettuce.

Nutritional Profile

PER SERVING	CLASSIC	MINIMAX
Calories	709	373
Fat (gm)	43	10
Saturated fat (gm)	14	2
Calories from fat	54%	25%
Cholesterol (mg)	110	64
Sodium (mg)	1184	532
Fiber (gm)	2	5

■ *Classic Compared: Fast-Food Burger*

SEAFOOD BURGERS

Serves 4
INGREDIENTS

8 ounces medium-sized shrimp (227 gm), boiled for 30 seconds, peeled and deveined
8 ounces orange roughy (227 gm), cut in small pieces
¼ teaspoon salt (1.25 ml)
¼ teaspoon cayenne pepper (1.25 ml)
3 green onions, finely chopped
4 medium white mushrooms
1 tablespoon fresh chopped dill (5 ml)
2 egg whites
¼ cup bread crumbs (59 ml)

NOW COOK

■ Preheat the oven to 400°F. (205°C). Place half of the shrimp and half of the roughy in a food processor and process 10 pulses; transfer to a large bowl. Repeat with the remaining shrimp and fish. Sprinkle with the salt and cayenne pepper.

■ Place the onions, mushrooms and dill in the processor and pulse 5 times. Add to the seafood, pour in the egg whites and mix well. Form into 4 patties and set aside.

■ Spread the bread crumbs out on a plate. Place the patties on top and press firmly, coating both sides with the crumbs, and transfer to a baking sheet. Bake for 10 minutes in the preheated oven.

■ To Serve: Serve 1 burger per diner, with a steamed vegetable like broccoli and mashed potatoes on the side.

NOTE: Orange roughy is a thick, dense white fillet of deep-water fish from the northeast coast of New Zealand that is readily available.

Nutritional Profile

PER SERVING	CLASSIC	MINIMAX
Calories	450	110
Fat (gm)	27	1
Saturated fat (gm)	6	0
Calories from fat	53%	10%
Cholesterol (mg)	46	80
Sodium (mg)	793	307
Fiber (gm)	1	1

■ *Classic Compared: Fast-Food Fish Sandwich*

SMOKING IN A POT

A universally popular food flavor comes from an ancient form of food preservation: smoking. Different regions of the world obviously had different aromatic woods, for example, the famous hickory, mesquite or alder. Other areas lacked wood altogether and used herbs or even tea for their smokes. I have adapted a Chinese tea smoke idea that imparts a very light, delicate, sweetish quality to poultry or fish.

The technique is extremely useful for Minimax cooks because the smoked flavors are unusual enough to absorb the diner's interest so that the dishes' very low fat content isn't immediately obvious. Then I surround the smoked meat with bright fresh crisp foods and a nonfat yogurt spread; the rich juiciness of the chicken or fish seems to actually tingle with added flavor.

Be careful what type of cookware you use to smoke. It must be either cast aluminum or cast iron. Please avoid bonded alloys—the dry heat can melt them, and you wind up with a giant hole in the pot and an ingot of metal forever welded to your stovetop!

With a little ingenuity and a deep heavy Dutch oven, you can balance a second expanding steamer platform on the first and double the amount of chicken or fish for larger dinner parties.

USES: So far I've used this technique on fish and chicken. I have no doubt that it could work well with veal, pork or even lamb. When once you've been bitten by the smoke bug and used different types of special woods as well as tea leaves mixed with rosemary or thyme—literally, the sky is the limit.

You may want to set aside a large Dutch oven exclusively for smoked foods. One last point: I suggest you swiftly wrap up the foil used in smoking and put it out in the trash. It does have a way of leaving residual aromas.

■ Lower the foil saucer into a cool pan. You can clearly see the rice, sugar and tea leaves . . . All simple to find in the average store. Turn the heat up high, cover closely and let it rip to build up a good smoke.

■ This is how the smoke ingredients look five minutes later . . . dark brown and bubbling; they give off dense, amber smoke. Simply put the lightly greased expanding steamer platform with the chicken breasts over the smoke and cover.

■ After another 11 minutes, the finished chicken will be a strong amber color outside and wonderfully moist inside . . . perfectly cooked and smoked.

BASIC RECIPE FOR A TEA SMOKE

In this case I remove the skin before smoking the chicken so that I can get an even color over the entire surface. By starting with the skinned side up I also avoid the little dimples caused by the steamer holes—these wind up underneath.

Enough smoke for 4 chicken breasts
INGREDIENTS

2 tablespoons raw brown rice (30 ml)
1 tablespoon brown sugar (15 ml)
4 whole cloves
Tea leaves from 2 Earl Grey tea bags, removed from packets

¼ teaspoon olive oil (1.25 ml)
Two 6-ounce boneless, skinless chicken breasts (170 gm each)

FIRST PREPARE

■ Take 3 sheets of heavy-duty aluminum foil 15 inches (38 cm) square and start rolling the edges under to form a circle that fits in the bottom of your Dutch oven—in our case, a foil saucer approximately 5 inches (13 cm) in diameter. When the edge is rolled to about 1 inch (2.5 cm) high, stop and flatten it. Then, depress the center to hold the smoke ingredients.

NOW COOK

■ In the depression of the aluminum foil saucer, first sprinkle the rice, then the sugar, cloves and the contents of the tea bags. The order of ingredients is very important. Place the foil dish in Dutch oven, cover tightly and cook over high heat until the ingredients in the foil start smoking—about 5 minutes.

■ Brush a steamer platform with the olive oil. Place the chicken on the platform, skinned side up. Put into the Dutch oven over the smoke ingredients, cover and continue smoking over high heat until done—about 11 minutes.

Nutritional Profile

PER SERVING	CLASSIC	MINIMAX
Calories	346	93
Fat (gm)	22	2
Saturated fat (gm)	11	1
Calories from fat	57%	21%
Cholesterol (mg)	107	43
Sodium (mg)	426	40
Fiber (gm)	0	0

■ *Classic Compared: Chicken with White Sauce*

SMOKED CHICKEN SANDWICHES

Serves 4
INGREDIENTS

8 slices whole wheat bread, toasted
4 tablespoons strained yogurt (60 ml)
(see page 85)
4 lettuce leaves, with 1 edge trimmed straight
2 beefsteak tomatoes, each cut into 4 slices
Four 6-ounce boneless skinless chicken breasts,
(170 gm each), smoked and sliced on the diagonal

GARNISH:
Freshly ground black pepper
Freshly ground salt
Fresh finely chopped parsley

NOW COOK

■ For Each Serving: Take 2 pieces of toast, hot from the toaster, and spread 1 side of each with ½ tablespoon (7.5 ml) of the yogurt.

■ Place the toast slices side by side on a dinner plate, yogurt side up. Layer 1 piece of toast with a generous-sized lettuce leaf, letting its edges flow over the sides of the toast, and 1 chicken breast. Sprinkle with black pepper, salt and parsley to taste.

■ On the other piece of toast, layer 2 slices of tomato and dust with parsley. Serve as an open-faced sandwich, with a knife and fork.

Nutritional Profile

PER SERVING	CLASSIC	MINIMAX
Calories	703	449
Fat (gm)	43	9
Saturated fat (gm)	17	3
Calories from fat	54%	17%
Cholesterol (mg)	153	133
Sodium (mg)	677	442
Fiber (gm)	2	6

■ *Classic Compared: Sliced Cold Chicken Sandwich*

SMOKED CATFISH ON A RAFT

Serves 4 as a first course
INGREDIENTS

Four 4-ounce catfish fillets (113 gm each)
Basic Tea Smoke ingredients
½ cup strained yogurt (118 ml) (see page 85)
¼ cup finely chopped pimento (59 ml)
12 fresh basil leaves, very finely sliced
1 teaspoon creamy prepared horseradish (5 ml)
⅛ teaspoon salt (0.6 ml)
1 head iceberg lettuce, cut into ½-inch (1.5-cm) thick slices

GARNISH:
Finely chopped pimento
2 tablespoons fresh finely sliced basil leaves (30 ml)
Half a lemon

NOW COOK

■ Cook the catfish fillets in the Basic Tea Smoke— about 10 minutes. (I cook all of the fillets at the same time, stacking 2 steamer platforms on top of each other.) Remove the fish with tongs and set aside.

■ In a food processor or blender, puree the strained yogurt, half of the pimento, the basil and horseradish until smooth. Stir in the remaining pimento and the salt.

■ To Serve: Place a lettuce "raft" on an individual serving plate and spread with 2 tablespoons (30 ml) of the yogurt puree. Place 1 fillet on top and garnish with a little chopped pimento, basil and fresh lemon juice. Use any remaining pimento and basil to scatter decoratively around the plate.

Nutritional Profile

PER SERVING	CLASSIC	MINIMAX
Calories	709	173
Fat (gm)	42	4
Saturated fat (gm)	7	1
Calories from fat	53%	22%
Cholesterol (mg)	101	68
Sodium (mg)	322	130
Fiber (gm)	3	1

■ *Classic Compared: Fried Catfish Fillets with French Fries*

RISOTTO

There can be no more wonderful innovation among the ways to cook rice than the northern Italian risotto. Unfortunately the classic risotto from Milan is an extraordinary vehicle for adding saturated fat to our diet. I've seen huge quantities of butter and cheese swallowed up in the elegant arborio rice. The result is soft, smooth and delicious but obviously very rich.

In these recipes, which use almost no oil, you'll see that it's entirely possible to enjoy a low-fat risotto when the recipe takes full advantage of some of the aroma, color and texture concepts of fat replacement.

In the following recipes, I've made a modern classic, using veal shank, a curried chicken risotto that has a Polynesian twist and, in Christmas Risotto, the best all-around rice dish I've ever tasted. It was suggested initially by Robert Prince, my senior food associate, who is almost wedded to squash. Together we worked and reworked the idea until it became an excellent example of Minimax: full of aroma, color and texture. It has mouthroundfullness and is low in fat, high in fiber and has almost no cholesterol, surely proving beyond doubt that a low-fat vegetarian dish can be a great food experience.

USES: This is a side dish that works very well when you want to reduce the quantity of meat in your meals. Once you've mastered the basic technique you will be able to springboard with your own favorite seasonings and garnishes and serve risotto in place of a whole raft of high-fat rice, potato and pasta side dishes.

■ With only ½ (2.5 ml) teaspoon of oil it is possible to release the volatile oils from the onion. Sauté for 2 minutes, then add the arborio rice and stir together.

■ The curious quality of arborio rice is that stirring extracts its starch into liquid, creating the creaminess that is the essence of this dish. You can't achieve this creaminess without stirring. When the rice is really stiff, add additional stock until all the liquid is absorbed and the risotto is completely done. Cook over medium heat, because if it's too hot, the liquid will evaporate before it can be absorbed.

■ I always add the cheese, salt and pepper first and stir them in thoroughly. Then I add the meat and let it heat through rapidly. When everything is steaming hot, I slip in the peas and let them heat through on their way to the table.

VEAL RISOTTO

Serves 4
INGREDIENTS

STOCK:

¼ teaspoon extra-light olive oil, with a dash of sesame oil (1.25 ml)

1 onion, peeled and coarsely chopped

½ cup celery tops

1 cup carrots, chopped

One 1½-pound veal shank (680 gm)

1 bay leaf

2 cloves

6 black peppercorns

2 quarts water (1.9 l)

RISOTTO:

½ teaspoon extra-light olive oil, with a dash of sesame oil (2.5 ml)

½ onion, peeled and finely chopped

1 cup raw arborio rice (236 ml)

1 cup de-alcoholized white wine (236 ml)

¹⁄₁₆ teaspoon saffron (0.36 ml)

1 quart veal stock (944 ml)

½ cup freshly grated Parmesan cheese (118 ml)

¼ teaspoon freshly ground salt (1.25 ml)

¼ teaspoon freshly ground black pepper (1.25 ml)

1 cup frozen peas (236 ml), thawed

GARNISH:

2 teaspoons lemon zest (10 ml), minced

4 fresh sage leaves, minced

NOW COOK

■ The Stock: Pour the oil into a large stockpot over medium heat, and sauté the onion, celery and carrots for 3 minutes. Add the veal shank, bay leaf, cloves and peppercorns; cover with the water, bring to a boil, reduce the heat and simmer 2 hours. Skim off any foam that rises to the surface. After 1 hour, add enough water to bring the liquid up to the original level—about 1 cup (236 ml). Remove the veal shank, pull off the meat and set aside—you should have 8 ounces (227 gm) of meat. Strain the broth and remove the surface fat. Pour the stock into a fat-strainer jug—you should have about 1 quart (944 ml) of stock. Pour it back into the stockpot and keep warm.

■ The Risotto: Pour the oil into a large heavy saucepan over medium heat and sauté the onion for 2 minutes. Add the rice and stir until well coated. Pour in the wine, add the saffron and stir well, then let the wine be absorbed into the rice, stirring occasionally—(about 5 minutes). When the rice seems "dry," add enough hot stock to cover the rice—about 1 cup (236 ml)—stirring and cooking until it's absorbed into the rice. Continue the process of adding stock and stirring until all of it is absorbed—about 30 minutes.

■ Add the cheese, salt and pepper and stir well. Fold in the reserved veal. Just before serving, stir in the peas and heat through.

■ To Serve: Divide among 4 dinner plates and sprinkle with the lemon zest and sage.

Nutritional Profile

PER SERVING	CLASSIC	MINIMAX
Calories	2478	419
Fat (gm)	128	8
Saturated fat (gm)	54	4
Calories from fat	46%	18%
Cholesterol (mg)	1100	70
Sodium (mg)	1365	460
Fiber (gm)	3	3

■ *Classic Compared: Veal Osso Bucco*

PINEAPPLE CHICKEN CURRY

Serves 4
INGREDIENTS

1 teaspoon extra-light olive oil, with a dash of sesame oil (5 ml)

1 onion, peeled and finely chopped

1 clove garlic, peeled, mashed and chopped

1 tablespoon curry powder (15 ml)

¼ teaspoon turmeric (1.25 ml) (optional)

1 pound chicken thighs (450 gm), skin on

1 cup raw arborio rice (236 ml)

5 cups chicken stock (1.2 l) (see page 34)

¼ teaspoon freshly ground salt (1.25 ml)

¼ teaspoon freshly ground black pepper (1.25 ml)

One 8-ounce can water-packed small pineapple chunks (227 gm), water reserved

GARNISH:

4 green onions, finely chopped

POP MIXTURE (See page 44):

Two 1-inch (2.5 cm) pieces of cinnamon stick

½ teaspoon freshly grated nutmeg (2.5 ml)

4 whole cloves

8 allspice berries

½ teaspoon cumin seed (2.5 ml)

¼ teaspoon cayenne pepper (1.25 ml) (optional: if you like your curry hot)

NOW COOK

■ Pour the oil into a medium-sized saucepan over medium-high heat and sauté the onion and garlic for 2 minutes. Add the curry powder, stir well and heat through—about 3 minutes. Remove from the heat and set aside. If you like a brighter yellow curry, add ¼ teaspoon (1.25 ml) of turmeric to the curry powder.

■ Preheat the oven to 350°F. (180°C). Place the chicken on a flat surface. Remove 2 tablespoons (30 ml) of the curried onion mixture and spread it under the chicken skin. Press down hard,

distributing the onion over the chicken as much as possible. Put the chicken on a rack in a roasting pan and bake 30 minutes.

■ In order for the risotto to be ready at the same time as the chicken, start the rice after the chicken's been baking 15 minutes. Return the saucepan with the remaining curried onion to medium heat, add the rice and stir until well coated. Pour in enough stock to cover the rice and cook until the liquid is absorbed, stirring occasionally. Continue adding the stock, cooking and stirring until the liquid is completely absorbed —about 30 minutes.

■ Remove the chicken from the oven and transfer to a flat surface. Keeping a bowl of ice water on the side to cool your fingers, remove the chicken skin and slice the meat off the bone, retaining the natural muscle structures. Trim off any visible fat. Set the chicken aside.

■ Stir the salt, pepper, and ¼ cup (59 ml) of the reserved pineapple juice into the risotto, then fold in the chicken and the pineapple chunks.

■ Make the POP Mixture, by putting all the spices in a small coffee mill and grinding them to a powder—you should have about 2 teaspoons (10 ml).

■ To Serve: Spoon the curry into individual serving bowls and sprinkle each with 1 chopped green onion and ½ teaspoon (2.5 ml) of the POP Mixture or "perfume of the palate."

Nutritional Profile

PER SERVING	CLASSIC	MINIMAX
Calories	896	377
Fat (gm)	30	7
Saturated fat (gm)	11	2
Calories from fat	30%	17%
Cholesterol (mg)	152	45
Sodium (mg)	355	252
Fiber (gm)	8	3

■ *Classic Compared: Chicken Curry*

CHRISTMAS RISOTTO

A gorgeous red and green—perfect for Christmas or any time of the year.

Serves 4
INGREDIENTS

One 2½-pound butternut squash (1.1 kg)

4 cups vegetable stock (944 ml) (see page 36)

1 teaspoon extra-light olive oil, with a dash of sesame oil (5 ml)

½ teaspoon ground cumin (2.5 ml)

¼ teaspoon cayenne pepper (1.25 ml)

¼ teaspoon ground allspice (1.25 ml)

½ onion, peeled and finely chopped

1 clove garlic, peeled, mashed and chopped

1 cup raw arborio rice (236 ml)

1 cup de-alcoholized white wine (236 ml)

½ cup freshly grated Parmesan cheese (118 ml)

¼ teaspoon freshly ground salt (1.25 ml)

¼ teaspoon freshly ground black pepper (1.25 ml)

1 sweet red bell pepper, finely diced

1 tablespoon finely chopped parsley stalks (15 ml)

FIRST PREPARE

■ Preheat the oven to 350°F. (180°C). Cut off the neck part of the squash. Trim off the stem and then cut the neck into 4 slices 1 inch (2.5 cm) thick—about 1 pound (454 gm). Place on a lightly greased baking sheet and bake in the preheated oven for 20 minutes, turn and bake 5 more minutes. Remove from oven. Set aside and keep warm. The rest of the squash is cut in half, peeled, seeded and diced small—about 1 pound (454 gm) of diced squash.

NOW COOK

■ Heat the vegetable stock in a medium-sized saucepan and keep warm. In a small bowl, mix together the cumin, cayenne and allspice. Pour the oil into a large saucepan over medium heat and fry the onion and garlic for 3 minutes. Add ½ teaspoon (2.5 ml) of the spice mixture and stir well. Add the diced squash, stir well, cover and cook 5 minutes. Pour in ½ cup (118 ml) of the warm stock and cook 5 more minutes. Remove from the heat and strain the squash juices through a sieve into the saucepan with the vegetable stock. Return the vegetables to their original saucepan.

■ Add the rice to the squash and shake together, to avoid stirring and breaking the squash pieces. Pour in the wine and 1 cup (236 ml) of the warm stock. Stir carefully and cook over medium heat until the liquid is absorbed. Continue adding the stock, cooking and stirring, until you've used all the stock—about 30 minutes.

■ Stir in the remaining spice mixture, the cheese, salt and pepper. Fold in the red pepper and parsley stalks.

■ To Serve: Peel the skin off of the baked squash neck slices. Place 1 slice on each plate and partially cover with the risotto, leaving half the slice exposed.

Nutritional Profile

PER SERVING	CLASSIC	MINIMAX
Calories	703	423
Fat (gm)	26	7
Saturated fat (gm)	10	3
Calories from fat	34%	16%
Cholesterol (mg)	41	8
Sodium (mg)	1629	385
Fiber (gm)	3	10

■ *Classic Compared: Risotto con Due Formaggi*

SPLIT SPUN SALADS

At first glance, from a fat-percentage point of view, dressed salads look devastatingly bad, but reflect for just one moment on the total calories in a salad.

In this section, there are three salads: the basic Split Spun with 35 percent of its calories from fat, the Tomato and Endive at 40 percent, and the Chou Chou with 20 percent. Two of the three might seem "bad" for you. But this is where the percentages are misleading. Take a look at their total calories: Split Spun has 82, Tomato and Endive 61, and Chou Chou 203. As you can see, the lower the calories, the higher the fat as a percentage tends to be.

By far the best way to check the healthfulness of a recipe is to note its total fat, in the case of these salads, 3 grams, 3 grams and 5 grams, respectively. Then keep a running total of how many grams of fat you're eating over a day.

Half your ideal weight in pounds is approximately the number of fat grams you could eat each day. For example, I'm 6 feet 2 inches tall and large boned. A good weight for me is about 180 pounds. Therefore 90 grams of fat would be the maximum I should consume in a day.

However, cooking for my wife, Treena, who is at high risk for heart disease, I usually take in less than 60 grams of fat for about 18 to 20 percent of my total daily calories from fat.

Even the salad with the highest amount of fat has only one twelfth of my daily total and I'm still left with 55 grams of fat to have fun with! The moral of the story is to eat lots of salad and please watch the dressing.

The basic idea in Split Spun Salad is to make a thin enough dressing to spin off or otherwise remove it after it has "seasoned" the salad.

The Chou Chou doesn't work that way, but it's so good, I had to put it somewhere—another defeat for legalism.

USES: The basic technique can be used with any thin dressing. Obviously it doesn't work with creamy mayonnaise or Thousand Island. Do try the oil and vinegar dressing on your own salad items . . . it may become your all-time favorite.

■ Here I've laid out some easy examples of "hard" and "soft" (leaf) vegetables. Please springboard with this idea and use your imagination and your favorite fruits as well as vegetables, herbs and greens in your salads.

■ By spinning the marinated vegetables, you can extract ⅛ cup (30 ml), which, compared with a typical oil and vinegar dressing, is going to reduce the salad from 41 to 3 grams of fat.

■ I only add the spun hard vegetables to the greens at the last moment—spinning them together to once again distribute the dressing and spin off the excess for later use.

SPLIT SPUN SALAD

Serves 4
INGREDIENTS

HARD INGREDIENTS (VEGETABLES):

8 green onions

4 plum tomatoes, cut into eighths

1 cucumber, peeled, seeded and thinly sliced, ¼ inch (0.75 cm)

1 carrot, cut into matchsticks

DRESSING:

2 tablespoons canola oil (30 ml)

1 teaspoon toasted sesame oil (5 ml)

½ cup rice wine vinegar (118 ml)

2 tablespoons brown sugar (30 ml)

¼ teaspoon freshly ground black pepper (1.25 ml)

SOFT INGREDIENTS (GREENS):

½ head iceberg lettuce

2 romaine lettuce leaves

GARNISH:

Freshly ground pepper to taste

NOW COOK

■ Chop the green onions in two where the green stem starts turning a dark color. Chop the white bulb coarsely and set aside. Coarsely chop the dark green tops diagonally and set aside separately.

■ Put all the hard ingredients except the dark green onion tops in a large serving bowl and toss well.

■ In a small bowl or blender, beat the dressing ingredients together—you'll have about ⅔ cup (156 ml) of dressing. Add to the hard ingredients, toss well and let sit 30 minutes. Drain off and reserve the dressing: you now have about ½ cup (118 ml).

■ Put the hard ingredients in a salad spinner set over a bowl and spin about 20 turns. You will spin off an extra ⅛ cup (30 ml) more of the dressing. Now you have only ⅛ cup (30 ml) of dressing on the hard ingredients. Transfer these vegetables onto a plate and set aside.

■ Tear the soft ingredients, the salad greens, into small, 2-inch (5-cm) pieces—a size that's easily handled on a fork—and wash them well. Put into the salad spinner and spin 20 times to remove excess liquid. Add the reserved green onion tops to the salad greens.

■ Just before serving put half the greens in the salad spinner, followed by the vegetables and finally the remaining greens. Pour in the dressing and spin 10 times. You extract about ½ cup (118 ml) of the dressing in this process, leaving only a total of ¼ cup (59 ml) coating the salad ingredients. Transfer the salad to a large bowl, sprinkle with the pepper and toss well. The surplus dressing can be stored in the refrigerator for another day, but should be used before the week is out. The recipe makes enough for 12 servings when spun off in this way.

■ To Serve: Divide among individual plates. Be sure to toss the vegetables with the greens at the last moment. This will protect the leaves from wilting.

Nutritional Profile

PER SERVING	CLASSIC	MINIMAX
Calories	413	82
Fat (gm)	41	3
Saturated fat (gm)	6	0
Calories from fat	89%	35%
Cholesterol (mg)	0	0
Sodium (mg)	160	25
Fiber (gm)	4	3

■ *Classic Compared: French Vinaigrette*

TOMATO AND ENDIVE SALAD

The tomatoes really need to be beautiful for the successful presentation of this salad.

Serves 4
INGREDIENTS

2 large beefsteak tomatoes, cored and cut into 8 thick slices
¼ teaspoon freshly ground black pepper (1.25 ml)
2 heads Belgian endive, ends trimmed, leaves separated
1 green onion, finely chopped

TREENA'S VINAIGRETTE:
1 clove garlic, peeled and smashed
2 tablespoons extra-light olive oil, with a dash of sesame oil (30 ml)
½ cup white wine vinegar (118 ml)
½ teaspoon dry mustard (2.5 ml)
2 tablespoons brown sugar (30 ml)
⅛ teaspoon cayenne pepper (0.6 ml), ¼ teaspoon (1.25 ml) if you like it hot.

NOW COOK

■ Place the tomato slices in a pie plate—you should be able to get 2 layers.

■ Make Treena's Vinaigrette by beating all the ingredients together in a blender until the garlic is dissolved—about 1 minute. Pour over the tomatoes, sprinkle with the pepper, then turn the top layer over so the pepper gets distributed throughout both layers and let sit for 5 minutes.

■ Arrange the tomatoes in an overlapping line down the center of a long serving platter. Put the Belgian endive leaves in the dressing and toss until coated. Tuck the endive leaves along either side of the tomatoes. Scatter with the chopped green onion and serve.

Nutritional Profile

PER SERVING	CLASSIC	MINIMAX
Calories	392	61
Fat (gm)	37	3
Saturated fat (gm)	5	0
Calories from fat	85%	40%
Cholesterol (mg)	0	0
Sodium (mg)	169	17
Fiber (gm)	4	2

■ *Classic Compared: Wine Vinaigrette*

CHOU CHOU SALAD

Serves 4

INGREDIENTS

2 carrots, peeled and cut into matchsticks

1 cauliflower head, just the florets, each cut in half

1 cucumber, peeled, seeded and sliced ¼ inch (0.75 cm) thick

2 large romaine lettuce leaves, very finely sliced

GARNISH:

2 tablespoons pine nuts (30 ml)

¼ cup raisins (59 ml)

DRESSING:

¼ teaspoon extra-light olive oil, with a dash of sesame oil (1.25 ml)

¼ teaspoon cayenne pepper (1.25 ml)

1 tablespoon mustard seed (15 ml)

1 teaspoon cumin seed (5 ml)

1 teaspoon turmeric (5 ml)

2 tablespoons brown sugar (30 ml)

¼ cup rice wine vinegar (59 ml)

¼ cup water (59 ml)

1 cup strained yogurt (236 ml) (see page 85)

1 heaping tablespoon fresh finely chopped cilantro (15 ml)

NOW COOK

■ Steam the carrots and cauliflower until tender—about 10 minutes.

■ To make a spice flavor base for the dressing, pour the oil into a small skillet over medium heat and sauté the cayenne, mustard seed, cumin seed and turmeric for 3 minutes. Add the sugar and mix until well incorporated. Add the vinegar and water, reduce the heat and simmer 30 minutes. Strain—you should have 3 tablespoons (45 ml) of highly concentrated flavor.

■ In a small bowl, gently stir the yogurt until you remove the lumps. Add the spice flavor base, and stir until it's the same consistency as a heavy mayonnaise. Fold in the cilantro until well incorporated.

■ Put the steamed vegetables in a large bowl, add the cucumber and toss well. Add the dressing and stir until the vegetables are well coated.

■ To Serve: Place a mound of the vegetables, nestled in a wreath of the finely sliced lettuce leaves, on each plate. Garnish with the pine nuts and raisins.

Nutritional Profile

PER SERVING	CLASSIC	MINIMAX
Calories	195	176
Fat (gm)	12	5
Saturated fat (gm)	7	1
Calories from fat	53%	24%
Cholesterol (mg)	38	1
Sodium (mg)	325	127
Fiber (gm)	5	9

■ *Classic Compared: Sour Cream Dressing*

STRAINED YOGURT SPREADS AND SALAD DRESSINGS

If I were to name one ingredient that I use more than any other in creative Minimax cooking, it would be strained yogurt. Incredibly simple to make, the straining process creates a thick, creamy yogurt "cheese" that's infinitely versatile, giving you a creative tool to achieve great Minimax results that won't call for heaps of salt, fat, refined sugars and starches.

Strained yogurt can be used as a creamy spread alternative to butter or margarine (without a single gram of fat), as a dressing for a new-era Caesar salad and last, but by no means least, as a hot white creamy coating sauce for all manner of main dishes.

Keep a regular supply of strained yogurt in your refrigerator, where it will last at least two weeks, and I think you'll cut your consumption of fat by at least 20 percent without even trying.

Even people who claim to be terrorized by yogurt are amazed at how well it works . . . and that just might be you!

■ For ultrasimplicity, all you need is my yogurt strainer set on top of an empty 32 ounce (907 gm) yogurt tub (it fits perfectly). Fill the sieve to the top with the yogurt, cover and put into the refrigerator for at least 5 hours or overnight.

■ It's really important to cover the yogurt during the straining time to prevent contamination. The whey that drains out is clear and greenish and can be added to grains such as oats to complete the protein or just discarded. The strained yogurt is usually halved in volume.

■ I find that plain strained yogurt is the perfect substitute for butter or margarine on my breakfast toast. I keep it covered in small containers that also look good on the table.

BASIC STRAINED YOGURT

Yields ¾ cup (177 ml), to serve 36
INGREDIENTS

1½ cups plain nonfat yogurt (354 ml)

4 English muffins, or 4 slices of bread, toasted
8 teaspoons marmalade or fruit spread (30 ml)

NOW COOK

■ Put the yogurt in the strainer over a bowl, or you can use a coffee filter, muslin or a paper towel and place in a small sieve over a bowl. Cover and let it drain in the refrigerator, for 5 hours or overnight. The liquid whey drains into the bowl, leaving you with a thick creamy yogurt "cheese."

■ To Serve: Spread 1 teaspoon (5 ml) of the strained yogurt on each toasted muffin half and spread with 1 teaspoon (5 ml) of the marmalade.

Nutritional Profile

PER SERVING	CLASSIC	MINIMAX
Calories	34	3
Fat (gm)	4	0
Saturated fat (gm)	2	0
Calories in fat	102%	3%
Cholesterol (mg)	10	0
Sodium (mg)	1	4
Fiber (gm)	0	0

■ *Classic Compared: Butter*

GARLIC SPREAD

A savory hors d'oeuvre dip or bread spread.

Serves 8
INGREDIENTS

1 whole head garlic
1 cup strained yogurt (236 ml)
1 tablespoon fresh chopped parsley (15 ml)
¼ teaspoon coarsely ground black pepper (1.25 ml)
¼ teaspoon freshly ground salt (1.25 ml)

1 medium loaf whole grain bread, thickly sliced

FIRST PREPARE

■ Preheat oven to 375°F. (190°C). Slice the top off the garlic head, about ½ inch (1.5 cm) from the top. Wrap the garlic head in aluminum foil and bake in the preheated oven for 35 minutes. Remove the aluminum foil and press the baked garlic until all the flesh squeezes out. You should have 1 heaping tablespoon (15 ml) of puree.

NOW COOK

■ Spoon the garlic puree onto a flat surface and use a knife to scrape it together with the yogurt until well incorporated. Scrape in the parsley, pepper and salt.

■ To Serve: Spread the garlic mixture thickly on slices of bread and serve as an hors d'oeuvre. Garlic spread also works well as a vegetable dip or as an alternative to butter for rolls, etc.

Nutritional Profile

PER SERVING	CLASSIC	MINIMAX
Calories	200	96
Fat (gm)	22	1
Saturated fat (gm)	3	0
Calories from fat	98%	9%
Cholesterol (mg)	16	1
Sodium (mg)	157	242
Fiber (gm)	0	2

■ *Classic Compared: Aïoli Mayonnaise Sauce*

CAESAR SALAD

Imagine Caesar salad without the risk of salmonella poisoning from raw egg yolks or artery clogging from high fat! It's here—and it's just what you remember from the classic: fresh, tangy and the perfect first course.

Serves 4
INGREDIENTS

2 slices of whole wheat bread
2 cloves garlic, peeled, mashed and chopped
2 anchovy fillets
¼ teaspoon coarsely ground black pepper (1.25 ml)
4 teaspoons freshly grated Parmesan cheese (20 ml)
½ cup strained yogurt (118 ml)
2 tablespoons de-alcoholized white wine (30 ml)
1 large head romaine lettuce, torn in 2-inch (5-cm) pieces. (Save the dark green top halves of the outer leaves for sandwiches and set the crisp inner leaves aside as a garnish for another dish.)

FIRST PREPARE

■ Preheat the oven to 350°F. (180°C). Make croutons by cutting the bread into ½ inch (1.5 cm) cubes. Put on a baking sheet and bake in preheated oven for 15 minutes or until light golden brown. Set aside.

NOW COOK

■ Working on a flat surface, scrape the garlic and anchovy fillets together with the blade of a knife (a mortar and pestle will also work well). Sprinkle with the pepper and keep scraping until well incorporated. The crumbly coarsely ground pepper is a gritty substance that helps combine all the ingredients.

■ Scrape in the cheese until well combined. (I've used Parmesan because this is readily available. Please feel free to use the dry cheese of your choice.) Transfer to a small bowl. Add the yogurt and mix well. Pour the wine on top and scrape together.

■ To Serve: Put the Romaine leaves in a large bowl. Spoon in the dressing and toss until each leaf is well coated. Sprinkle with the croutons and toss again. Divide onto individual serving plates and bring to the table for your fortunate guests.

Nutritional Profile

PER SERVING	CLASSIC	MINIMAX
Calories	741	91
Fat (gm)	69	1
Saturated fat (gm)	16	1
Calories from fat	84%	14%
Cholesterol (mg)	49	4
Sodium (mg)	1372	214
Fiber (gm)	3	2

■ *Classic Compared: Lemony Caesar Salad*

UPPER CRUSTS AND LOWER CRUSTS

*H*igh up on the health risk list comes everyone's favorites: pie, quiche and cheesecake. Surprisingly, it isn't always the filling that delivers the fat punch, but rather the crusts, which often have as much as 70 percent of their calories from fat.

So what to do about these favorites? For pie, I've invented a flaky crust with wheat germ that will suit either sweet or savory pies. The quiche is made with a rice and cheese crust that is, to say the least, unique! Then the cheesecake is wrapped in a fig and cookie crust, which delivers aroma, color and texture without the fat. What follows are many offerings, some basic hints and nine variations on the theme of "lower crusts."

Wheat Germ Crusts

*M*y father was a Scot, my mother, English, and I was born in London, England. I'm a Brit to my roots, and my love of savory pies of any kind confirms the fact!

I started with an old five-minute (to make) flaky pie crust recipe and replaced butter with stick *margarine,* reducing the quantity by one third. Then I boosted the plain flour with wheat germ, which added a nutty "warm" flavor and a pleasing freckled appearance.

The final touch came when I tried to reduce the volume of pastry by baking only a lid and setting it on top of a good stew or casserole. Please understand me: I know it isn't a pie, but it does provide the pleasure of having a crisp crust to crunch and mingle with the tender meat and it avoids the all-too-often pallid, soggy, raw pastry bottoms for which "we" (I mean the royal "we" here, representing the British nation) are supposed to be famous.

■ Smooth the margarine over your fingers with your thumb. You're not making crumbs, but distributing thin flecks of margarine throughout the crust.

■ It mixes quickly into a malleable dough, so please don't overwork it.

■ This folding and rolling process helps distribute the margarine more completely and gives you a lighter, flakier final product.

WHEAT GERM CRUST

Covers the top of a 9 inch pie (23 cm);
serves 8

INGREDIENTS

1½ cups all-purpose flour (354 ml)

¼ cup wheat germ (59 ml)

6 tablespoons polyunsaturated stick margarine (90 ml), cut into 12 small pieces and well chilled in the freezer for 2 hours

5 tablespoons ice water (75 ml)

1 tablespoon 2% fat milk (15 ml)

NOW COOK

■ Sift the flour into a bowl and stir in the wheat germ. Pinch the margarine pieces into the flour with the tips of your fingers until it's completely distributed.

■ Pour in the ice water and mix the dough with your fingers until it sticks together and forms a small ball.

■ Preheat the oven to 425°F. (220°C). Turn the dough out onto a floured board and roll into a long rectangle, about ⅛ inch (0.5 cm) thick. Fold the bottom third over the middle and the top third

over that and repeat the process twice more. Finally, roll the dough out into a circle and place a pie plate on top, upside down. Cut along the outside edge of the pie plate with a sharp knife to get the perfect size circle. Roll it up over the rolling pin and unroll it onto a baking sheet covered with parchment paper. If you're making a pie top with the dough, you might want to score the dough with serving lines that make the crust easier to slice after it's baked. It does make a very crisp, flaky crust. Bake for 10 minutes. For a tasty stew to serve under your Wheat Germ Crust, see Hearty Vegetable Stew Seasoned With Beef, page 19.

Nutritional Profile

PER SERVING	CLASSIC	MINIMAX
Calories	348	176
Fat (gm)	21	9
Saturated fat (gm)	13	2
Calories from fat	55%	47%
Cholesterol (mg)	123	0
Sodium (mg)	183	5
Fiber (gm)	1	1

■ *Classic Compared: Sweet Buttery Crust*

BRITISH CLAY BOWL SALMON PIE AND SWEET CORN SAUCE

Just to let you know that my birthright still means a great deal to me, I have invented the British Clay Bowl Salmon Pie, presented in a crust case that stays wonderfully crisp. Tender and tasty, pink, yellow and white, it is a lunch pie with a nutty-tasting crust.

Serves 4
INGREDIENTS

1 Wheat Germ Crust
One 7½ ounce can water-packed salmon (213 gm), sodium free if possible, or 8 ounces fresh salmon (213 gm)
2 teaspoons capers (10 ml)
1 teaspoon fresh chopped dill (5 ml)
¼ teaspoon freshly ground black pepper (1.25 ml)
1 cup cooked white rice (236 ml)
½ cup frozen corn (118 ml)

SAUCE:

1 cup frozen corn (236 ml)
1 cup de-alcoholized white wine (236 ml)
1 teaspoon cornstarch (5 ml), mixed with 2 teaspoons de-alcoholized white wine (10 ml)
½ cup strained yogurt (118 ml) (see page 85)
1 teaspoon fresh chopped dill (5 ml)

FIRST PREPARE

■ Prepare the Wheat Germ Crust to the final rolling-out step. Lightly grease a 5½-inch (14-cm) wide, 2 cups (472 ml) in volume, ovenproof clay bowl with margarine. Drop the pastry over the bowl, pressing it lightly to line the bottom and sides. There will be three folds. Just pinch the folded dough together until it thins and comes off easily. Carefully press the remaining dough together to obscure the pinch marks. Cut the excess dough away from the bowl rim.

■ Use the excess dough to make the pie top. Press all the pieces on top of each other then roll out about ⅛ inch (0.5) cm thick.

NOW COOK

■ Preheat the oven to 350°F. (180°C). In a small bowl, mix the salmon, capers, half the dill and half the pepper. In another bowl, mix the rice, corn, remaining dill and remaining pepper.

■ Spoon half of the rice mixture into the crust-lined bowl and press down firmly. Follow with half the salmon, the remaining rice and finally the remaining salmon.

■ Moisten the pastry on the rim of the bowl with water. Cover with the pie top, press the edges lightly together, cut off the excess and crimp the edges tight. Cut a few steam vents and bake the pie 50 minutes. Don't be fooled—this crust doesn't turn golden brown . . . but it will shrink back and be wonderfully crisp.

■ The Sauce: In a large saucepan, mix the corn and wine, bring to a boil and remove from the heat. Strain, reserving the liquid and solids separately. Put all the corn in a processor or blender and add enough liquid to puree until smooth. Strain back into the saucepan, pushing gently on the solids to extract all the juices and add the reserved liquid. Add the cornstarch slurry, return to the heat, bring to a boil and stir until thickened—about 30 seconds. Remove from the heat and let cool.

■ Put the yogurt in a small bowl and stir gently to remove the lumps. Add the cooled sauce and stir until completely incorporated. Stir in the dill.

■ To Serve: Invert the bowl over a serving plate. Hold the bowl firmly to the plate and give it a sharp shake. Cut the pie into 4 wedges and serve with the sauce spooned on top.

Nutritional Profile

PER SERVING	CLASSIC	MINIMAX
Calories	591	494
Fat (gm)	38	17
Saturated fat (gm)	16	3
Calories from fat	58%	31%
Cholesterol (mg)	173	25
Sodium (mg)	853	77
Fiber (gm)	2	5

■ *Classic Compared: Crisp-Crusted Fish and Green Pepper Pie*

CRUNCHY TOP TURKEY

Serves 4

INGREDIENTS

½ recipe Wheat Germ Crust

2 teaspoons extra-light olive oil, with a dash of sesame oil (10 ml)

2 onions, peeled and finely chopped

1 teaspoon caraway seed (5 ml)

1 teaspoon dill seed (5 ml)

1 pound turkey thigh meat (454 gm), fat trimmed and cut off the bones into large slices, following the muscle lines

1 cup beef stock (236 ml) (see page 35)

1 cup de-alcoholized red wine (236 ml)

4 ounces fresh mushrooms (113 gm)

1 tablespoon arrowroot (15 ml), mixed with 2 tablespoons de-alcoholized red wine (30 ml)

1 pound broccoli (454 gm), florets trimmed

4 medium sweet potatoes, baked and kept warm

FIRST PREPARE

■ Make half the recipe for Wheat Germ Crust. After it's baked, cut into 4 wedges, one for each person.

NOW COOK

■ To a large skillet over high heat, add half of the oil and cook the onions, caraway and dill seeds, letting them sit without stirring for 2 minutes. Now that they're browning nicely, turn the heat down to medium and cook 3 minutes more. Remove and set aside.

■ To the same skillet, add the remaining oil and distribute the turkey, piece by piece, flat on the pan, to brown for 2 minutes on one side. Add the cooked onions and stir until well incorporated. Cook over medium heat for 5 minutes, stirring occasionally.

■ Pour in the beef stock, scraping the pan residues completely into the liquid. Pour in the wine, stir well and simmer, uncovered, for 15 minutes. Add the mushrooms and simmer 10 minutes more. Remove from the heat, add the arrowroot slurry, return to the heat and stir until thickened.

■ At the same time you add the mushrooms, put the broccoli on to steam until tender—about 10 minutes.

■ To Serve: Place a baked sweet potato and some broccoli on each plate. Spoon on the turkey and vegetables and top with a pastry wedge.

Nutritional Profile

PER SERVING	CLASSIC	MINIMAX
Calories	566	570
Fat (gm)	32	19
Saturated fat (gm)	13	4
Calories from fat	51%	30%
Cholesterol (mg)	136	71
Sodium (mg)	992	119
Fiber (gm)	5	8

■ *Classic Compared: Turkey Pot Pie*

Rice Crusts

This is another new technique to eliminate the fat reservoirs found in classic pastry crusts. It's a savory crust made with steamed rice seasoned with just a hint of cheese and molded into a "dough" with egg white.

It does need a short time to precook before adding the filling. I've created an egg-substitute filling in order to provide a flavor very much like custardy quiche.

Please note the radical difference in the fat content: this rice crust makes those nostalgic summer-picnic pies possible, regardless of the cholesterol wars!

The outer exposed rice rim will be crusty and unusual in texture—don't let it throw you. It's only a small piece of the overall crust and it's good to have a chew every now and again!

■ The rice must be carefully cooked to make a good crust. I cook long grain white rice for 10 minutes in boiling water, and turn it directly into a *metal* hand sieve or strainer. Put it over 1 inch of boiling water and cover with a lid. Continue to steam for an extra 5 minutes and it's ready.

■ Turn the rice into a bowl and immediately add the cheese, salt and pepper, and stir very well. Then add the beaten egg white and blend thoroughly. The internal temperature reaches over 180°F. (82°C), so the egg white cooks completely.

■ Turn the seasoned rice-and-cheese ball into a nonstick pie pan and press it firmly into the pan starting at the center and moving out. Raise the sides about ½ inch (1.5 cm) above the rim. The crust is now ready to be prebaked before filling.

PIQUENIQUE PIE

Serves 6

INGREDIENTS

BASIC RICE CRUST:

2 cups cooked white rice

¼ cup freshly grated Parmesan cheese (59 ml)

½ teaspoon freshly ground salt (2.5 ml)

¼ teaspoon freshly ground black pepper (1.25 ml)

1 lightly beaten egg white

FILLING:

1 teaspoon extra-light olive oil, with a dash of sesame oil (5 ml)

1 large yellow onion, peeled, and finely sliced

4 large red new potatoes (about 1¼ pounds or 567 gm), sliced paper thin

1½ teaspoons fresh chopped thyme leaves (7.5 ml)

Freshly ground salt

Freshly ground black pepper

1 cup beef stock (236 ml) (see page 35)

1 cup liquid egg substitute (236 ml)

Garnish with freshly grated Parmesan cheese

FIRST PREPARE

■ The Rice Crust: Preheat the oven to 375°F. (190°C). Pour about 1 inch (2.5 cm) of water into a medium-sized saucepan and bring to a boil. Put the cooked rice in a sieve and place over the boiling water, cover and steam 5 minutes. This process gives you separate, fluffy grains—essential for the rice crust.

■ Transfer the warm rice to a medium-sized bowl and work in the cheese, until the grains are all a pale, uniform yellow. Add the salt and pepper and stir well. Pour in the egg white and stir until the rice clumps together. Shape it into a large ball and transfer to a 9-inch nonstick pie pan.

■ Keeping a bowl of ice water on the side to prevent your fingers from becoming too sticky, press the rice into a thin, uniform layer around the bottom and sides of the pie pan. Start on the bottom, moving to the sides and up to the rim. The crust rim should extend about ½ inch (1.5 cm)

beyond the top of the pie pan. This crust shrinks a lot in the baking process. Bake until just slightly brown—about 25 minutes. Remove and set aside.

NOW COOK

■ The Filling: Pour the oil into a large skillet over medium heat, add the onion and cook until just translucent, but not limp—about 5 minutes. Remove and set aside.

■ Set aside a quarter of the potato slices for the top of the pie. In the same skillet as the onion, layer one third of the remaining potatoes and sprinkle with ½ teaspoon (2.5 ml) of the thyme, a dusting of salt and a dusting of black pepper. Repeat the process with the remaining two thirds of the potatoes and seasonings. Pour in the stock, cover and simmer 10 minutes. The potatoes will not have absorbed all of the stock, so it will help to approach the next step with a slotted spoon so as not to add any stock liquid to the pie.

■ Preheat the oven to 375°F. (190°C). Layer one third of the potatoes and onion on the bottom of the prepared crust and pour on one third of the egg substitute. Repeat the process until the crust is full. Decorate the top with a wreath of overlapping slices from the reserved raw potato. Liberally brush with the remaining skillet juices and bake for 35 minutes—until the top potatoes are translucent, the custard set and the color golden. You might see little driblets of liquid in the center, but that's just the moisture from the stock and potatoes.

■ To Serve: It's the best excuse for a picnic—serve at room temperature, sprinkled with cheese.

Nutritional Profile

PER SERVING	CLASSIC	MINIMAX
Calories	448	279
Fat (gm)	23	2
Saturated fat (gm)	10	1
Calories from fat	46%	7%
Cholesterol (mg)	35	3
Sodium (mg)	286	348
Fiber (gm)	4	4

■ *Classic Compared: Potato Onion Pie*

LEEK AND MUSHROOM QUICHE

Serves 6
INGREDIENTS

1 Basic Rice Crust, baked

FILLING:

2 pounds leeks (907 gm) to yield 1 pound (454 gm) white bulbs only, greens discarded

1 teaspoon extra-light olive oil, with a dash of sesame oil (5 ml)

1 tablespoon fresh chopped thyme (15 ml)

8 ounces fresh mushrooms (227 gm), sliced

¼ teaspoon freshly ground salt (1.25 ml)

¼ teaspoon freshly ground pepper (1.25 ml)

1 cup liquid egg substitute (236 ml)

½ cup 2% fat milk (118 ml)

1 tablespoon freshly grated Parmesan cheese (15 ml)

NOW COOK

■ Cut the white bulbs of the leeks in half lengthwise, rinse well, then slice thinly.

■ Into a large casserole over medium heat, pour half of the oil, add the leeks, stir until well coated and cook 10 minutes, stirring occasionally. Add the thyme and cook an additional 5 minutes. The leeks should be just turning brown. Remove the leeks from the pan.

■ Preheat the oven to 375°F. (190°C). Pour the remaining oil into the same pan, add the mushrooms and cook over low heat for 8 minutes, stirring occasionally. Stir in the leeks, salt and pepper, increase the heat to medium and cook for 2 minutes. Remove from the heat and transfer into the prepared crust.

■ In a bowl, mix together the egg substitute and milk and pour gently over the cooked vegetables. Bake for 30 to 35 minutes until the custard is just set. Remove from the oven and let stand 10 minutes before slicing.

■ To Serve: Sprinkle the pie with the Parmesan cheese and serve with a fresh green salad. (See Helpful Hints and Observations, page 145, for a recipe.)

Nutritional Profile

PER SERVING	CLASSIC	MINIMAX
Calories	604	169
Fat (gm)	46	2
Saturated fat (gm)	24	1
Calories from fat	69%	13%
Cholesterol (mg)	248	5
Sodium (mg)	883	445
Fiber (gm)	1	3

■ *Classic Compared: Mushroom Quiche*

SEAFOOD PIE

Serves 6
INGREDIENTS

1 Basic Rice Crust, baked

FILLING:

8 ounces fresh mushrooms (227 gm)

4 ounces shallots (113 gm)

1 teaspoon extra-light olive oil, with a dash of sesame oil (5 ml)

¼ teaspoon freshly ground salt (1.25 ml)

¼ teaspoon freshly ground pepper (1.25 ml)

½ teaspoon fresh chopped thyme (2.5 ml)

12 ounces scallops (340 gm), cut in half

8 ounces sole (227 gm), cut into fingers

8 ounces shrimp (227 gm) (41 to 50 count to a pound), peeled and deveined

Juice of ½ lemon (about 4 teaspoons or 20 ml)

1 cup liquid egg substitute (236 ml)

1 tablespoon freshly grated Parmesan cheese (15 ml)

NOW COOK

■ Preheat the oven to 375°F. (190°C). In a food processor, pulse the mushrooms and shallots at the lowest speed until very finely minced, but not pureed—about 30 seconds.

■ Pour the oil into a large skillet over medium heat, add the minced mushrooms and shallots, sprinkle with the salt and pepper and cook until reduced in volume by half—about 5 minutes. Stir in the thyme and cook 3 minutes more. If there is any surplus liquid at this stage, be sure to press it out and strain from the pan.

■ Add the seafood to the cooked mushroom mixture, add the lemon juice and stir well. Cook for 5 minutes to remove excess moisture.

■ Pour half the egg substitute into the prepared crust. Cover with half of the seafood mixture, then the remaining egg substitute and seafood. Sprinkle with the cheese and bake for 30 to 35 minutes. You will see some liquid surfacing on the top of the quiche. Do not worry, when you remove it from the oven, the liquid will be reabsorbed. Let the quiche stand for 10 minutes before serving.

■ To Serve: In cold weather, it's ideal to have small new potatoes and some freshly steamed broccoli with the pie. When it's warm, there is nothing better than a good Split Spun Salad (page 80).

Nutritional Profile

PER SERVING	CLASSIC	MINIMAX
Calories	435	270
Fat (gm)	22	4
Saturated fat (gm)	13	1
Calories from fat	22%	13%
Cholesterol (mg)	212	93
Sodium (mg)	1163	674
Fiber (gm)	1	2

■ *Classic Compared: Shrimp Pie*

Fig Crusts

I've used rice and a little cheese for the crust in savory pies and quiches, a lighter crust with wheat germ to substitute for flaky pastry and, most unusual of all, is this fig and crumb crust for great no-bake cheesecakes.

The examples I've given using the fig crust are for a chocolate cheesecake, a spicy butternut squash cheesecake and, perhaps the oddest idea in the whole book, a dessert log, with a chocolate fig crust and creamed rice and mincemeat filling that's a spin-off of the British sausage roll (puff pastry encased sausages).

Remember, with figs you get no fat and so much fiber you could wind up feeling like a coconut. You may need a small food processor to help you work the figs, because it's very hard work with a knife.

■ Here you can see the white figs and crackers before and after their 30-second pulse. They have completely combined into a smooth "dough" that doesn't need cooking.

■ Always smooth the crust into the pan base first and work out from the center. When the base is less than ¼ inch (0.75 cm) thick, start to move up the sides; trim flush with the top.

■ Pour the filling into the fig crust until it reaches the brim. Refrigerate for 2 to 3 hours until perfectly set.

CHOCOLATE CHEESECAKE WITH FIG CRUST

Serves 12

INGREDIENTS

BASIC FIG CRUST:

18 dried white figs, stalk ends removed

1 cup graham cracker crumbs (236 ml)

FILLING:

¾ cup brown sugar (177 ml)

1 cup evaporated skim milk (236 ml)

4 envelopes unflavored gelatin

4 tablespoons unsweetened cocoa powder (60 ml)

2 teaspoons vanilla (10 ml)

3 cups 2% fat cottage cheese (708 ml)

GARNISH:

Paper-thin orange slices or orange zest

NOW COOK

■ The Fig Crust: In a processor, pulse the figs and graham crackers until they clump together in a sticky ball—about 30 seconds (on my Oster Kitchen Center, half speed does the job perfectly). Don't process too long or the crackers will lose their texture. Transfer to a small bowl and press the mass into roughly the same shape as the cheesecake pan.

■ Lightly grease a high-sided 7 inch (18 cm) springform cheesecake pan. Press the crust mixture into the bottom and completely up the sides of the pan. Dip your fingers into a bowl of cold water to alleviate any stickiness. Smooth the crust over the bottom of the pan completely first, work out from the center, then build up the sides, bringing the crust up to and beyond the rim of the pan; finally, trim the crust with a small sharp knife for a clean presentation.

■ The Filling: In a small pan, mix the gelatin with the evaporated milk and warm on low heat until the gelatin is dissolved—about 3 minutes. In a blender, puree the evaporated milk and gelatin mixture, the sugar, cocoa and vanilla until completely incorporated—about 30 seconds.

■ Add the cottage cheese one cup at a time, keeping one cup in reserve. Because I like a bit of texture in my filling, I leave the mixture in the food processor until it is completely smooth and then turn it into a bowl, stirring in the last cup of cottage cheese unprocessed.

■ Pour the filling into the prepared crust, pop into the refrigerator and chill until set—about 2 to 3 hours.

■ To Serve: Unmold, slice with a warm knife and garnish each piece with a paper-thin orange slice or blanched orange zest.

Nutritional Profile

PER SERVING	CLASSIC	MINIMAX
Calories	413	210
Fat (gm)	28	3
Saturated fat (gm)	17	1
Calories from fat	61%	11%
Cholesterol (mg)	118	6
Sodium (mg)	241	292
Fiber (gm)	2	3

■ *Classic Compared: Chocolate Cheesecake*

BUTTERNUT SQUASH CHEESECAKE WITH A CHOCOLATE CRUST

Serves 12
INGREDIENTS

BASIC FIG CRUST:

18 dried white figs, stalk ends removed

1 cup crushed chocolate wafers (236 ml)

FILLING:

1 small butternut squash to yield 2 cups (472 ml) cooked squash

4 envelopes unflavored gelatin, completely dissolved in 1 cup warmed water (236 ml)

¾ cup brown sugar (177 ml)

2 cups 2% fat cottage cheese

½ teaspoon cinnamon (2.5 ml)

½ teaspoon ground cloves (2.5 ml)

½ teaspoon ginger (2.5 ml)

1 cup plain nonfat yogurt (236 ml)

GARNISH:

1 heaping tablespoon (15 ml) orange zest, cut into strips, or 12 paper-thin orange slices.

FIRST PREPARE

■ Preheat oven to 350°F. (180°C). Cut the squash in half, remove the seeds, place face down on a baking sheet and bake in the preheated oven for 40 minutes. Remove and let cool. Scoop 2 cups (472 ml) of the flesh out and puree for this recipe and freeze the rest for future use.

NOW COOK

■ Make the Fig Crust, substituting chocolate wafers for the graham cracker crumbs, and press into a springform pan.

■ The Filling: In a blender, puree all the ingredients except the squash and yogurt until smooth and creamy—about 2 minutes, gradually increasing the speed. Stir if necessary to complete the incorporation. Turn this mixture into the reserved squash and stir thoroughly. Then fold in the yogurt until just combined.

■ Pour the filling into the prepared crust, pop into the refrigerator and chill until set—about 2 to 3 hours.

■ To Serve: Unmold, slice with a warm knife and garnish each piece with orange zest or a thin orange slice.

Nutritional Profile

PER SERVING	CLASSIC	MINIMAX
Calories	366	249
Fat (gm)	27	4
Saturated fat (gm)	16	1
Calories from fat	65	13
Cholesterol (mg)	120	10
Sodium (mg)	267	252
Fiber (gm)	1	4

■ *Classic Compared: Butternut Cheesecake*

YULE STICKIES

A merry Minimax alternative to Christmas cookies. Make them at your leisure, then freeze until you're ready to serve them. Joyeux Noël for both the busy hostess and her guests!

Makes about 27 stickies

INGREDIENTS

FILLING:

½ cup raw pearl rice (118 ml)
2 cups 2% fat milk (472 ml)
2 tablespoons mincemeat pie filling (30 ml)
1 tablespoon orange zest (15 ml), in strips
¼ teaspoon cinnamon (1.25 ml)
¼ teaspoon ground nutmeg (1.25 ml)
¼ teaspoon ground ginger (1.25 ml)
¼ teaspoon ground allspice (1.25 ml)

BASIC FIG CRUST:

12 dried white figs, stalk ends removed
1 cup crushed chocolate wafers (236 ml)

COATING:

2 tablespoons Minimax Seed Mix (30 ml), finely ground (see page 113)
1 teaspoon all-purpose flour (5 ml)

NOW COOK

■ The Filling: Make a risotto with the rice and milk. First pour the milk into a small saucepan, bring just to the boiling point and remove from the heat. Put the rice in a medium-sized saucepan over medium-high heat, add enough of the milk to cover and stir until the liquid is absorbed—about 7 minutes. Cover with milk again and repeat the process until all the milk is absorbed and the rice is tender and creamy—a total of about 30 minutes. Remove from the heat and let cool.

■ In a large bowl, mix the cooled cooked rice, mincemeat, orange zest and spices until well incorporated.

■ Make the Basic Fig Crust, substituting the ingredients listed above.

■ Transfer the crust onto a piece of plastic wrap on a flat surface and shape it into a long, flat rectangle about 12 inches (30 cm) long and 5 inches (13 cm) wide. Pressing firmly with your fingers, push from the center out to the sides until the strip is ⅛ inch (0.5 cm) thick. Trim the edges neatly with a knife. Use the trimmings by pressing them onto either end of the rectangle, continuing the strip lengthwise. The final trimmed rectangle should be about 20 inches (51 cm) long.

■ Spoon the rice filling along the center of the crust rectangle, using a knife to firmly press the sides smooth and about 1 inch (2.5 cm) high. Lift the long sides of the plastic to bring the fig crust edges together in a long cylinder. Pinch the edges tightly closed, cutting off any excess filling and crust. Pull off the plastic wrap. Cut the log in half, wrap both pieces in plastic and put into the freezer until ready to serve. The log will stiffen, but not freeze hard.

■ To Serve: Mix the Minimax Seed Mix with the flour and spread on a flat surface. Roll the log in the seeds until well coated. Using a sharp, serrated knife and a sawing motion, cut the log into ¾ inch (2 cm) slices and arrange on a serving plate. This is great, sweet, sticky, finger food; just provide cocktail napkins and you're all set!

Nutritional Profile

PER SERVING	CLASSIC	MINIMAX
Calories	106	78
Fat (gm)	4	2
Saturated fat (gm)	1	1
Calories from fat	36%	21%
Cholesterol (mg)	18	4
Sodium (mg)	91	49
Fiber (gm)	1	1

■ *Classic Compared: Chocolate Fruit Bars*

MUFFINS

Without doubt, the muffin can be one of the key elements in changing our eating habits. It's a universally enjoyed and much-appreciated morning carbohydrate, but unfortunately, it traditionally comes loaded with fat, eggs and sugar, and what appears to be healthful may actually present a major risk.

I've taken a stab at resolving two muffin problems. The first assumes that very few of us will tumble out of bed early, in order to whip up a batch of muffins from scratch. But what, I reasoned, if the batter could be made up completely the evening before, and then in the morning spooned into muffin cups, and simply slipped into the oven for twenty-five minutes? The recipes I've given you in this section will do this for you.

Secondly, I wanted to use ingredients that pack added nutrient benefits, such as beta-carotene. In the recipes that follow, you've got butternut squash and sweet potatoes, the undisputed "King of the Roots." I've seasoned these carefully with ground ginger, cinnamon and lemon zest to add excitement and applesauce to keep the moisture and texture with much less fat. These muffins are a particular help with fiber and also "good energy," the kind that's derived from calories that come complete with macro- and micronutrients . . . so much so that the nutritional comparisons speak for themselves.

As with every muffin, they are best when served warm from the oven. Make them soon as a great way to please and care for your family.

USES: The technique is really basic and you'll see how it can be modified to incorporate vegetables as well as fruit purees. This type of muffin is less fluffy and leans to a finer texture, but is full of taste and nourishment. Try eating Minimax muffins instead of breakfast Danish—lots of calorie savings if you do.

■ The egg whites and sugar or, as in this case, golden molasses —are beaten together into a light froth. This is the moment to add the applesauce.

■ I never stir the wet and dry ingredients together more than 20 turns—the less handled the better. At this point, add the frozen raspberries and fold twice, carefully. Transfer immediately to the muffin cups and bake. If you make the batter the night before, keep the addition of the raspberries until you are ready to bake.

■ Here we have three muffins. Ours is the golden-brown muffin in the middle, with 1 gram of fat and 149 calories. On its left is a store-bought muffin that is double the volume, but contains 960 calories and a whopping 20 grams of fat. On the right is a store-bought dark raisin bran muffin, a more reasonable size, but it will bring you 480 calories and 10 fat grams.

GOLDEN BRAN AND RASPBERRY MUFFINS

The bright note of the raspberry is designed to startle your taste buds in mid-bite.

Makes 6 large muffins
INGREDIENTS

1 cup cake flour (236 ml)
1 cup wheat bran (236 ml)
2 teaspoons baking powder (10 ml)
½ teaspoon baking soda (2.5 ml)
2 egg whites
¼ cup molasses (59 ml)
¾ cup unsweetened applesauce (177 ml)
¼ cup evaporated skim milk (59 ml)
½ cup frozen unsweetened raspberries (118 ml), thawed but not mushy

NOW COOK

■ Line your muffin tin with paper or foil muffin cups and preheat the oven to 350°F. (180°C). In a large bowl, mix the flour, bran, baking powder and baking sodas until well incorporated.

■ In a medium-sized bowl, whisk the egg whites and molasses until frothy. Whisk in the applesauce and milk.

■ Pour the liquids on top of the dry ingredients and stir until just incorporated, but do not overstir. At this point you can cover the batter and leave in the refrigerator overnight. The fruit should be added just before baking.

■ Very gently fold in the raspberries, trying to prevent the fruit from breaking. Spoon a heaping ¼ cup (59 ml) of the batter into each muffin cup, filling each completely; the muffins do rise, but not as much as their high-fat cousins. Bake for 25 minutes until golden brown. Remove the muffins from the tin and transfer to a wire rack to cool for 5 minutes.

■ To Serve: Take them to the table while still warm. No need for added fat, preserve or jelly. The muffin's complete in itself.

Nutritional Profile

PER SERVING	CLASSIC	MINIMAX
Calories	352	149
Fat (gm)	16	1
Saturated fat (gm)	3	0.7
Calories from fat	42%	4%
Cholesterol (mg)	72	0
Sodium (mg)	294	201
Fiber (gm)	6	6

■ *Classic Compared: Bran Muffins*

SQUASH AND GINGER MUFFINS

Ginger is a fresh, lively addition to these muffins, but make sure you measure it absolutely flat and level so you don't overwhelm the muffins with its distinctive flavor. The baked squash should be somewhat crumbly, not completely smooth, so that it flecks throughout the batter.

These muffins are also great for dinner with a pot of chili. Just before baking, grate a teaspoonful (5 ml) of cheese on top.

Makes 6 large muffins
INGREDIENTS

1¾ cups cake flour (413 ml)
2 teaspoons baking powder (10 ml)
½ teaspoon baking soda (2.5 ml)
1 teaspoon ginger (5 ml)
2 egg whites
¼ cup brown sugar (59 ml)
¾ cup unsweetened applesauce (177 ml)
¼ cup evaporated skim milk (59 ml)
1 small butternut squash (about 1 pound or 454 gm), baked and flesh removed. You need ¾ cup (177 ml) for this recipe.

NOW COOK

■ Line your muffin tin with muffin cups and preheat the oven to 350°F. (180°C). In a large bowl, whisk the flour, baking powder, baking soda, and ginger together until well incorporated. The whisking process eliminates the need for sifting.

■ In a medium-sized bowl, whisk the egg whites together with the brown sugar until just frothy. Whisk in the applesauce and milk. Mash the squash with a fork and stir into the liquid mixture until distributed evenly.

■ Add the liquid mixture all at once over the top of the dry ingredients and stir until just combined —it's important not to overstir. Spoon a heaping ¼ cup (59 ml) of the batter into each muffin cup; each should be full and well rounded. Bake for 25 minutes or until golden brown. Turn the muffins out onto a wire rack to cool for 5 minutes.

■ To Serve: Once again, these muffins don't need butter or jams. They also can be served as a biscuit alternative with casserole dishes.

Nutritional Profile

PER SERVING	CLASSIC	MINIMAX
Calories	362	183
Fat (gm)	11	0
Saturated fat (gm)	6	1
Calories from fat	27%	2%
Cholesterol (mg)	78	0
Sodium (mg)	244	191
Fiber (gm)	2	2

■ *Classic Compared: Sweet Potato Maple Muffins*

SWEET POTATO AND RAISIN MUFFINS

It's so vital to incorporate beta-carotene–rich vegetables into your life, and I can think of few more pleasant ways than with this colorful muffin.

Makes 7 large muffins
INGREDIENTS

1¾ cups cake flour (413 ml)
2 teaspoons baking powder (10 ml)
½ teaspoon baking soda (2.5 ml)
½ teaspoon cinnamon (2.5 ml)
2 egg whites
2 tablespoons brown sugar (30 ml)
¾ cup unsweetened applesauce (177 ml)
¼ cup evaporated skim milk (59 ml)

2 medium sweet potatoes, baked and flesh removed to yield ¾ cup (177 ml) of mashed potato
1 tablespoon lemon zest (15 ml), finely chopped
2 tablespoons freshly squeezed lemon juice (30 ml)
½ cup dark raisins (118 ml)

NOW COOK

■ Line your muffin tin with paper or foil muffin cups and preheat the oven to 350°F. (180°C). In a large bowl, whisk the flour, baking powder, baking soda and cinnamon until well incorporated.

■ In a medium-sized bowl, beat the egg whites with the sugar until just frothy. Stir in the applesauce and milk, then the mashed sweet potato, lemon zest, lemon juice and raisins, stirring until well combined.

■ Add the liquid mixture all at once over the top of the dry ingredients and stir until *just* combined. Spoon a heaping ¼ cup (59 ml) of the batter into each muffin cup, each should be full and well rounded. Bake for 25 minutes or until golden brown. Turn the muffins out onto a wire rack to cool for 5 minutes.

Nutritional Profile

PER SERVING	CLASSIC	MINIMAX
Calories	362	216
Fat (gm)	11	0
Saturated fat (gm)	6	0
Calories from fat	27%	2%
Cholesterol (mg)	78	0
Sodium (mg)	244	171
Fiber (gm)	2	3

■ *Classic Compared: Sweet Potato Maple Muffins*

COCOA

*C*hocolate is my downfall. If Treena ever brings it into the house, I have a nose like a truffle hound for the stuff and I'll find it.

My best Minimax defense against chocolate consumption has been unsweetened cocoa powder, which, while not fat free, does have substantially less fat than chocolate. You will probably note that I use it quite frequently. This is in the hope that, like me, you might gradually adjust to its use and save yourself substantial exposure to a short-term pleasure with a potential long-term risk.

I've given you a hot fudge type sauce and a cold milky chocolate flowing sauce for waffles or frozen yogurt. The obvious missing ingredient is cocoa butter, you will feel the powdery finish and may miss the rich, smooth, almost cloying taste of chocolate.

One or two experiments later, however, and you'll be on your way, and even more importantly, your kids and grandchildren will get a fresh new start that can develop a much less potent habit.

USES: The flavor and color of chocolate are very much alive in this cocoa technique. With a can of good Dutch cocoa on your shelf, you will be ready to add it to cake mixes, custards, nonfat milk, even sprinkled in your morning coffee. The more you establish cocoa's flavor in your diet, the more it is likely to win as a new habit alternative to chocolate.

■ I wanted you to see this in order to convince you that indeed it is thick, rich, smooth, dark and glossy, and I urge you to make it to see for yourself that the taste is also a classic hot fudge.

■ Cold milk cocoa sauce combines brown sugar, cocoa powder and strained yogurt. In moments, it's ready.

■ It looks fairly obvious. I anointed low-fat frozen yogurt with hot drizzled fudge sauce— terrific! The waffle has the benefit of the cocoa sauce as well as a few discreet chocolate morsels hurled into the batter with reckless abandon.

BASIC HOT FUDGE SAUCE

Makes 12 tablespoons (177 ml)
INGREDIENTS

5 tablespoons warm water (75 ml)
3 tablespoons unsweetened cocoa powder (45 ml)
4 tablespoons brown sugar (60 ml)
1 tablespoon arrowroot (15 ml), mixed with
2 tablespoons water (30 ml)

■ Pour the water, cocoa powder and sugar into a small saucepan and stir over low heat until dissolved. Remove from the heat, stir in the arrowroot slurry, return to the heat and whisk until thickened. Remove from the heat and whisk until smooth.

Nutritional Profile: Basic Hot Fudge Sauce

PER SERVING	CLASSIC	MINIMAX
Calories	477	75
Fat (gm)	20	1
Saturated fat (gm)	12	1
Calories from fat	37%	15%
Cholesterol (mg)	23	0
Sodium (mg)	59	5
Fiber (gm)	3	2

■ *Classic Compared: Hot Fudge Sauce*

HOT FUDGE SUNDAE

Serves 4
INGREDIENTS

16 ounces nonfat vanilla frozen yogurt (454 grams)
1 recipe Basic Hot Fudge Sauce (236 ml)
1 cup frozen cherries (236 ml)

■ Scoop 4 ounces (113 gm) of the yogurt into a parfait glass. Top with 3 tablespoons (59 ml) of the Basic Hot Fudge Sauce and garnish with a few of the cherries.

Nutritional Profile: Hot Fudge Sundae

PER SERVING	CLASSIC	MINIMAX
Calories	744	227
Fat (gm)	38	3
Saturated fat (gm)	23	2
Calories from fat	46%	12%
Cholesterol (mg)	90	6
Sodium (mg)	142	75
Fiber (gm)	3	2

■ *Classic Compared: Hot Fudge Sundae*

BASIC COOL COCOA SAUCE

Makes 12 tablespoons (177 ml)
INGREDIENTS

2 tablespoons unsweetened cocoa powder (30 ml)
3 tablespoons brown sugar (45 ml)
2 tablespoons nonfat milk (30 ml)
1 teaspoon vanilla (5 ml)
1 cup strained yogurt (236 ml) (see page 85)

■ In a small bowl, mix together the cocoa and sugar, stir in the milk until completely dissolved, then stir in the vanilla. In a medium-sized bowl, stir the yogurt until smooth, but do not overstir or it will become too thin. Gently stir in the cocoa mixture until well incorporated. You can stir just until you have a striped effect, or take it all the way to a creamy light brown.

Nutritional Profile: Basic Cool Cocoa Sauce

PER SERVING	CLASSIC	MINIMAX
Calories	396	87
Fat (gm)	19	1
Saturated fat (gm)	12	1
Calories from fat	43%	10%
Cholesterol (mg)	35	1
Sodium (mg)	79	54
Fiber (gm)	2	1

■ *Classic Compared: Creamy Chocolate Sauce*

CHOCOLATE WAFFLES

If you prefer, the Basic Cool Cocoa Sauce can be served as a Warm Cocoa Sauce on top of the waffles—it's your choice.

Serves 4

INGREDIENTS

WAFFLES:

1¾ cups all-purpose flour (413 ml)

1 tablespoon baking powder (15 ml)

⅛ teaspoon salt (0.6 ml)

3 tablespoons granulated sugar (45 ml)

½ cup unsweetened cocoa powder (118 ml)

2 cups nonfat milk (472 ml)

1 whole egg

3 egg whites

2 tablespoons extra-light olive oil (30 ml)

4 teaspoons chocolate morsels (20 ml)

1 Recipe Basic Cool Cocoa Sauce

NOW COOK

■ In a large bowl, stir together the flour, baking powder, salt, sugar and cocoa powder until well incorporated.

■ In another bowl, mix the milk, whole egg and oil. Stir the wet ingredients into the dry mix and beat until smooth and creamy.

■ Just before cooking, beat the egg whites in a copper bowl until they form soft peaks. Gently fold the meringue into the waffle batter, one third at a time, until just incorporated.

■ Preheat the waffle iron according to the manufacturer's directions, or until a drop of water sizzles and bounces. Brush grids lightly with the plain olive oil, then pour approximately ½ cup (118 ml) of the batter per waffle square, or enough to fill the entire iron. It will depend on the type of waffle iron you have. Sprinkle with ½ teaspoon (2.5 ml) of the chocolate morsels and cook for 3 minutes. If the waffles are not crisp enough for you, put them on a wire rack and toast for a minute under a hot oven broiler.

■ To Serve: Present the waffles "hot from the iron" with the Basic Cool Cocoa Sauce on the side. If you can't serve them immediately, lay them out on oven racks to keep crisp at 250°F. (120°C). Please *never, ever* stack them, as they steam and go limp!

Nutritional Profile

PER SERVING	CLASSIC	MINIMAX
Calories	544	487
Fat (gm)	27	14
Saturated fat (gm)	9	5
Calories from fat	44%	26%
Cholesterol (mg)	86	50
Sodium (mg)	426	457
Fiber (gm)	4	7

■ *Classic Compared: Extra-Rich Chocolate Waffles with Hot Fudge Sauce*

SWEET AND SAVORY TOPPINGS

*C*ontinuing *in our series of cooking methods that meet fat head on, we come to two classic fat-collecting points: the dessert topping, where stiffly whipped heavy cream reigns supreme; and the side order of sour cream that accompanies so many baked potatoes and innumerable Mexican dishes.*

What versatile Minimax ingredient comes to the rescue? Once again I utilize strained yogurt (see page 85). In sweet toppings, you'll see that its sharp-edged, acidic quality is rounded off with honey. And here, to provide a further distraction, I add some pureed raspberries to introduce an unusual pink color.

In the savory topping, I was delighted to hit on the idea of using a hint of maple syrup. It doesn't show up on the tongue as sweet, it simply makes the taste more complex and "rounder." A final touch of minced, fresh green herb stalks provides both color and texture.

The point, as always, is to replace the missing fat mouthroundfullness ingredients with foods that provide vivid aromas, colors and textures.

One important point: because there is no fat in the yogurt it does not cling together for a long period after being beaten. If you overstir strained yogurt it will lose its creamy mouthfeel and become thin. This is why I suggest that you smooth out its lumps with gentle stirring and mix all the other ingredients together separately before stirring them into the yogurt . . . again, gently.

USES: So often when we decide to lower fat in our diet, we exclude any form of whipped or sour cream on anything! With these two toppings you have the freedom to enjoy nonfat dairy garnishes that look and taste like no-no's. So . . . wherever you thought you couldn't, now you can!

■ You can use your own favorite fruit to make a pure, non-gritty puree. One of my spoon spurtles in a stainless-steel fine-mesh sieve does the job perfectly. When stirred into the strained yogurt with a touch of honey . . . it's the best.

■ I used two simple herbs: chives and parsley for the savory topping. Parsley stems have amazing texture and taste that make them a very important Minimax garnish.

■ Here you have the two toppings served over pie and burritos, and remember, ZERO fat. On the left, the topping coats a piece of black cherry pie, and on the right, a burrito, where it takes the place of sour cream.

BASIC SWEET TOPPING

Yield 1½ cups (354 ml)
INGREDIENTS

1 cup frozen unsweetened raspberries (236 ml), thawed

2 tablespoons honey (30 ml)

¼ teaspoon vanilla (1.25 ml)

¾ cup strained yogurt (177 ml) (see page 85)

NOW COOK

■ Push the raspberries through a fine sieve into a small bowl to make ¼ cup (59 ml) of puree. Stir in the honey and vanilla. In another bowl, stir the strained yogurt gently with a spoon to flatten the small lumps. Combine with the sweetened raspberry puree and you've made a *great* topping.

■ To Serve: Spoon 2 tablespoons (30 ml) of the topping over the dessert of your choice.

Nutritional Profile: Basic Sweet Topping

PER SERVING	CLASSIC	MINIMAX
Calories	217	89
Fat (gm)	17	0
Saturated fat (gm)	10	0
Calories from fat	70%	4%
Cholesterol (mg)	61	1
Sodium (mg)	17	36
Fiber (gm)	3	3

■ *Classic Compared: Whipped Cream*

BASIC SAVORY TOPPING

Yield 1 cup (236 ml)
INGREDIENTS

¾ cup strained yogurt (177 ml) (see page 85)

1 tablespoon fresh minced parsley stalks (15 ml)

1 tablespoon fresh minced chives (15 ml)

½ teaspoon pure maple syrup (2.5 ml)

⅛ teaspoon coarsely ground black pepper (0.6 ml)

1 tablespoon de-alcoholized white wine (15 ml) (optional)

NOW COOK

■ Gently stir the yogurt in a small bowl to remove the lumps. Stir in the parsley stalks, chives, maple syrup and pepper. It's your choice whether or not to splash with the de-alcoholized wine.

■ To Serve: Spoon 2 tablespoons (30 ml) of the topping over baked potatoes, for example.

Nutritional Profile: Basic Savory Topping

PER SERVING	CLASSIC	MINIMAX
Calories	89	31
Fat (gm)	8	0
Saturated fat (gm)	5	0
Calories from fat	84%	3%
Cholesterol (mg)	29	1
Sodium (mg)	18	36
Fiber (gm)	0	0

■ *Classic Compared: Sour Cream*

OPEN-FACED BAKED POTATO SANDWICH

Serves 4
INGREDIENTS

4 medium russet potatoes

¾ cup Basic Savory Topping

4 ounces diced smoked turkey or any lean meat (113 gm)

½ cup finely diced plum tomato (118 ml)

GARNISH:

4 teaspoons freshly grated dry Monterey Jack cheese (20 ml)

Freshly chopped parsley

Freshly ground black pepper

NOW COOK

■ Bake the potatoes at 375°F. (190°C) for approximately 1 hour or until a fork inserts easily into the flesh.

■ While the potatoes are baking, make the Basic Savory Topping.

■ To Serve: Cut each potato in half lengthwise. Score the potato flesh with a knife and cover completely with a quarter of the topping. Sprinkle with the meat and tomato. Garnish each with 1 teaspoon (5 ml) of the cheese, chopped parsley, and black pepper to taste.

Nutritional Profile

PER SERVING	CLASSIC	MINIMAX
Calories	321	225
Fat (gm)	13	3
Saturated fat (gm)	8	1
Calories from fat	36%	10%
Cholesterol (mg)	35	22
Sodium (mg)	639	336
Fiber (gm)	5	4

■ *Classic Compared: Stuffed Baked Potatoes*

PEAR COMPOTE

Serves 4
INGREDIENTS

Four 8-ounce fresh pears (227 gm) (Comice or Bartletts are good)
Juice of ½ lemon
1½ quarts water (1.4 l)
2 whole cloves
One 1-inch piece of cinnamon stick (2.5 cm)
¼ cup brown sugar (59 ml)
1 tablespoon cornstarch (15 ml), mixed with 2 tablespoons water (30 ml)
1 recipe Basic Sweet Topping (236 ml)

FIRST PREPARE

■ Peel, core and quarter the pears, reserving the peels and cores separately. Submerge the pears in cool water, to which you've added the lemon juice to prevent browning, until ready to use.

NOW COOK

■ In a large saucepan, cover the reserved pear peels and cores with the water, add the cloves and cinnamon stick. Bring to a boil and simmer for 30 minutes. Strain, return the liquid to the same saucepan, add the brown sugar, bring to a boil and remove from the heat. Add the pears, return to the heat and poach until tender—about 25 minutes. Remove from the heat and drain, reserving both the pears and liquid.

■ Pour 2 cups (472 ml) of the reserved pear-poaching liquid back into the same saucepan and reduce by half. Pour the remaining liquid and the poached pears into a bowl and put in the refrigerator to cool.

■ Off the heat, stir the cornstarch slurry into the reduced pear poaching liquid, return to the heat, bring to a boil and stir until thickened—about 30 seconds. Remove from the heat and put in the refrigerator to cool.

■ When both pears and syrup are cold, remove the pears and chop into neat squares.

■ Make the Basic Sweet Topping.

■ To Serve: In a medium-sized bowl, toss the chopped pears with the cold syrup and spoon into 4 serving bowls. YOUR CHOICE: serve the sweet topping in the middle of the table and dip the poached pear pieces like fondue or give each person their own individual dipping bowl of dessert topping.

Nutritional Profile

PER SERVING	CLASSIC	MINIMAX
Calories	708	224
Fat (gm)	25	1
Saturated fat (gm)	15	0
Calories from fat	32%	4%
Cholesterol (mg)	59	1
Sodium (mg)	127	54
Fiber (gm)	4	6

■ *Classic Compared: Pears Hélène*

Minimax Recipes

BLUEBERRY, BANANA, AND BRAN MUFFINS

If changes in food were a parade, then it would have to be led by a bran muffin. Reducing the effects of excess fat consumption means "fat down, fiber up," and originally the bran muffin promised both. Of course, it didn't take long before the fats counterattacked, and now we hear about "muffins you would die for!" I set out to see if I could win back some popularity for the pioneer. This muffin should be served fresh from the oven or "nuked" for a few seconds in the microwave. No butter or fat spread, please. Instead, try the Blueberry, Banana, Yogurt Spread suggested in the recipe.

Nutritional Profile

PER SERVING	CLASSIC	MINIMAX
Calories	225	132
Fat (gm)	10	1
Saturated fat (gm)	2	0
Calories from fat	41%	8%
Cholesterol (mg)	36	0
Sodium (mg)	208	110
Fiber (gm)	3	4

■ *Classic Compared: Bran Muffins*

Time Estimate: Hands on, 20 minutes; unsupervised, 25 minutes

Cost Estimate: Low

Makes 12 muffins

INGREDIENTS

2 tablespoons brown sugar (30 ml)

2 egg whites

½ cup skim milk (118 ml)

¼ cup molasses (59 ml)

½ cup applesauce (118 ml)

1 teaspoon vanilla (5 ml)

1 cup cake flour (236 ml)

½ cup whole wheat flour (118 ml)

1 cup bran (236 ml)

2 teaspoons baking powder (10 ml)

½ teaspoon baking soda (2.5 ml)

1 cup fresh or frozen (not thawed) blueberries (236 ml)

2 tablespoons flaked almonds (30 ml)

1 teaspoon cinnamon (5 ml)

½ banana, sliced

Foil muffin cups

BLUEBERRY, BANANA, YOGURT SPREAD

Yield: 1¼ cups

½ cup mashed blueberries (118 ml)

1 medium banana, mashed

¼ cup plain nonfat yogurt (59 ml)

NOW COOK

■ Preheat the oven to 400°F. (205°C). In a large bowl, whisk the brown sugar and egg whites until frothy. Stir in the milk, molasses, applesauce and vanilla.

■ In a medium bowl, combine the flours, bran, baking powder and baking soda. Stir in the blueberries, almonds and cinnamon. Add the banana slices, keeping them separated and making sure each slice is completely coated with the flour mixture.

■ Gently add the wet ingredients to the flour mixture. Don't overmix—it took me approximately 40 stirs to incorporate.

■ Line the muffin tins with the foil muffin cups. Fill each cup two-thirds full and bake in the preheated oven for 25 minutes. If you use paper cups, the muffins really stick to the paper. I believe this is due to the low fat content of the batter.

■ The Blueberry, Banana, Yogurt Spread: While the muffins are baking, mix the blueberries, banana and yogurt together until well incorporated.

■ To Serve: Place each muffin on its own plate—remember: only one per serving—and spoon a tablespoon (15 ml) of the spread on the side.

Helpful Hints and Observations

I ran an experiment to see how much butter or margarine was "normally" added to a muffin. It averaged 1¼ teaspoons (6.25 ml), which contain 4.8 grams of fat. Add this to the muffin numbers and you begin to return the muffin to the high-fat numbers.

Our Blueberry, Banana, Yogurt Spread has 0.11 grams of fat per tablespoon (15 ml) and adds only 23 calories.

About the Ingredients:

BRAN. Bran is the outermost covering of the wheatberry, or seed. Although it looks like sawdust, bran is unusually high in fiber, minerals and especially the B vitamins. Store it in tightly covered containers in the refrigerator and it will last up to a year.

BLUEBERRIES. Like other berries, blueberries should be firm and plump and covered with a powdery dust called the "bloom." If you can't get fresh blueberries because of the season, don't hesitate to try a frozen product: blueberries freeze very well and the frozen ones substitute marvelously in most recipes.

POIPU BEACH BREAKFAST

$\mathscr{I}$ was quite content with my mornings until we spent some time on the Hawaiian Island of Kauai at Poipu Beach. One morning I raided the buffet ($19) selecting only granola, yogurt, kiwi fruit and strawberries. I topped it off with granola . . . terrific! My mornings were transformed! For a complete breakfast add ½ cup (118 ml) of fresh grapefruit juice and perhaps one of my Blueberry, Banana, and Bran Muffins (see page 108). All together this would add up to lots of energy and variety, so why not?

Nutritional Profile

PER SERVING	CLASSIC	MINIMAX
Calories	855	261
Fat (gm)	40	6
Saturated fat (gm)	16	1
Calories from fat	42%	23%
Cholesterol (mg)	0	0
Sodium (mg)	246	63
Fiber (gm)	11	6

■ *Classic Compared: Granola*

Time Estimate: Hands on, 20 minutes

Cost Estimate: Medium

Makes twelve ½ cup servings (118 ml)

INGREDIENTS

MINIMAX GRANOLA:

1 cup Grape-Nuts cereal (236 ml)

1 cup raisins (236 ml)

2 cups uncooked rolled oats (472 ml)

1 cup toasted wheat germ (236 ml)

1 cup dried banana chips (236 ml)

½ cup raw sunflower seeds (118 ml)

¼ cup sliced almonds (59 ml)

BREAKFAST FOR TWO:

1⅓ cups plain nonfat yogurt (314 ml)

4 teaspoons honey (20 ml)

1 cup Minimax Granola (236 ml)

2 kiwi fruit, peeled and thinly sliced

2 strawberries, stemmed and thinly sliced

GARNISH:

1 kiwi fruit, peeled and thinly sliced

1 strawberry, stemmed and thinly sliced

2 sprigs of mint (optional)

FIRST PREPARE

■ The Minimax Granola: In a large bowl, combine all the granola ingredients. Store in a sealed container in the refrigerator until ready to use.

NOW COOK

■ In a small bowl, mix the yogurt and honey.

■ For each serving, scoop ½ cup (118 ml) of the granola into a bowl. Spread slices of kiwi fruit and strawberry over the top. Spoon ⅔ cup (156 ml) of the yogurt mixture over the fruit. Garnish with 2 slices each of the kiwi fruit and the strawberry and a mint sprig.

If you like your cereal "soggy" (some folks do), then add ¼ cup (59 ml) of skim milk per bowl of granola before adding the fruit and yogurt.

Helpful Hints and Observations

SEEDS, NUTS AND WHEAT GERM. Oil is a source of energy for the plant to use as fuel for growth. Unfortunately these oils can go rancid over time, and, therefore, seeds and nuts should be purchased from people who know enough to keep them cool.

About the ingredients

FIREWEED HONEY. Honey varieties are named after the flower from which the honey is made. In the northwestern United States, honey made from the wildflower fireweed is readily available. If you can't find fireweed honey, don't let this discourage you. Substitute clover or alfalfa. Remember that honey is a refined sugar, refined by bees which turn flower nectar into a mixture of fructose and glucose. Honey is natural, but is somewhat similar to white sugar. It provides almost empty calories, so use it sparingly.

MINIMAX SEED ROLLS

This recipe has multiple uses. First, use it as a small dinner roll that is obviously different and sends a clear signal—homemade. If you've never made a bread roll, then this is step one on a fascinating journey. Please take it. The same recipe can be used to make the Minimax Pirogen (see page 114): basically a Slavic bread roll filled with a savory meat and vegetable filling. Why not start with the dinner rolls and then branch out? This is recreational weekend cooking in action. I serve them with my yogurt and herb spread on the side. This sidesteps the possibility that fresh, warm rolls may become a perfect platform for slathers of butter.

Nutritional Profile

PER SERVING	CLASSIC	MINIMAX
Calories	102	136
Fat (gm)	6	3
Saturated fat (gm)	17	0
Calories from fat	49%	18%
Cholesterol (mg)	6	0
Sodium (mg)	256	43
Fiber (gm)	1	1

■ *Classic Compared: Crescent Rolls*

Time Estimate: Hands on, 45 minutes; unsupervised, 2 hours 20 minutes

Cost Estimate: Low

Makes 16 rolls

INGREDIENTS

1 (0.6 oz) cake compressed yeast
1 cup lukewarm skim milk (236 ml)
3¾ cups all-purpose flour (885 ml)
⅝ cup liquid egg substitute (150 ml)
⅛ teaspoon freshly ground salt (0.6 ml)
⅛ teaspoon freshly ground black pepper (0.6 ml)
1 teaspoon sugar (5 ml)
1 tablespoon extra-light olive oil, with a dash of sesame oil (15 ml)
⅜ cup Minimax Seed Mix (90 ml) (see below), roughly chopped
1 tablespoon skim milk (15 ml)

NOW COOK

■ Crumble the cake of yeast into a small bowl and stir in ¼ cup (59 ml) of the lukewarm milk until the yeast is dissolved. Slowly stir in the rest of the milk.

■ Sift 3 cups (708 ml) of the flour into a large bowl, pour in the yeast-milk mixture and stir with a wooden spoon until the dough holds together. Knead the dough in the bowl with your hands until it no longer sticks to your fingers. Shape into a small bread loaf and set on a plate. Rinse out the bowl with warm water, dry, put the dough back in, cover with plastic wrap and let stand in a warm place for 1 hour.

■ Uncover the dough and pierce deep holes into it with a knife. Pour the egg substitute into the holes. Sprinkle the loaf with ½ cup (118 ml) of the flour, the salt, pepper, sugar, oil and ¼ cup of the Minimax Seed Mix. Mix together by cutting into the dough with a knife. When loosely combined, use your fingers to blend thoroughly.

■ Using part of the remaining ¼ cup (59 ml) of flour, flour a board. Transfer the dough to the floured board and knead it until it no longer sticks to your hands. Put dough back in the bowl, cover it and let stand in a warm place for 30 minutes.

■ Place the dough back on the floured pastry board and cut into quarters, then cut each quarter into quarters again, to give you 16 pieces. Fold each piece into a rough ball, put your hand down flat over the top, then roll the dough around until you form a smooth ball. Brush the tops with a little of the 1 tablespoon (15 ml) milk, dip each roll into the remaining Minimax Seed Mix and place on a baking sheet. Cover and let stand until almost doubled—about 30 minutes.

■ Bake the rolls in a preheated 350°F. (180°C) oven for 20 minutes.

Helpful Hints and Observations

MINIMAX SEED MIX. Oh, the tantalizing texture this mixture will impart to your recipes! Make a big batch and keep it tightly covered in the refrigerator for handy use. Just combine equal measures of sunflower seeds, unhulled sesame seeds, green pumpkin seeds and sliced almonds, with a half measure of flax seeds. I sprinkle some on my cereal every morning.

About the Ingredients

YEAST. Yeast is a fungus, more specifically, a sugar fungus. When mixed with sugar and warm liquid, it will start to grow. The by-product of this is a bubbling of carbon dioxide, which tries to escape from the dough, thus making it rise. There are different types of baking yeasts: compressed, or active dry. There're interchangeable; just follow the package instructions.

MINIMAX PIROGEN

*I*n many Slavic nations there is a common way of encasing a meat or vegetable filling with an egg-enriched bread dough, either baking or deep frying the package and serving instantly. I have, as usual, made some major changes, and the result is a bread crust spiked with seeds and a filling sparked by Worcestershire sauce. It has a very different taste, but the concept is intact.

Nutritional Profile

PER SERVING	CLASSIC	MINIMAX
Calories	613	370
Fat (gm)	26	9
Saturated fat (gm)	10	2
Calories from fat	39%	21%
Cholesterol (mg)	307	26
Sodium (mg)	331	301
Fiber (gm)	4	5

■ *Classic Compared: Russian Pastry with Meat*

Time Estimate: Hands on, 90 minutes; unsupervised, 3 hours 30 minutes

Cost Estimate: Low

Serves 6

INGREDIENTS

1 recipe Minimax Seed Rolls dough (see page 112)

FILLING:

½ teaspoon extra-light olive oil, with a dash of sesame oil (2.5 ml)

1 medium onion, peeled and minced

8 ounces cooked loin pork (227 gm)

2 tablespoons dried European mushrooms (30 ml), soaked in ½ cup boiling water (118 ml) for 30 minutes and chopped

3 tablespoons Worcestershire sauce (45 ml)

1 teaspoon dried dill weed (5 ml)

⅛ teaspoon freshly ground salt (0.6 ml)

¼ teaspoon freshly ground black pepper (1.25 ml)

1 cup shredded green cabbage (236 ml)

1 tablespoon skim milk (15 ml)

¼ cup Minimax Seed Mix (59 ml) (see page 113)

SIDE DISH: BEET SALAD

One 16-ounce can beets (454 gm), drained

⅓ cup cider vinegar (78 ml)

1 teaspoon fresh chives (5 ml)

½ cup strained yogurt (118 ml) (see page 85)

1 tablespoon fresh chopped parsley (15 ml)

FIRST PREPARE

■ The Pirogen: Prepare the dough according to the instructions, up to the point where the dough sits until it's almost doubled in size.

■ The Beet Salad: In a large bowl, mix the beets, vinegar and chives and marinate for 30 minutes. Strain, discarding the marinade. Place the beets back into the bowl and stir in the yogurt and parsley.

NOW COOK

■ The Filling: Heat the oil in a medium-sized sauté pan and cook the onion until soft and slightly translucent—about 5 minutes. Remove.

■ Mince the pork and cooked onion through a meat grinder (see Helpful Hints, Bread Trick) and into a large bowl. Add the mushrooms, Worcestershire sauce, dill weed, salt, pepper and cabbage.

■ To Assemble: Roll each dough piece into a short, thin oval, about 5 inches (13 cm) long and ⅛ inch (0.5 cm) thick. Spoon 3 tablespoons (45 ml) of filling on one half of each oval. Fold the other half over and crimp the edges. Turn the half oval onto its side on a baking sheet, crimped edge facing up. Cover and let stand 30 minutes.

■ Preheat the oven to 450°F. (230°C). Brush the tops of the pirogen with the milk. Scatter the seed mix evenly over the pirogen, pressing the seeds gently into the surface of the dough. Bake in the preheated oven for 15 minutes.

■ To Serve: Serve the pirogen hot out of the oven with the beet salad on the side.

Helpful Hints and Observations:

BREAD TRICK. After putting all the meat and onion into the grinder, follow it with a slice (or heel) of bread. When you see the bread coming through, you'll know you've left nothing to waste!

SPECIAL EDGE CRIMPER. I worked with my fellow designers to produce a large-sized pastry crimper to make the sealing task easier for pirogen, small calzone and other dumpling dishes. It looks like an odd set of false teeth, but it's remarkably effective.

About the Ingredients

BEETS. A terrific addition to Minimax dishes, beets offer a rich purple color, crunchy texture and light, sweet taste. Here I've used a pickled beet in keeping with Eastern European tradition and flavor. When you buy them fresh in the market, look for beets without dents or bruises and with crisp leaves. Select the smaller ones as the larger ones can be tough.

DRIED EUROPEAN MUSHROOMS. When I saw that the classic recipe for pirogen contained an ingredient called "dried European wild mushrooms," I thought, "That's not much of a description." After all, there are many types of European mushrooms. However, my local supermarket actually had a bottle labeled "Dried European Wild Mushrooms" on the shelf. If you're not so lucky as to find the same, substitute any dried mushroom. Happy foraging.

SOOKE SOUP

This is a remarkable example of microregional food. Sooke Soup is a dish that traces its creation to a very small area on the west coast of Vancouver Island in British Columbia, to the town of Sooke Harbour, which is indeed famous for the cuisine developed at the Sooke Harbour House by Sinclair Philip, his wife, Fredrica, and their superb team of chefs. Here you find the brilliance of invention coupled with the freshest of foods. Sooke Harbour is also immersed in its own beauty and is well worth a visit.

Nutritional Profile

PER SERVING	CLASSIC	MINIMAX
Calories	173	232
Fat (gm)	9	4
Saturated fat (gm)	5	1
Calories from fat	48%	17%
Cholesterol (mg)	92	21
Sodium (mg)	164	228
Fiber (gm)	4	6

■ *Classic Compared: Cream of Winter Kale and Apple Soup*

Time Estimate: Hands on, 55 minutes

Cost Estimate: Medium

Serves 6
INGREDIENTS

YOGURT SAUCE

¼ cup strained yogurt (59 ml) (see page 85)

1 tablespoon de-alcoholized white wine (15 ml)

½ teaspoon fresh chopped thyme (2.5 ml)

1 teaspoon fresh chopped chives (5 ml)

¼ teaspoon freshly ground black pepper (1.25 ml)

⅛ teaspoon freshly ground salt (0.6 ml)

¼ teaspoon freshly ground nutmeg (1.25 ml)

SOUP:

2 Granny Smith apples, cored and peeled

1 tablespoon extra-light olive oil, with a dash of sesame oil (15 ml)

⅓ cup chopped onion (78 ml)

1 clove garlic, peeled, smashed and diced

6 cups chicken stock (1.4 l) (see page 34)

½ teaspoon fresh chopped thyme (2.5 ml)

4 cups frozen peas (944 ml), thawed

2 cups curly kale leaves (472 ml)

¼ cup cornstarch (59 ml), mixed with ½ cup nonfat milk (118 ml)

8 ounces smoked black cod (227 gm), chopped in small pieces

GARNISH:

1 tablespoon fresh chopped chives (15 ml)

1 tablespoon fresh chopped thyme (15 ml)

¼ teaspoon cayenne pepper (1.25 ml)

FIRST PREPARE

■ The Yogurt Sauce: In a small bowl, combine the yogurt, de-alcoholized white wine, thyme and chives, stirring until all lumps have disappeared. Stir in the pepper, salt and nutmeg and set aside.

■ *Slice* one Granny Smith apple and *dice* the other.

NOW COOK

■ In a large high-sided stewpot, heat the oil and sauté the onion and garlic for 2 minutes. Add the *sliced* apple, stirring to coat. Add the chicken stock and thyme, bring to a boil and simmer for 10 minutes. Add the peas.

■ In a steamer, cook the kale leaves for 3 to 4 minutes. The kale will turn a beautiful bright green. Remove and cut into very fine strips. Keep cool for later use.

■ Pour the soup into the container of a food processor or blender and puree. Pass the pureed soup through a mesh sieve and return the sieved puree to the stewpot. Stir in the cornstarch paste and bring just to a boil, stirring constantly until thickened. Add the *diced* apple, cod and kale; heat through until the cod is firm.

■ To Serve: Spoon the soup into individual serving bowls and garnish with the chives, thyme and cayenne pepper. Dollop a spoonful of Yogurt Sauce on top and enjoy!

Helpful Hints and Observations

THE GRIT RINSE. Kale has decidedly crinkled leaves that seem designed to hold grit—a simple rinse just doesn't do it. Be sure to hold each leaf under running water (unless there's a shortage) and avoid ruining the special experience of a great green.

About the Ingredients

SMOKED BLACK COD. This fish is best prepared in the smokehouses of the Pacific Northwest. It is smoked to a creamy amber color, with flavor that rolls right off of your tongue. If it is not available, try smoked scallops or trout.

KALE. Kale grows quite easily in a garden, and our friends at the Sooke Harbour House take advantage of this, picking it fresh as they need it. It's a member of the cabbage family, with large, green leaves that are quite curly along the edges. Serve it by itself as a side dish, steamed and sprinkled with lemon juice and pepper, or cut it up and enjoy it in soups and casseroles—either way, kale is a winner.

MINESTRONE

Minestrone may be the world's best-known soup. In Italy it changes from region to region. The northern versions are unusually light, possibly due to the heavier main dishes that follow. In the south, they add sausage, ham and pig's trotters with meat broth. I've adapted the Genoa method for a delicious main-dish soup. I would like to encourage you to serve soup for one main meal a week. This is a great way to test if such a meal satisfies your family. With good whole grain bread on the side, it provides all the nourishment and pleasure you'll need.

Nutritional Profile

PER SERVING	CLASSIC	MINIMAX
Calories	516	329
Fat (gm)	22	5
Saturated fat (gm)	4	2
Calories from fat	39%	15%
Cholesterol (mg)	7	5
Sodium (mg)	252	511
Fiber (gm)	10	11

■ *Classic Compared: Minestrone alla Genovese*

Time Estimate: Hands on, 45 minutes

Cost Estimate: Medium

Serves 6

INGREDIENTS

BASIL PESTO:

2 tablespoons fresh chopped basil leaves (30 ml)

2 tablespoons pine nuts (30 ml)

1 clove garlic, peeled and crushed

1 tablespoon freshly grated Pecorino Romano cheese (15 ml)

OR

PARSLEY PESTO:

2 tablespoons fresh chopped parsley (30 ml)

1 tablespoon dried basil (15 ml)

⅛ teaspoon extra-light olive oil, with a dash of sesame oil (0.6 ml)

2 tablespoons pine nuts (30 ml)

1 clove garlic, peeled and crushed

1 tablespoon freshly grated Pecorino Romano cheese (15 ml)

SOUP:

1 teaspoon extra-light olive oil, with a dash of sesame oil (5 ml)

1 onion, peeled and diced into ¼-inch (0.75-cm) pieces

2 stalks celery, finely diced

4 carrots, finely diced

8 ounces red new potatoes (227 gm), quartered

7 cups water (1.65 l)

4 ounces small raw pasta shells (113 gm)

2 zucchini, quartered and sliced

2 tablespoons pesto (30 ml) (see recipes below)

One 15-ounce can cannellini (white kidney) beans (425 gm), drained and well rinsed

2 cups peeled, seeded and chopped plum tomatoes (472 ml)

½ teaspoon freshly ground salt (2.5 ml)

¼ teaspoon freshly ground black pepper (1.25 ml)

GARNISH:

1 tablespoon fresh chopped basil (15 ml)

6 tablespoons freshly grated Pecorino Romano cheese (90 ml)

FIRST PREPARE

■ The Basil Pesto: Place the basil on a cutting board. Smash the pine nuts and press together with the back of a knife to form a thick paste. Using the back of the knife, scrape and mix the basil, pine nuts, garlic and cheese together into a well-combined paste.

OR

■ The Parsley Pesto: On a cutting board, use a knife to chop the parsley, basil and oil together into a paste. Smash the pine nuts, pressing with the back of the knife to form a thick paste and add to the parsley, along with the garlic and cheese.

NOW COOK

■ In a large pot or Dutch oven, heat the oil and sauté the onion until soft—about 2 minutes. Add the celery and carrots and cook 3 minutes. Add the potatoes and water and bring to a boil. Add the pasta shells and simmer for 10 minutes. Add the zucchini and simmer for 10 minutes more.

■ Transfer 1 cup (236 ml) of the soup into a small bowl. Stir in the pesto until blended, then return this mixture to the soup pot. Add the beans, tomatoes, salt and pepper and cook until heated through.

■ To Serve: Spoon the Minestrone into individual serving bowls. Garnish with basil and cheese.

Helpful Hints and Observations

PESTO. My pesto is very lean. Pine nuts and Pecorino cheese contribute some fat, but their flavor is so concentrated that only a smattering is needed.

About the Ingredients

PECORINO CHEESE. I've used a well-aged Pecorino Romano, which, through the aging process, becomes very hard and is excellent for grating. Pecorino is made of sheep's milk and can come in soft styles such as Pecorino Tuscano and Percorino Sardo. Pecorino Romano can be found in most supermarkets, while the other varieties are available in better cheese shops.

CANNELLINI BEANS. These classic white beans can be found fresh, canned or dried. Many of the canned brands are very high in quality and are suitable for most recipes. Just rinse the canned beans to remove excess sodium.

SANDWICHES: BRITISH BACON & TOMATO AND ROAST LAMB

*A*ll the world loves a sandwich and some of them have become quite famous: the Reuben, with corned beef, sauerkraut and Swiss cheese; the BLT, with bacon, lettuce and tomato; and the club, with layers of meat, lettuce, tomato, three slices of bread and lots of mayonnaise. My two contributions to the world of sandwiches feature a zesty Garlic and Herb Yogurt Spread and both hold the fat and calories down.

Nutritional Profiles

PER SERVING	CLASSIC	MINIMAX BRITISH BACON & TOMATO	MINIMAX ROAST LAMB
Calories	482	237	285
Fat (gm)	22	6	7
Saturated fat (gm)	21	1	2
Calories from fat	41%	24%	23%
Cholesterol (mg)	164	15	42
Sodium (mg)	707	742	421
Fiber (gm)	2	6	6

■ *Classic Compared: Club Sandwich*

Time Estimates:
   British Bacon & Tomato Sandwich: Hands on, 15 minutes; unsupervised, 35 minutes
   Roast Lamb Sandwich: Hands on, 25 minutes; unsupervised, 35 minutes

Cost Estimates: Medium for both sandwiches

Serves 4
INGREDIENTS

GARLIC AND HERB YOGURT SPREAD:

1 large head garlic

2 teaspoons fresh rosemary leaves (10 ml)

12 juniper berries

12 black peppercorns

½ cup strained yogurt (118 ml) (see page 85)

6 sun-dried tomatoes, soaked in hot water for 30 minutes and finely chopped

BRITISH BACON & TOMATO SANDWICH

SANDWICH CONDIMENT:

¼ cup balsamic vinegar (59 ml)

1 tablespoon extra-light olive oil, with a dash of sesame oil (15 ml)

4 plum tomatoes

½ cup radish or alfalfa sprouts (118 ml)

⅛ teaspoon freshly ground salt (0.6 ml)

¼ teaspoon freshly ground peppercorns (1.25 ml)

8 slices whole wheat bread

4 ounces Canadian bacon (113 gm), thinly sliced

ROAST LAMB SANDWICH

1 teaspoon extra-light olive oil, with a dash of sesame oil (5 ml)

8 ounces leg of lamb (or chicken breast) (227 gm), boneless and lean, cut into ¼-inch (0.75-cm) slices

⅛ teaspoon freshly ground salt (0.6 ml)

¼ teaspoon freshly ground black peppercorns (1.25 ml)

2 pita breads

2 lettuce leaves, shredded

4 plum tomatoes, sliced

FIRST PREPARE

■ The Garlic and Herb Yogurt Spread: Roast the garlic by slicing the top off the garlic head, about ½ inch (1.5 cm) from the top. Wrap the garlic head in aluminum foil and bake at 375°F. (190°C) for 35 minutes.

■ While the garlic is roasting, in a small coffee grinder, whiz the rosemary, juniper berries and black peppercorns.

■ When the garlic is done, squeeze the soft flesh out of the roasted skin and mash. Mix with the strained yogurt, sun-dried tomatoes and 4 teaspoons (20 ml) of the "whizzed" herb mixture. Reserve the excess herb mixture.

NOW COOK

BRITISH BACON & TOMATO SANDWICH

■ The Sandwich Condiment: Combine the vinegar and the oil and shake well. Slice the tomatoes and place on a dinner plate. Sprinkle with the sprouts, salt, pepper and the oil and vinegar and let marinate for at least 15 minutes. Place another serving plate on top of the tomatoes and, holding the plates vertically, squeeze them together, allowing the excess juices to drain into a small bowl. (These juices can be added to any salad dressing.)

■ The Sandwich: Spread one side of the bread slices with the Garlic and Herb Yogurt Spread. Layer one bread slice with Canadian bacon, the marinated sprouts and tomato slices. Place another slice of bread on top and press down hard.

■ To Serve: Slice off the crusts, and cut the sandwiches into quarters. Serve with extra sprouts on the side, if you like. (Of course, slicing off the crusts is just a habit from my British heritage. Keep them on if you prefer.)

ROAST LAMB SANDWICH

■ In a medium skillet, heat the oil and brown the lamb quickly—about 2 minutes total. Season with the salt and pepper and set aside.

■ Cut each pita bread in half, to form 2 pockets. Spread the inside of each pocket with 1½ teaspoons (7.5 ml) of the Garlic and Herb Yogurt Spread. Fill each half with lettuce, tomato and lamb. Dust with the reserved "whizzed" herbs and serve hot.

MEXICAN SCRAMBLED EGGS AND SALSA

$\mathcal{B}$runch is a wonderful meal and a terrific way for the weekend cook to get a round of applause and be part of a great family memory. This classic Mexican egg dish is substantially changed and yet has many complex tastes that make up a medley for the memory. (How's that for purple prose?) I serve two tortillas to each adult, one to children. To keep the heat down, I suggest you add only half the habañeros sauce and serve a small bottle on the side for those who like to make others gasp before they go purple!

Nutritional Profile

PER SERVING	CLASSIC	MINIMAX
Calories	448	372
Fat (gm)	32	3
Saturated fat (gm)	9	0
Calories from fat	64%	8%
Cholesterol (mg)	385	0
Sodium (mg)	313	591
Fiber (gm)	5	16

■ *Classic Compared: Mexican Scrambled Eggs*

Time Estimate: Hands on, 35 minutes; unsupervised, 30 minutes

Cost Estimate: Medium

Serves 4
INGREDIENTS

SALSA:

One 15-ounce can black beans (425 gm), drained and rinsed

1 cup unpeeled, finely chopped, plum tomatoes (236 ml)

4 green onions, chopped in ¼-inch (0.75-cm) pieces

2 tablespoons fresh chopped cilantro (30 ml)

½ teaspoon green habañeros chili sauce (2.5 ml)

½ cup corn kernels (118 ml), frozen or fresh

2 tablespoons freshly squeezed orange juice (30 ml)

⅛ teaspoon freshly ground salt (0.6 ml)

¼ teaspoon ground cumin seed (1.25 ml)

½ teaspoon arrowroot (2.5 ml), mixed with 1 tablespoon water (15 ml)

SCRAMBLED EGGS:

1 cup chopped unpeeled plum tomatoes (236 ml)

½ teaspoon extra-light olive oil, with a dash of sesame oil (2.5 ml)

1 cup peeled and chopped onion (236 ml)

½ teaspoon seeded and chopped serrano chilies (2.5 ml)

1 tablespoon fresh chopped cilantro (15 ml)

1½ cups liquid egg substitute (354 ml)

¼ cup chopped green onion tops (59 ml), roughly chopped on the diagonal

8 soft corn tortillas

4 tablespoons strained yogurt (60 ml) (see page 85)

FIRST PREPARE

■ The Salsa: In a large bowl combine the black beans, tomatoes, green onions, cilantro, habañeros sauce, corn and orange juice. Season with the salt and cumin and let sit for 30 minutes. Strain, reserving both the vegetables and the liquid, separately.

■ Heat the reserved salsa liquid to a simmer, remove from the heat and add the arrowroot slurry.

■ In a small bowl, combine the reserved salsa solids and the thickened salsa liquid. The salsa now has a beautiful gloss and is ready to serve.

NOW COOK

■ The Scrambled Eggs: Put the chopped tomatoes in a strainer and drain off any excess liquid. In a large sauté pan, heat the oil and quickly sauté the onion and tomatoes until the onion is soft—about 5 minutes. Add the serrano chilies, cilantro, egg substitute and green onion tops. Cook the eggs, scrambling slowly and gently, until firm—about 4 minutes.

■ To Serve: Heat the corn tortillas by laying them flat on one half of a large piece of aluminum foil. Fold the other half over the tortillas until they are completely covered, crimping the edges until well sealed. Pop into a 350°F. oven for 10 minutes. Spoon the scrambled eggs onto the tortillas, reserving 4 spoonfuls for garnish, and then roll the tortillas in order to enclose the egg mixture. Place 2 tortillas on each plate, with a spoonful of salsa on one side and a dollop of strained yogurt on the other. Finish with another spoonful of scrambled eggs on top and . . . olé!

About the Ingredients

HABAÑERO. Recently Treena and I went to a new restaurant on the shores of Lake Washington, near Seattle. The Cactus specializes in Latin and South American cuisines and serves, with some distinction and appropriate warning, this hottest of all chilies in a brilliant green bottled sauce.

The habañero is estimated at 200,000 on the Scoville Scale, against the jalapeño, with only 5,000. A Scoville Unit is the percentage of pain experienced by a game panel of tender tongues who put science before sense and spent several days licking peppers and recording their reactions.

If you cannot locate this "green war" product, try Tabasco sauce: it is tamer and certainly easier to find.

SERRANO. This is a small dark green chili that turns red when it ripens. Serranos are very hot, hotter than the common jalapeño. Look for a smooth shiny skin and flesh that is firm to the touch. If serranos are unavailable in your area, substitute jalapeños. Remember, never rub your eyes when working with hot chilies; the volatile oils need soap and water to remove them from your hands.

PEANUT BUTTER SPREADIN'DIPITY (THREE RECIPES IN ONE!)

This is literally the "hop, skip and jump" of the kitchen. I lead off with a simple combination of flavors added to peanut butter which gives a spread that has almost 20 percent fewer calories from fat. Then I add some great flavor to make a dip and finally move on to a marinating and basting sauce for chicken on a skewer.

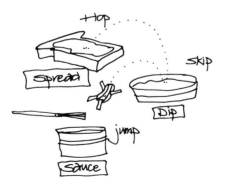

Nutritional Profiles

PER SERVING	*The Spread*	
	CLASSIC	MINIMAX
Calories	162	108
Fat (gm)	9	4
Saturated fat (gm)	2	0
Calories from fat	49%	30%
Cholesterol (mg)	1	1
Sodium (mg)	203	155
Fiber (gm)	1	3

■ *Classic Compared: Peanut Butter*

The Spread
Time Estimate: Hands on, 5 minutes

Cost Estimate: Low

Skewered Chicken		
PER SERVING	CLASSIC	MINIMAX
Calories	362	167
Fat (gm)	25	5
Saturated fat (gm)	10	1
Calories from fat	62%	29%
Cholesterol (mg)	56	54
Sodium (mg)	642	457
Fiber (gm)	2	1

■ *Classic Compared: Chicken with Peanut Sauce*

**The Sauce and Chicken
Time Estimate: Hands on, 12 minutes;
unsupervised, 17 minutes**

Cost Estimate: Low

Makes 24 tablespoons (360 ml)
INGREDIENTS

SPREAD:

½ cup strained yogurt (118 ml) (see page 85)
½ cup creamy peanut butter (118 ml)
1 banana, peeled and mashed

DIP:

2 teaspoons fresh chopped cilantro (10 ml)
¼ teaspoon cayenne pepper (1.25 ml)

SAUCE:

2 tablespoons freshly squeezed lemon juice (30 ml)
4 teaspoons low-sodium soy sauce (20 ml)

SKEWERED CHICKEN:

Serves 4

4 cloves garlic, peeled and smashed
1 teaspoon sesame oil (5 ml)
4 teaspoons low-sodium soy sauce (20 ml)
Four 3½-ounce boneless, skinless chicken breasts
(100 gm each), cut into ½-inch (1.5 cm) cubes

FIRST PREPARE

■ Spread: In a small bowl, combine the strained yogurt, peanut butter and mashed banana. Enjoy 1 tablespoon (15 ml) of this spread on a slice of whole wheat bread, muffin or even a waffle.

■ Dip: Now let's take that spread and move it up to the dipping level. Add the cilantro and cayenne and let sit for 5 minutes. Allow 7 ounces (198 gm) of fresh vegetables for each of your guests to dip. There is enough dip to serve 10 at a party.

■ Sauce: The final variation is the creation of a sauce. Add the lemon juice and soy sauce to the dip. I recommend you use this sauce with Skewered Chicken.

NOW COOK

■ The Skewered Chicken: In a small bowl, mix the garlic, oil and soy sauce. Brush the chicken pieces until well coated and let stand for 10 minutes.

■ Preheat the broiler. Divide the chicken pieces equally among 4 skewers, place on a rack in a roaster pan and broil for 5 minutes. Remove from the broiler, turn the skewers, brush the chicken with the sauce and put back under the broiler for 2 minutes. Serve with the rest of the sauce on the side, for dipping.

Helpful Hints and Observations

UNLOCKING PEANUT PROTEIN. Peanut butter supplies protein, but also more than enough fat. I've designed these recipes to minimize the fat while maximizing the protein absorption. For your body to use the protein that is provided by peanut butter it needs to be eaten with complementary proteins, such as those from whole grain breads or low fat meats, such as chicken.

A SPREAD THAT LASTS. Peanut Butter Spreadin'dipity will last for a week in a refrigerated, covered jar.

About the Ingredients

PEANUT BUTTER. I suggest that you avoid the brand-name spreads, which contain hydrogenated vegetable oil as a stabilizer, and buy a *natural* peanut butter. The only consequence of not having a stabilizer is that the oil separates from the ground peanut solids. Don't worry; all you have to do is stir it back together before using. I also suggest that you refrigerate these peanut butters because the cold temperature solidifies the oil, and you won't have to stir it up as frequently.

BANANA. Choose bananas that are firm and uniform in size, but don't worry if they're green. Bananas are picked green but will ripen easily at home over a couple of days, to a mottled yellow color and their full sweetness.

ALL-AMERICAN PICNIC: OVEN FRIED CHICKEN AND POTATO SALAD

Fried chicken and potato salad have to be the ultimate American picnic food. I set out to find a way to make them available to the heart-conscious eater who loves picnics, fresh air and mossy banks beside sylvan streams. With about 12 percent of its calories from fat, this version meets the need and tastes great! Don't forget the insect repellent.

uh, graham...

Nutritional Profile

PER SERVING	CLASSIC	MINIMAX
Calories	1251	530
Fat (gm)	95	7
Saturated fat (gm)	14	2
Calories from fat	68%	12%
Cholesterol (mg)	340	77
Sodium (mg)	1535	360
Fiber (gm)	5	5

■ *Classic Compared: Southern Fried Chicken and Potato Salad*

Time Estimate: Hands on, 30 minutes; unsupervised, 35 minutes

Cost Estimate: Medium

INGREDIENTS

POTATO SALAD:

1½ pounds red new potatoes (680 gm), steamed and quartered

¼ cup finely chopped green onions (59 ml)

1 tablespoon finely chopped parsley stalks (15 ml)

1 tablespoon finely chopped parsley leaves (15 ml)

¼ red onion, peeled and finely diced

1 stalk celery, finely diced

¾ cup strained yogurt (177 ml) (see page 85)

4 teaspoons Dijon mustard (20 ml)

1 teaspoon dark brown sugar (5 ml)

¼ teaspoon freshly ground black pepper (1.25 ml)

CHICKEN:

½ cup cornmeal (118 ml)

½ teaspoon cayenne pepper (2.5 ml)

½ cup bread crumbs (118 ml)

½ teaspoon dried tarragon (2.5 ml)

½ teaspoon ground ginger (2.5 ml)

¼ teaspoon freshly ground salt (1.25 ml)

¾ cup liquid egg substitute (177 ml)

½ cup all-purpose flour (59 ml)

One 3-pound fryer chicken (1.4 kg), quartered, (1 whole breast, split, and 2 whole legs), skin and fat removed

NOW COOK

■ The Potato Salad: In a large bowl, combine the potatoes, green onions, parsley stalks and leaves, red onion and celery.

■ In a small bowl, mix the strained yogurt, Dijon mustard and brown sugar and stir into the potatoes until well combined. Stir in the black pepper.

■ The Chicken: Preheat the oven to 350°F. (180°C). Line a baking sheet with parchment paper to help keep the batter from sticking to the baking sheet. In a medium-sized bowl, combine the cornmeal, cayenne, bead crumbs, tarragon, ginger and salt. Pour the egg substitute into a small bowl and place it next to the bowl with the cornmeal mixture. Put the flour in a large bowl.

■ Dip the chicken pieces in the flour, turning until they are completely covered. Next dip the chicken in the egg substitute and then in the cornmeal. When completely coated with the cornmeal, place the chicken pieces on the baking sheet, round side down.

■ Bake in the preheated oven for 20 minutes. Turn the pieces over, return to the oven and cook 15 minutes more.

■ You can eat the Oven Fried Chicken hot out of the oven along with the Potato Salad, or save them for a picnic. To prepare the chicken for later use, cool it rapidly on a rack in the refrigerator. When cold, put the chicken and potato salad into sealed plastic containers and refrigerate until ready to leave for your picnic.

Helpful Hints and Observations

FLIP IT . . . HALFWAY. The chicken skin has been removed, the fat trimmed and the usual egg yolks and oil are nonexistent. What fat there is in the chicken pieces will emerge gradually and move "downhill." To help this fat do its thing, start the cooking round side down. After twenty minutes, just flip the pieces and allow that apparent "fried look" to grace both sides.

PARCHMENT PAPER. Because of the lack of fat in the cooking process it's helpful to have a layer of paper between the batter-coated chicken and the baking sheet to prevent sticking. Parchment paper is treated to withstand high temperatures without burning. Look for it in your supermarket or a kitchen shop. Otherwise, use aluminum foil.

About the Ingredients

CORNMEAL. There are so many uses for this delightful grain besides making corn bread! Just as one example, in this recipe you can see how cornmeal provides the base for a marvelous breading that crisps without fat. Because of its high oil content, cornmeal can go rancid quickly. Store it in an airtight container in the refrigerator.

DIJON MUSTARD. What gives it that special tang? This mustard is blended with grape juice! Its name comes from its place of origin: Dijon, France.

BRAISED CHICKEN WITH PEPPER SAUCE AND POLENTA

*A*nother great "food of the people" (or bistro-food idea). These braised chicken legs are succulent, tender and full of pepper, onion, garlic and anchovy flavor. The sauce is dark with bright flashes and very aromatic. The polenta is yellow and studded with reds and greens. I love to serve this chicken on a bed of steamed mixed greens, with the polenta served either in a wedge or as a moist mound surrounded with the sauce. It really is a great dish.

Nutritional Profile

PER SERVING	CLASSIC	MINIMAX
Calories	1343	523
Fat (gm)	76	15
Saturated fat (gm)	22	6
Calories from fat	51%	26%
Cholesterol (mg)	217	97
Sodium (mg)	3096	729
Fiber (gm)	7	11

■ *Classic Compared: Polenta and Chicken*

Time Estimate: Hands on, 60 minutes

Cost Estimate: Medium High

Serves 4

INGREDIENTS

THE POLENTA:

7 cups cold water (1.65 l)

2 cups yellow cornmeal (472 ml)

½ teaspoon freshly ground salt (2.5 ml)

¼ teaspoon freshly ground black pepper (1.25 ml)

2 ounces Gorgonzola cheese (57 gm)

1 red bell pepper, seeded and diced

1 tablespoon fresh chopped parsley (15 ml)

THE CHICKEN WITH PEPPER SAUCE:

1 teaspoon extra-light olive oil, with a dash of sesame oil (5 ml)

2 pounds chicken (907 gm)—4 whole legs weighing 8 ounces (227 gm) each

1 cup peeled and chopped onions (236 ml)

3 cloves garlic, peeled, smashed and finely diced

2 tablespoons tomato paste (30 ml)

1 red bell pepper, seeded and finely diced

1 tablespoon fresh chopped rosemary (15 ml)

2 bay leaves

½ cup de-alcoholized white wine (118 ml)

4 anchovy fillets, finely chopped

2 cups chicken stock (472 ml) (see page 34)

1 tablespoon arrowroot (15 ml), mixed with 2 tablespoons de-alcoholized white wine (30 ml)

¼ teaspoon grated lemon zest (1.25 ml)

GREENS:

3 cups collard leaves, washed, thick stems removed (708 ml)

2 cups kale leaves, washed, thick stems removed (472 ml)

2 cups loosely packed mustard greens, washed, thick stems removed (472 ml)

NOW COOK

■ The Polenta: In a large saucepan, bring the water to a rapid boil. Stir the water rapidly, while sprinkling in the cornmeal. Do not let the water come off the boil. When all the cornmeal is in, sprinkle in the salt and pepper. Adjust the heat to maintain the boil, stirring and scraping the sides and bottom of the saucepan. Lower the heat if the mixture starts to stick. When done, the polenta will be a thick porridge that pulls cleanly from the sides of the saucepan, and a spoon will stand up in it. This takes about 25 minutes.

■ Transfer 4 cups (944 ml) of the polenta into a large bowl. Stir in the cheese, red pepper and

parsley. Refrigerate and save the unused polenta for breakfast with honey, or baked as a snack cake.

■ The Chicken with Pepper Sauce: Preheat the oven to 350°F. (180°C). On top of the stove, heat the oil in a large ovenproof stewpot and brown the chicken on both sides. Remove the chicken to a cutting board; take off the skin and discard, using paper towels to absorb any excess fat from the meat. Set aside.

■ Put the onions and garlic in the stewpot and sauté until softened—about 5 minutes. Stir in the tomato paste and cook briskly until its color darkens. Add the red pepper, rosemary, bay leaves and wine, scraping the bottom of the stewpot in order to deglaze it. Add the anchovy fillets, chicken and chicken stock and bring to a boil. Place the stewpot in the preheated oven and bake 35 minutes.

■ Transfer the cooked chicken to a cutting board. Trim off the exposed leg and thigh bones (see Helpful Hints). Stir the arrowroot slurry into the pepper sauce, return to low heat on the stovetop and stir until thickened. Return the chicken to the sauce. Stir in the lemon zest and heat through.

■ The Greens: In a large pot, bring 2 cups water to a boil and steam the greens, covered, for 4 minutes.

■ To Serve: Place a whole chicken leg on each dinner plate and surround with ¼ cup (59 ml) of the polenta and one quarter of the greens. Drizzle the chicken with the pepper sauce.

Helpful Hints and Observations

LESS FAT? You can reduce the fat content by cutting out the Gorgonzola cheese. The polenta is obviously less rich, but it still carries the day when served with this excellent sauce. In this way, you can drop the fat by 4 grams per serving and that gets the percentage of calories from fat down to 21 percent.

About the Ingredients

POLENTA. Polenta is actually a "dish" rather than an ingredient, but over the ages it has become synonymous with its main ingredient, cornmeal. Soon after corn arrived in Italy from the Americas it was ground and used in porridgelike dishes, and polenta was born! Polenta lends itself to many springboarding experiments—try some of your own favorite vegetable combinations.

POLLO DI PRINCE

This is a wonderful dish. It's my own invention with, of course, lots of help from Robert Prince, my ever-supportive Food Associate. Please serve it as suggested: crisp the bread in the oven, if necessary (it should be neither rock hard nor soggy). If you've never had a good creamy goat cheese, then this is a real treat, but watch how you use the rest—it has 5 grams of fat per tablespoon. I suggest you serve a good salad on the side (see page 80 for a suggestion).

Fresh
goat cheese
As recommended
by graham kerr

Nutritional Profile

PER SERVING	CLASSIC	MINIMAX
Calories	685	408
Fat (gm)	24	8
Saturated fat (gm)	9	2
Calories from fat	32%	18%
Cholesterol (mg)	208	63
Sodium (mg)	858	618
Fiber (gm)	13	7

■ *Classic Compared: Cotoletta di Pollo*

Time Estimate: Hands on, 60 minutes

Cost Estimate: Medium High

Serves 4
INGREDIENTS

FRENCH BREAD:

4 teaspoons goat cheese (20 ml)

1 teaspoon fresh chopped basil (5 ml)

⅛ teaspoon cayenne pepper (0.6 ml)

Four slices French bread, 3 inches (8 cm) thick ×
4 inches (10 cm) wide

TOMATO SAUCE:

1 teaspoon extra-light olive oil, with a dash of
sesame oil (5 ml)

1 cup peeled and finely chopped onions (236 ml)

1 clove garlic, peeled, smashed and chopped

2 medium carrots, peeled and diced

2 tablespoons low-sodium tomato paste (30 ml)

One 28-ounce can peeled Italian tomatoes (794
gm), chopped, with juice

2 tablespoons fresh chopped basil (30 ml)

⅛ teaspoon freshly ground salt (0.6 ml)

¼ teaspoon freshly ground black peppercorns
(1.25 ml)

CHICKEN:

Four 4-ounce boneless chicken breasts
(113 gm each), with skin

⅛ teaspoon freshly ground salt (0.6 ml)

¼ teaspoon freshly ground black pepper (1.25 ml)

1 teaspoon extra-light olive oil, with a dash of
sesame oil (5 ml)

8 ounces fresh mushrooms (227 gm), thickly sliced

1 tablespoon fresh chopped sage leaves (15 ml)

1 tablespoon freshly squeezed lemon juice (15 ml)

⅛ teaspoon cayenne pepper (0.6 ml)

½ cup de-alcoholized white wine (118 ml)

1 tablespoon arrowroot (15 ml), mixed with 2
tablespoons de-alcoholized white wine (30 ml)

2 tablespoons fresh chopped parsley (30 ml)

GARNISH:

½ cup fresh chopped parsley (118 ml)

FIRST PREPARE

■ The French Bread: In a small bowl, mix the goat
cheese with the basil and cayenne pepper. Hollow
out each bread slice by removing some of the inner
dough, leaving a ¼-inch (0.75-cm) wall. Spread a
quarter of the goat cheese mixture in the hollowed-
out portion of each slice.

NOW COOK

■ The Tomato Sauce: Heat the oil in a large skillet
and sauté the onions, garlic and carrots for
2 minutes. Add the tomato paste and cook until it
has deepened in color. (See Maillard Reaction
technique, page 17.)

■ Stir in the tomatoes, basil, salt and pepper and
bring to a vigorous boil. Reduce the heat, cover
and simmer for 10 minutes, or until the carrots
have softened.

■ The Chicken: Sprinkle the breasts with the salt
and pepper. Heat the oil in a small frying pan and
cook the chicken 4 minutes on each side. Add the
mushrooms and sage, cover and cook 2 more
minutes.

■ Remove the mushrooms to a small bowl.
Sprinkle them with the lemon juice and cayenne
pepper and set aside.

■ Transfer the chicken breasts to a warm plate
and remove and discard the skin. Tip the fat out of
the frying pan and discard. With a piece of paper
toweling blot out the fat remaining in the pan;
repeat this process, blotting the excess fat from the
skinned chicken as well. Place the pan back on the
burner and deglaze with the wine. Add the warmed
wine from the pan to the tomato sauce.

■ Remove the tomato sauce from the heat, stir in
the arrowroot slurry, return to the heat and stir
until thickened. Add the parsley and heat through.

■ To Serve: Spread the garnish parsley out on a
flat plate or surface. Pour a bed of the tomato
sauce on each dinner plate. Take a French bread
slice, press the hollowed-out side into the tomato
sauce and then into the finely chopped parsley,
creating a green rim around the hollowed center.
Place a piece of bread, parsley side up, in the
center of each plate. Place a chicken breast in the
hollow of the bread and spoon the reserved
mushrooms over the top. Garnish with a sprinkle of
parsley.

About the Ingredients

GOAT CHEESE. Soft and tangy, cheeses made from
goat's milk are becoming more widely available.
They come in many different varieties: spiked with
fresh herbs or zesty with garlic. When you go
shopping, read the labels and pick the one you like
best. Goat cheese is also called *chèvre*.

CHICKEN AND RED BELL PEPPER PASTA

I think I'm genuinely embarrassed. (Sometimes I find it hard to judge!) Treena and I often visit the Beach Café at Yarrow Bay on Lake Washington, near Seattle. Almost always I order the same dish, yet I keep on proposing "variety, variety." My only defense is that this is one of the best pasta dishes I've ever eaten! So, embarrassed or not, I keep going back to the same thing. Now you can, too!

Nutritional Profile

PER SERVING	CLASSIC	MINIMAX
Calories	893	258
Fat (gm)	50	5
Saturated fat (gm)	24	1
Calories from fat	50%	18%
Cholesterol (mg)	279	57
Sodium (mg)	1291	203
Fiber (gm)	5	6

■ *Classic Compared: Red Bell Pepper Fettucine with Grilled Chicken*

Time Estimate: Hands on, 45 minutes

Cost Estimate: Medium High

INGREDIENTS

13 sun-dried tomato halves

One 3-pound chicken (1.4-kg), quartered, or
1 whole breast, split, and 2 whole legs

½ teaspoon black peppercorns (2.5 ml)

½ teaspoon allspice berries (2.5 ml)

4 whole cloves

1 tablespoon fresh chopped thyme (15 ml)

⅛ teaspoon freshly ground salt (0.6 ml)

4 cups loosely packed spinach leaves (944 ml)

1 teaspoon extra-light olive oil, with a dash of
sesame oil (5 ml)

One 14½-ounce can chicken stock (435 ml)

1 bouquet garni (see page 36)

½ cup roasted sweet red peppers (118 ml)

2 tablespoons fresh chopped parsley (30 ml)

1 tablespoon arrowroot (15 ml), mixed with 2
tablespoons de-alcoholized white wine (30 ml)

8 ounces raw fettucine (227 gm)

NOW COOK

■ Slice 3 of the sun-dried tomato halves in half
and reserve. Reconstitute the other 10. Put them in
a small saucepan and cover with water. Bring to a
boil, then take off the heat and let soak 30 minutes.
Drain and cut each tomato in half. Set aside.

■ While the tomatoes are soaking, remove bones
from chicken pieces, keeping the skin on. Use the
leftover bones for chicken stock.

■ Put the black peppercorns, allspice berries,
cloves, thyme, salt, and reserved tomatoes into a
small grinder and whiz to a powder. Sprinkle the
spice powder liberally over both sides of the
chicken, evenly packing the spices under the skin.

■ Wash the spinach leaves well and chop off the
stems. Slice the leaves to match the fettucine's
width. Set aside.

■ In a large skillet, heat the oil and brown the
chicken pieces for 5 minutes on both sides.
Remove from the pan and cut off and discard the
skin. Slice the chicken meat into bite-size pieces
and set aside. Drain the fat from the skillet.

■ In a saucepan, bring the chicken stock to a boil,
add the bouquet garni and simmer for 5 minutes.
Remove the bouquet garni. Pour the stock into the
skillet used to brown the chicken. Stir in the
reconstituted sun-dried tomatoes, red peppers and
parsley and cook over medium heat for 5 minutes.
Stir in the chicken, remove the skillet from the
heat, stir in the arrowroot slurry, return to the heat
and stir until thickened.

■ Drop the fettucine into a large pot of boiling
water and cook for 8 minutes. Drain over a large
bowl. Discard the water and now you have a
beautifully warmed bowl ready to serve your pasta!
Put the fettucine in the bowl.

■ Toss the fettucine with the sliced raw spinach.
Pour in the chicken and red pepper sauce, toss
well and serve.

Helpful Hints and Observations

WHIZZED SEASONINGS. It's really like having an
electronic pestle and mortar. What happens is that
solid spices, with flavors locked in and ready to go,
can give their all to a dish when whizzed up in an
electric coffee mill or small processor. (See POP
technique, page 44.)

About the Ingredients

SUN-DRIED TOMATOES. The main issue when
buying sun-dried tomatoes is whether or not
they're packed in oil. I prefer those that have not
been soaked in oil. I've even found one type that
actually isn't sun dried, it's oven dried. A
manufacturer in Sonoma, California, dries tomatoes
in ovens the size of a large shed. The tomatoes are
laid out in trays and wheeled into the ovens and
dried for 24 hours. They are then cooled and
packaged for sale. It's an unusual approach, but
one that works quite well.

ROASTED SWEET RED PEPPERS (PIMENTO). I
prefer using pimento from a jar rather than the
tinned variety for this simple reason: you can see
what you are getting. Quality differs immensely.
Pimento should be free of any skin and black
roasting marks. I've run across quite a nice product
from Greece. The peppers are left whole and for
the most part are blemish-free. If you cannot find
pimentos in a jar, the tinned will still work well.
You just might have to trim off some of the edges.

THAI CHICKEN SALAD

*H*ere's a radically different chicken salad, combining some Asian ideas with the Western love of lettuce and tomatoes. Salads are usually associated with light diet eating, but in reality an amazing amount of fat is often carried in the salad dressing. Let's get smart together on delicious, low-fat salads like this one.

Nutritional Profile

PER SERVING	CLASSIC	MINIMAX
Calories	484	283
Fat (gm)	29	7
Saturated fat (gm)	7	1
Calories from fat	54%	23%
Cholesterol (mg)	78	47
Sodium (mg)	340	240
Fiber (gm)	5	3

■ *Classic Compared: Curried Chicken Salad*

Time Estimate: Hands on, 30 minutes

Cost Estimate: Medium

Serves 4
INGREDIENTS

DRESSING:

½ cup rice wine vinegar (118 ml)

½ cup water (118 ml)

2 tablespoons sugar (30 ml)

SALAD:

6 ounces raw Chinese rice noodles (170 gm)

½ head iceberg lettuce, finely shredded

4 plum tomatoes, seeded and finely diced

2 tablespoons fresh chopped cilantro (30 ml)

¼ teaspoon salt (1.25 ml)

1 tablespoon extra-light olive oil, with a dash of sesame seed oil (15 ml)

4 green onions, separated into white and green parts, both cut into ¼-inch (0.75-cm) pieces

4 "quarter-size" slices of fresh gingerroot

2 cloves garlic, peeled, smashed and chopped

12 ounces boneless chicken breast (340 gm), sliced lengthwise in ¼ x 2-inch strips (0.75 x 5 cm)

⅛ teaspoon red pepper flakes (1.25 cm)

1 cup bean sprouts (236 ml)

Juice of 1 large lime

GARNISH:

½ cup uncooked long grain white rice (118 ml)

1 thin slice of fresh gingerroot 3 x ¼ inches (8 x 0.75 cm)

FIRST PREPARE

■ In a medium-sized bowl, combine the ingredients for the dressing and set aside.

■ For the Salad: Cook the rice noodles according to the package instructions. Drain and run under cold water to stop the cooking process and keep moist. Let the noodles sit in a sieve or colander for 5 minutes, allowing any excess moisture to drain.

■ Combine the noodles with the lettuce, half of the tomatoes, half of the dressing, half of the cilantro and the salt.

■ For the Garnish: Add the rice and ginger to a small dry pan and cook over medium heat, stirring frequently, until the rice turns nutty brown. Transfer to a small coffee mill, grind to a coarse texture and set aside.

NOW COOK

■ Pour the oil into a large skillet or wok over medium-high heat, add the white parts of the green onions, the gingerroot and garlic and cook for 1 minute. (This is the beautiful perfume of bao syang; see page 47.) Add the chicken and red pepper flakes and cook for 6 minutes. Add the green onion tops, the remaining tomatoes and the bean sprouts and cook for 1 minute, stirring frequently. Add the remaining dressing and the lime juice and remove the pan from the heat.

■ To Serve: Divide the noodle salad into 4 deep bowls and top with equal amounts of the chicken mixture. Now sprinkle each portion with some of the remaining cilantro and 1 teaspoon (5 ml) of the rice garnish.

Helpful Hints and Observations

TRUE GRIT. Thai salads often have a gritty textural finish provided by rice roasted with galangal, a rhizome similar to ginger, but with the flavor of eucalyptus. I've used the more readily available fresh gingerroot. It's a garnish that really delivers a different texture.

About the Ingredients

BEAN SPROUTS. These crunchy, delicate-flavored sprouts are the early growth of the mung bean. Choose sprouts that are firm and light in color. Brown ends are a sign of old age, and the sprouts should be discarded. Bean sprouts are quite versatile and can be used in many different salads and soups.

RICE NOODLES. Look for these dried rice-flour noodles in Asian grocery stores. They come in a variety of thicknesses, so the cooking time may vary—just check the package for exact directions. If you cannot find this type of noodle in your grocery store, you can substitute angel hair pasta and still achieve similar results.

CHOP SUEY

This is not a Chinese dish: It was created in the United States by Chinese Americans. But it could well be the source of worldwide enthusiasm for the stir-fry as we know it today. As with all speedily cooked dishes using fresh foods, your time will be taken up beforehand, cutting and slicing, but the sheer fun of putting it all together is well worth it. Simply make sure that the family is seated before you begin to cook since the process goes so quickly. Serve a good deep bowl of boiled rice on the side. I love to eat Chop Suey with chopsticks and share good conversation!

Nutritional Profile

PER SERVING	CLASSIC	MINIMAX
Calories	580	366
Fat (gm)	22	6
Saturated fat (gm)	4	1
Calories from fat	34%	14%
Cholesterol (mg)	58	29
Sodium (mg)	1053	843
Fiber (gm)	7	7

■ *Classic Compared: Chop Suey*

Time Estimate: Hands on, 30 minutes

Cost Estimate: Medium High

Serves 4
INGREDIENTS
RICE:

1 cup uncooked short grain white rice (236 ml)

1½ cups cold water (354 ml)

CHOP SUEY:

6 green onions

One 8-ounce boneless chicken breast (227 gm)

1 cup chicken stock (236 ml) (see page 34)

3 tablespoons low-sodium soy sauce (45 ml)

2 tablespoons cornstarch (30 ml)

1 tablespoon extra-light olive oil, with a dash of sesame oil (15 ml)

1 teaspoon freshly grated gingerroot (5 ml)

2 cloves garlic, peeled, smashed and chopped

1 large onion, peeled and thinly sliced

1 large green bell pepper, cored, seeded and sliced

½ cup canned sliced bamboo shoots (118 ml)

One 5-ounce can whole water chestnuts (142 gm), each sliced into 3 pieces

1 cup quartered fresh mushrooms (236 ml)

2 cups bean sprouts (472 ml)

2 red pimentos, sliced

¼ cup frozen green peas (59 ml)

FIRST PREPARE

■ Trim the withered bits off the green onions and cut the green ends into 1-inch (2.5-cm) pieces and the white bulbs into 1½-inch (4-cm) pieces.

■ Slice the chicken into thin strips, cutting across the breast.

■ Combine the chicken stock, soy sauce and cornstarch.

NOW COOK

■ The Rice: Rinse the rice gently until the water is quite clear of all milkiness and drain well in a sieve or colander. Put the drained rice in a heavy 2½-quart (2.4-l) saucepan. Pour in the 1½ cups (354 ml) water and bring to a boil. Cover, reduce the heat and simmer for 15 minutes. Turn off the heat and let stand 15 minutes. Then check to make sure all the water has been absorbed.

■ The Chop Suey: Heat 1 teaspoon (5 ml) of the oil in a large wok or skillet and sauté the green onion ends, ginger and garlic for 30 seconds. Turn out onto a plate and set aside.

■ Heat another 1 teaspoon (5 ml) of oil in the wok and sauté the chicken, stirring constantly, for 1 minute. Add the remaining oil and stir in the white bulbs of the green onions, the onion and green pepper. Add the cooked green onions, ginger and garlic, the bamboo shoots, water chestnuts and mushrooms. Sprinkle the bean sprouts, pimentos, and peas over the top and cook for 1 more minute.

■ Pour in the chicken stock mixture and stir gently until evenly combined. Cook until the sauce boils and thickens.

■ To Serve your inscrutable dinner guests: Spoon the Chop Suey onto dinner plates with the cooked rice on the side.

Helpful Hints and Observations

BAO SYANG OR MARINADE? In the original recipe, the chicken is often marinated in lemon juice with ginger and green onions. I prefer to introduce these seasonings in the bao syang ("explosion of fragrance") technique (see page 47) by adding garlic and literally scalding the three in very hot oil. This method produces a unique and special aroma, which returns later on in the cooking, after the major items, the chicken and onions in this case, have been tossed together.

About the Ingredients

BAMBOO SHOOTS. Unfortunately, bamboo shoots are rarely seen fresh outside of Asia. You can purchase them canned in the oriental foods section of your supermarket. Rinse them under cold running water to help remove any "tinny" flavor. Leftover shoots can be put in water and kept fresh in the refrigerator for up to two weeks. Just change the water every couple of days.

CHINESE SHORT GRAIN RICE. Sometimes called "sticky" or "sweet" rice, this short grain rice is very popular in southwestern China and Thailand. Look for it in the oriental foods section of supermarkets or specialty stores. Rinsing the rice is very important because it washes away excess rice starch. If Chinese short grain rice is not available, short grain or pearl rice can be substituted.

BRAISED TURKEY AND CELERY

T *have made several dishes from turkey breast, which has caused some to ask, "What about the leftover thighs?" Not wishing to have a segregated kitchen or a fridge full of hindquarters, I have made this dish out of fresh thighs which, when braised with celery hearts, rosemary and sage, are delicious. It's full of flavor, easy to prepare and lets me cook the breast separately without guilt.*

Nutritional Profile

PER SERVING	CLASSIC	MINIMAX
Calories	1048	516
Fat (gm)	28	10
Saturated fat (gm)	11	3
Calories from fat	24%	17%
Cholesterol (mg)	301	76
Sodium (mg)	1085	331
Fiber (gm)	11	11

■ *Classic Compared: Turkey Breast Pot Roast*

Time Estimate: Hands on, 75 minutes; unsupervised, 20 minutes

Cost Estimate: Medium High

Serves 4

INGREDIENTS

Two 13-ounce whole turkey legs (369 gm each), yielding 12 ounces (340 gm) of thigh meat

1 teaspoon extra-light olive oil, with a dash of sesame oil (5 ml)

1 large onion, peeled and diced

⅔ cup de-alcoholized red wine (156 ml)

2 celery hearts, trimmed to 4 inches (10 cm) and cut in half lengthwise

1 sprig rosemary

1 fresh sage leaf

3 cups turkey broth (708 ml) (see page 34)

3 tablespoons arrowroot (45 ml), mixed with ¼ cup of de-alcoholized red wine (59 ml)

SIDE DISH: STEAMED VEGETABLES

8 red new potatoes

12 baby carrots

¼ teaspoon freshly ground nutmeg (1.25 ml)

1 turnip, peeled and finely sliced

¼ teaspoon freshly ground black pepper (1.25 ml)

⅛ teaspoon freshly ground salt (0.6 ml)

FIRST PREPARE

■ To separate the turkey thigh from the drumstick: Feel on the inside of the turkey leg. Run your finger down from the exposed ball-and-socket joint at the top of the thigh and you will find a joint about 4 inches (10 cm) away, depending on the size of the turkey. Press the knife down through the joint, separating the thigh from the drumstick. Repeat with the other whole leg and set aside. Freeze the turkey drumsticks for later use.

NOW COOK

■ Preheat the oven to 350°F. (180°C). In a large stewpot, on top of the stove, heat the oil and sauté the onion until slightly soft—about 3 minutes. Remove the onion and set aside.

■ Place the turkey thighs, cut side down, (the cut side is the side opposite the skin side), into the stewpot. Brown well on each side for 2 minutes. Remove the browned thighs, take off the skin and discard. Put the thighs back into the stewpot and lightly brown the area from which the skin was removed—about 1 minute. Remove the thighs and set aside.

■ Wipe a paper towel around the stewpot to blot up the excess grease, then deglaze the pot with ⅓ cup (78 ml) of the wine and add the cooked

onion, celery hearts, rosemary and sage. Lay the thighs, cut side up, on top. Pour in the turkey broth and the remaining ⅓ cup (78 ml) wine and bring to a boil. Remove from the heat, cover and bake in the preheated oven for 40 minutes.

■ About 20 minutes before the turkey is done, cook the side vegetables: Place the potatoes in a steamer and steam for 15 minutes. After 6 minutes, place the carrots in the steamer and sprinkle with the nutmeg. After 4 minutes, spread the turnip slices on a steamer rack, sprinkle with pepper and salt and steam for 5 minutes.

■ Remove the stewpot from the oven. Spoon out the celery hearts and the turkey. Cut the turkey thighs into 4 pieces. Strain the remaining pan juices into a bowl. Pour the juices into a fat separator, waiting for the fat to rise to the top. Pour the separated juices back into the stewpot, keeping the fat in the separator.

■ In the stewpot, bring the pan juices to a boil. Remove from the heat, add the arrowroot paste, return to the heat and stir until thickened. Add the braised celery hearts and turkey pieces and warm through.

■ To Serve: Place a quarter of the turkey pieces, 1 piece of the celery, 2 potatoes, 3 carrots and several slices of turnip on each plate. Drizzle the thickened pan juices on top.

Helpful Hints and Observations

TURKEY BROTH. Because the whole idea behind this recipe is to utilize the tougher legs in a dish separate from the more tender breast, it follows that at one time the turkey had it all together and was dismembered, leaving both the giblets, the neck, wings and the breast and backbones. From these can be made a great turkey stock—please don't throw them out! (See page 34.)

VEGETABLE TIMES. I'm very keen on multiple-level steamers. (See Stack and Steam technique, page 62.)

About the Ingredients

TURKEY. With fewer calories and less fat, turkey has become a popular choice for people who are Minimaxing their lives. No longer do you have to buy a huge whole turkey if you don't want to; in recent years, turkey has begun to be sold packaged in parts: breasts, thighs, drumsticks, even ground. In this latter case, you do need to watch to see that skin fat is *excluded,* or at least greatly reduced. If no reference to fat is given on the package, I suggest you leave it alone.

SEA BASS BAKED IN PARCHMENT

*A*ffectation or a real benefit? I admit I've asked the question about foods baked in parchment. Now that every scrap of food is important I've decided that it really works wonders. The food is sealed and cooks in the aromatic steam created in the confines of the parchment, without the need of fat-laden pastry or obscuring sauces. I cook up to four portions in a single wrap and then cut along the straight folded edge so that the contents can be slipped out onto a serving platter to receive its final garnish. I don't try to serve wrapped portions as single servings; there's too much inedible paper left on the plate and it winds up looking messy.

Nutritional Profile

PER SERVING	CLASSIC	MINIMAX
Calories	806	613
Fat (gm)	47	7
Saturated fat (gm)	21	1
Calories from fat	52%	10%
Cholesterol (mg)	389	60
Sodium (mg)	732	470
Fiber (gm)	1	5

■ *Classic Compared: Pompano en Papillote*

Time Estimate: Hands on, 45 minutes

Cost Estimate: Celebrate

INGREDIENTS

4 green onions

1 red bell pepper, seeded and cut into matchsticks

1 tablespoon lime zest (15 ml), in strips

4½ cups fish stock (1.1 l) (see page 36)

1 cup uncooked long grain white rice (236 ml)

¼ cup uncooked wild rice (59 ml)

4 tablespoons fish sauce (60 ml) (found in Asian food stores)

1⅛ teaspoons extra-light olive oil, with a dash of sesame oil (5.6 ml)

4 thin slices gingerroot

1 large turnip, peeled and cut into matchsticks

4 inches of lemon grass, cut into 2 x ⅛-inch (5 x 0.5-cm) pieces, or substitute 1 tablespoon very narrow strips of lemon peel (15 ml)

4 green onions, cut green tops in narrow strips and white ends diagonally

1 dried red chili pepper, finely chopped

Two 4-ounce white fish fillets (113 gm each), (sea bass is preferable)

1 tablespoon arrowroot (15 ml), mixed with 2 tablespoons water (30 ml)

FIRST PREPARE

■ Cut a 2-foot (61-cm) piece of parchment paper and fold it in half. Starting at the top of the folded edge, cut a half circle that uses as much paper as possible. Unfold, and you have an oval.

■ Starting with the bulb, slice the green onions on the diagonal, up to 3 inches (8 cm) from end of the green part. Chop the remaining 3 inches (8 cm) of the green part into very thin strips, similar in diameter to the lemon grass.

■ In a small bowl, combine the red pepper matchsticks with the green onion strips, add the lime zest and divide the mixture in half: one half for the fish topping and one for the sauce.

NOW COOK

■ Preheat the oven to 350°F. (180°C). In a large saucepan, heat 1½ cups (354 ml) of the fish stock, add the white rice and bring to a boil. Stir once and cover. Reduce the heat to low and cook for 25 minutes.

■ In a small saucepan, heat 1 cup (236 ml) of the fish stock, add the wild rice, 2 tablespoons (30 ml) of the fish sauce and bring to a boil. Reduce the heat, cover loosely and cook for 45 minutes. Drain and add the wild rice to the cooked white rice.

■ In a large frying pan, heat 1 teaspoon (5 ml) of the oil and sauté the ginger, turnip, lemon grass, the diagonal slices of green onion and the red chili for about 2 minutes. Pour in the remaining fish stock and the remaining fish sauce, bring to a boil and reduce by half. Remove from the heat and strain, reserving the broth and cooked vegetables separately.

■ Lay the parchment paper circle on a baking sheet. On half of the circle, near the center fold, make a bed out of the reserved vegetables and place the fish fillets on top. Sprinkle with half of the red pepper and green onion mixture. Fold the parchment paper over the fish and turn the whole thing so that the open edges face you. Starting at one end, fold over about 3 inches (8 cm) of the edge. Crease the middle of the fold, and make another 3-inch (8-cm) fold that overlaps the first one. Continue this overlapping folding around the entire edge. Finish off the last fold with a slight twist to secure it all together. Make sure you leave some air space inside the paper packet, allowing steam to expand but remain contained. Bake the fish in the preheated oven for 15 minutes.

■ While the fish cooks, make the sauce: In a small saucepan, heat the reserved fish broth. Remove from the heat, add the arrowroot slurry, return to heat and stir until thickened. Add the remaining red pepper and green onion mixture and heat through.

■ To Serve: Tear open the parchment packet along the folds. Slip each fillet out onto a dinner plate and coat with the sauce. Spoon out the vegetables and serve on the side.

FISH 'N' CHIPS 'N' PEAS

*W*ithout doubt, this is England's most famous dish. Always deep fried, the fish is mostly cod, and the batter made with eggs, milk and flour. Liberally salted, the fish and chips are traditionally doused with malt vinegar and wrapped in newspaper, so that everything goes limp. My recipe is designed not to flaunt tradition, but to make the taste available to those who count fat grams for good reason. My method delivers this "grease heaven" for a mere 13 grams of fat per serving . . . or 23 percent calories from fat. The peas are definitely not "classic"—they simply don't behave well in a newspaper . . . but then, who does?

Nutritional Profile

PER SERVING	CLASSIC	MINIMAX
Calories	1104	516
Fat (gm)	57	13
Saturated fat (gm)	19	2
Calories from fat	46%	23%
Cholesterol (mg)	150	63
Sodium (mg)	2264	546
Fiber (gm)	8	8

■ *Classic Compared: Fish and Chips*

Time Estimate: Hands on, 45 minutes

Cost Estimate: Low

Serves 4

INGREDIENTS

CHIPS:

2 tablespoons extra-light olive oil, with a dash of sesame oil (30 ml)

2 large russet potatoes, each sliced lengthwise into 9 even "sticks"

½ teaspoon freshly ground salt (2.5 ml)

FISH:

½ cup cornmeal (118 ml)

½ cup bread crumbs (118 ml)

½ teaspoon cayenne pepper (2.5 ml)

½ teaspoon freshly ground salt (2.5 ml)

1 tablespoon fresh finely chopped parsley (15 ml)

1 tablespoon fresh finely chopped dill (15 ml)

½ cup 2% fat milk (118 ml)

¼ cup sifted all-purpose flour (59 ml)

1 tablespoon extra-light olive oil, with a dash of sesame oil (15 ml)

Four 4-ounce cod fillets (113-gm each), skin removed

PEAS:

¼ cup water (59 ml)

2 cups frozen peas (472 ml)

⅛ teaspoon freshly ground salt (0.6 ml)

1 small sprig of fresh mint

1 teaspoon sugar (5 ml)

GARNISH:

4 sprays watercress, washed and dried well

1 lemon, cut into wedges

NOW COOK

■ The Chips: Preheat the oven to 500°F. (260°C). In a large frying pan, heat the oil and fry the potato sticks until brown on all sides—about 13 minutes. Transfer the potatoes to a roaster pan and bake for 10 minutes. Remove from oven and sprinkle with the salt.

■ The Fish: In a small bowl, combine the cornmeal, bread crumbs, cayenne, salt, parsley and dill. Spread the mixture out on a large plate.

■ Pour the milk, flour and oil out, each onto its own large plate. Set all 4 plates side by side.

■ Dip the fillets first into the milk and then into the flour, turning until completely covered. Next dip the fish back into the milk, then into the bread crumb mixture and through the oil. Place the breaded cod on a baking sheet and bake for 8 minutes (you can time the fish to cook for the last 8 minutes with the chips).

■ The Peas: In a medium saucepan, bring the water to a boil and simmer the peas, salt, mint and sugar until the peas are tender—about 3 minutes.

■ To Serve: Divide fish and chips among 4 dinner plates. I serve this classic with a "handy" wedge of lemon (easy to squeeze), peas and, if available, a good spray of watercress. It's the combination of golden browns and vivid greens and lemon yellow that makes such a great picture.

Helpful Hints and Observations

BIG CHIPS. The bigger the better! We experimented for some time with the idea that the larger the french fry the lower its fat content would be. It's simply a matter of exposed surface area. By cutting a large russet potato lengthwise into three slices both ways, you'll get nine potato sticks between ½ and ¾ inch (1.5 and 2.2 cm) thick. When they are cooked, you'll experience a completely new and fabulous taste—potato, almost free of grease.

About the Ingredients

COD. Cod has beauty, flavor and texture—what more could a fish ask for? It's also widely available! There are Atlantic and Pacific cods, along with many smaller catches, such as arctic cod, tomcod, pollock and walleye pollock. I think the cod that sets the standard is the Atlantic. Look for fresh fillets that are firm, with a true white flesh. By the way, because of its popularity, there are many fish that are falsely given the name cod, such as black cod, sablefish and the ling cod, which is actually a member of the greenling family.

SALMON HASH

*B*radley Ogden of Lark's Creek Inn near San Francisco, California, has a wonderfully delicious salmon hash and graciously collaborated with me to make it available to folks who love great hash but can't manage the fat levels. Here is the result— and it's delicious! This is great brunch food—or perhaps for a late supper? With crusty French bread, another one of those fantastic salads full of greens and herbs and a tangy dressing, it would be hard to beat.

Nutritional Profile

PER SERVING	CLASSIC	MINIMAX
Calories	515	311
Fat (gm)	38	9
Saturated Fat (gm)	14	2
Calories from fat	66%	27%
Cholesterol (mg)	286	28
Sodium (mg)	300	283
Fiber (gm)	2	4

■ *Classic Compared: Salmon Hash*

Time Estimate: Hands on, 50 minutes

Cost Estimate: Medium

Serves 4
INGREDIENTS

12 ounces fresh salmon fillet (340 gm)

½ teaspoon freshly ground black pepper (2.5 ml)

2 tablespoons freshly squeezed lemon juice (30 ml)

1 pound small red new potatoes (454 gm), diced into ¼-inch (0.75-cm) cubes

4 teaspoons extra-light olive oil, with a dash of sesame oil (20 ml)

½ cup green onion pieces (118 ml), ¼ inch long (0.75 cm), cut diagonally

¾ cup green bell pepper matchsticks (177 ml), cut 2 inches (5 cm) long

¾ cup red bell pepper matchsticks (177 ml), cut 2 inches (5 cm) long

5 teaspoons fresh chopped thyme (25 ml)

2 tablespoons fresh chopped flat-leaf parsley (30 ml)

¼ cup de-alcoholized white wine (59 ml)

¼ cup water (59 ml)

1¼ cup liquid egg substitute (295 ml)

⅛ teaspoon salt (0.6 ml)

¼ teaspoon cayenne pepper (1.25 ml)

2 tablespoons capers (30 ml)

FIRST PREPARE

■ Preheat oven to 350°F. (180°C). Remove the skin, fat and small bones from the salmon. Slice into very thin strips and place on a plate. Sprinkle with the black pepper and half of the lemon juice. Keep in the refrigerator until ready to use.

NOW COOK

■ In a large bowl, toss the potatoes and 2 teaspoons (10 ml) of the oil until the potatoes are well coated. Spread them out on a nonstick baking sheet and bake in preheated oven for 20 minutes. Remove potatoes and turn the oven temperature to warm. Transfer the potatoes back into the same bowl and toss in any residual oil.

■ Pour the remaining oil into a large wok over medium heat and cook the green onions and green and red peppers until they are just limp—about 3 minutes. Gently stir in the potatoes, the thyme and half the parsley. Transfer the vegetable mixture into the bowl used for the potatoes and keep warm in the oven.

■ Rinse the wok until cool, then return it to the burner. Pour in the wine and the water and bring to a breaking boil (small bubbles just break through the surface). Poach the salmon strips, one half at a time—about 4 minutes for each batch. Transfer the salmon to an ovenproof plate and put in the oven to keep warm with the potatoes.

■ Pour the egg substitute into a hot medium-sized skillet and cook, stirring and scraping the bottom, until just firm—about 4 minutes. Remove from the heat and set aside.

■ To Serve: Nestle separate mounds of the potatoes, eggs and salmon next to each other on a large serving platter or individual plates. Sprinkle with the salt, the remaining lemon juice and the cayenne pepper, and garnish with the remaining parsley and the capers.

Helpful Hints and Observations

THE WEARING OF THE GREEN (FOR SALADS). Not just green, but mixed with red and white, when you use any of the following great salad greens and herbs: arugula, chervil, salad burnet, basil, endive, red leaf lettuce and butter lettuce.

TANGY SALAD DRESSING. Beat together 1 chopped shallot, ¼ cup (59 ml) de-alcoholized red wine, 1 tablespoon (15 ml) olive oil, 1 tablespoon (15 ml) sugar and ¼ teaspoon (1.25 ml) freshly ground black pepper.

About the Ingredients

OMEGA-3 FATTY ACIDS. Omega-3 fatty acids are found in fish and marine plants. Scientists believe they are a substance that can help protect us against heart disease. Studies have shown that cultures with a diet high in fish, such as the Japanese and the Eskimos of Greenland, have a very low incidence of heart disease. Salmon, mackerel, sardines and bluefish are all excellent sources of omega-3 fatty acids.

EGG SUBSTITUTE. I use Fleischmann's Egg Beaters. They are 99 percent egg whites. Egg Beaters are a great way to avoid cholesterol but still enjoy eggs for meals and in your baking. Follow the carton directions and you'll have a great result every time. Egg substitute is found in the freezer section of supermarkets.

SALMON MUMMIES

Catch 35 is a wonderful, mainly seafood, restaurant in downtown Chicago. Here you can eat very fresh fish in an upbeat environment and enjoy simple elegance. Chef-owner, Eak Prukpitikul, is a trained architect who sketches out his dish before he cooks. This recipe is basically his idea, with some considerable springboarding from our kitchen. The major change is in the use of bok choy in place of hard-to-find banana leaves.

Nutritional Profile

PER SERVING	CLASSIC	MINIMAX
Calories	529	258
Fat (gm)	26	6
Saturated fat (gm)	5	1
Calories from fat	44%	22%
Cholesterol (mg)	68	36
Sodium (mg)	460	147
Fiber (gm)	0.7	2

■ *Classic Compared: Catch 35 Salmon*

Time Estimate: Hands on, 60 minutes

Cost Estimate: Celebrate

Serves 4

INGREDIENTS

MARINATED VEGETABLES:

1 red bell pepper, seeded and cut into matchsticks

2 stalks bok choy, cut into matchsticks (the same size as the red pepper)

12 cilantro leaves, finely chopped

4 tablespoons rice wine vinegar (60 ml)

¼ teaspoon toasted sesame oil (1.25 ml)

RICE:

5 green onions

½ teaspoon toasted sesame oil (2.5 ml)

One 2-inch (5-cm) piece of gingerroot, peeled and bruised

4 tablespoons fresh chopped cilantro stalks (60 ml)

1 lemon, zested in strips, zest bruised

¼ teaspoon freshly ground salt (1.25 ml)

⅛ teaspoon cayenne pepper (0.6 ml)

2 cups water (472 ml)

1 cup uncooked long grain white rice (236 ml)

SALMON:

12 large bok choy leaves, stems removed (or Savoy cabbage)

1¼ pounds salmon fillet (567 gm), skin and bones removed, fillet cut into 4 equal pieces

4 slivers of gingerroot

FIRST PREPARE

■ The Marinated Vegetables: In a large bowl, combine the sliced red pepper, bok choy stalks and cilantro leaves with the vinegar and sesame oil and set aside.

NOW COOK

■ The Rice: Cut 1-inch (2.5-cm) pieces off the green ends of the onions and set aside. Cut the rest of the green onions in a thin diagonal slice.

■ In a large saucepan, heat the sesame oil and quickly sauté the green ends of the onion, the ginger, cilantro stalks and lemon zest for 2 minutes. Add the salt, cayenne and water and simmer 10 minutes. Strain, catching the liquid in a bowl. Return the liquid to the saucepan and bring to a boil. Add the rice, cover and simmer for 12 minutes. Take out ½ cup (118 ml) of the cooked rice and reserve. Stir the rest of the rice into the marinating vegetables.

■ The Salmon: Steam the bok choy leaves until just limp—about 30 seconds.

■ Spread the reserved rice out on a large plate. Roll one of the salmon pieces in the rice, giving it a light rice crust. Then wrap in steamed bok choy leaves. Repeat for the remaining 3 salmon pieces. Steam the Salmon Mummies for 8 minutes.

■ To Serve: Place one of the remaining steamed bok choy leaves on each dinner plate and make a mound of a quarter of the marinated rice and vegetables on the stem end. Cut the Salmon Mummies in half and nestle 2 halves in the rice on each plate, cut side up, to reveal the moist, salmon interior to your dinner guests.

Helpful Hints and Observations

HOW DOES HE FOLD THOSE BOK CHOY LEAVES?

1. Spread 2 steamed bok choy leaves on a cutting board, stems overlapping about 2 inches (5 cm) at the middle.

2. Place salmon in the center with a ginger sliver on top.

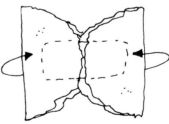

3. Fold the ends of the leaves over the salmon.

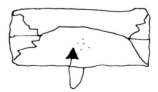

4. Roll Salmon Mummies like a burrito.

BROILED SALMON STEAK AND CREAMY CUCUMBER SAUCE

In February 1991, we had some very dear friends pay us a visit. I really wanted to do my best, but time was against an elaborate menu (sound familiar?). This recipe was the result. It worked perfectly—simple and delicious and less than thirty minutes to do the whole thing!

Nutritional Profile

PER SERVING	CLASSIC	MINIMAX
Calories	692	537
Fat (gm)	34	15
Saturated fat (gm)	11	3
Calories from fat	44%	24%
Cholesterol (mg)	108	82
Sodium (mg)	1366	296
Fiber (gm)	4	5

■ *Classic Compared: Salmon with Cream Sauce*

Time Estimate: Hands on, 30 minutes

Cost Estimate: Celebrate

Serves 4

INGREDIENTS

SIDE DISHES: STEAMED NEW POTATOES AND ASPARAGUS

6 cups water (1.4 l)

15 red new potatoes (about 1¼ pounds or 567 gm)

1 pound asparagus (454 gm), stems cut off 2 inches (5 cm) below the tips

2 teaspoons fresh chopped dill (10 ml)

CUCUMBER SAUCE:

2 cups peeled, seeded and diced cucumbers (472 ml)

1 tablespoon fresh chopped dill (15 ml)

1 teaspoon fresh chopped mint (5 ml)

⅛ teaspoon freshly ground white peppercorns (0.6 ml)

⅛ teaspoon freshly ground salt (0.6 ml)

½ cup de-alcoholized white wine (118 ml)

1 tablespoon cornstarch (15 ml), mixed with 2 tablespoons de-alcoholized wine (30 ml)

1 cup strained yogurt (236 ml) (see page 85)

SALMON:

Two 1 pound king salmon steaks (454 gm each)

1 teaspoon extra-light olive oil, with a dash of sesame oil (5 ml)

⅛ teaspoon freshly ground white peppercorns (0.6 ml)

⅛ teaspoon freshly ground salt (0.6 ml)

NOW COOK

■ The Side Dishes: Pour the water into a large stewpot, bring to a boil and steam the potatoes, covered, for 20 minutes. Remove and set aside. Steam the asparagus tips in the same stewpot, covered, for 5 minutes. Sprinkle with the dill just before serving.

■ The Sauce: While the potatoes and asparagus are steaming, in a medium saucepan, combine the cucumbers, dill, mint, pepper and salt and cook over low heat for 10 minutes. Add the wine, increase the heat to high and bring to a boil. Add the cornstarch slurry and stir until sauce is thickened—about 30 seconds. Remove from the heat and let cool, until you can just put your finger in it without saying ouch. Stir in the strained yogurt.

■ The Salmon: Preheat the broiler. Remove the free bones from the salmon (see Helpful Hints). Pour the oil onto a plate and sprinkle with the pepper and salt. Season both sides of the salmon steaks by wiping them through the oil on the plate. Place the steaks on a rack in a broiler pan. Arrange an oven rack 3 to 4 inches (8 to 10 cm) from the broiling element. Broil the salmon steaks for 8 minutes on each side.

■ Take the salmon out of the broiler and put on a cutting board. Peel off the skin; then, using a small pair of strong tweezers or needle-nosed pliers, pull out the ribs and backbone.

■ To Serve: Cut each salmon steak in half. Spoon a bed of sauce onto each dinner plate and place one of the pieces of salmon in the middle. Drizzle more sauce in a narrow band down the center of the salmon. Serve with the new potatoes and asparagus on the side.

Helpful Hints and Observations

BONELESS SALMON. Before you broil the salmon, remove the "free" bones. They fan out on either side of the backbones in a V shape. Press down on either side of the bone ends as this will make them protrude. Using a pair of fine needle-nosed pliers, pull out the bones and discard. After the fish is cooked, strip off the outer skin and carefully remove the ribs and backbone.

DOUBLE STEAMER. (See Stack and Steam technique, page 62.)

TURNING THE SALMON. I use the double grill-rack method. Use two equal-sized wire broiler racks that fit your broiler pan. Remove the rack with the salmon from the pan to the counter, then place the other rack upside down on top of the salmon steaks. Hold racks firmly together and invert. Return the salmon to the broiler pan. You can also turn the salmon over with two large fish servers, but this requires somewhat superhuman dexterity.

About the Ingredients

KING SALMON. King salmon, also known as Chinook, is a Pacific fish, and I think the most flavorful of the five American salmon species. My favorite Kings come from the Copper River in Alaska, where they spawn from May until June. If you happen to be in the Northwest during their spawning time, don't miss trying them!

SMOKED BLACK COD WITH BARLEY PILAF

O*ne of the truly great taste experiences of the Pacific Northwest is the locally caught and lightly smoked black cod. I've used the same fish, but given it a light tea smoke and a Pacific Rim garnish that is a blend of Asian and European cuisine. This dish has great color, texture and taste, with a definite aroma of fresh ginger. Serve the Barley Pilaf in a small bowl on the side—this is real eating!*

Nutritional Profile

PER SERVING	CLASSIC	MINIMAX
Calories	655	181
Fat (gm)	32	4
Saturated fat (gm)	8	0
Calories from fat	44%	22%
Cholesterol (mg)	122	79
Sodium (mg)	1814	127
Fiber (gm)	2	2

■ *Classic Compared: Fried Cod*

Time Estimate: Hands on, 35 minutes; unsupervised, 82 minutes

Cost Estimate: Medium High

Serves 4
INGREDIENTS

BARLEY PILAF:

2 leeks, dark green tops only

1 teaspoon extra-light olive oil, with a dash of sesame oil (5 ml)

⅛ teaspoon toasted sesame oil (0.6 ml)

2 cloves garlic, peeled and smashed

1 cup uncooked long grain brown rice (236 ml)

½ cup pearl barley (118 ml)

2⅞ cups water (682 ml), mixed with ⅛ cup of fish sauce (30 ml)

SMOKE:

2 tablespoons raw brown rice (30 ml)

1 tablespoon brown sugar (15 ml)

4 whole cloves

Tea leaves from 2 Earl Grey tea bags, removed from packets

COD:

Four 6-ounce black cod fillets (170 gm each)

1 teaspoon extra-light olive oil, with a dash of sesame oil (5 ml)

MARINATED VEGETABLES:

2 leeks, light green parts only

½ red bell pepper, seeded and cut lengthwise into ¼-inch (0.75-cm) slices

½ green bell pepper, seeded and sliced lengthwise into thin matchsticks

⅛ large red onion, thinly sliced

4 sprigs of Italian flat-leaf parsley

¼ cup rice wine vinegar (59 ml)

¼ teaspoon toasted sesame oil (1.25 ml)

4 cups water (944 ml)

One 2 x 3-inch (5 x 8-cm) piece of fresh gingerroot, bruised

FIRST PREPARE

■ The Leeks: Cut each leek into three 3-inch (8-cm) pieces, separating the pieces into 3 groups: the white bulbs, the light green and the dark green tops. Slice the white bulbs in half lengthwise; the light green parts into matchsticks; dice the dark green tops.

NOW COOK

■ The Barley Pilaf: In a small saucepan, heat the oils and sauté the diced dark green leek tops and garlic for 2 minutes. Stir in the rice, barley, water

and fish sauce, cover and cook over medium heat for 45 minutes.

■ The Smoke: See Smoking in a Pot, page 73.

■ The Cod: Brush the cod with the oil and place on a steamer platform. Set the platform in a cast iron pot over the smoke ingredients, cover and cook over high heat for 10 minutes.

■ Marinated Vegetables: In a large bowl, combine the light green leek matchsticks, red pepper, green pepper, red onion and parsley. Stir in the vinegar and sesame oil and let rest for 15 minutes.

■ Pour the water into a steamer, add the ginger and bring to a boil. Put the white leek halves on a steamer platform, place the platform in the steamer, cover and steam for 12 minutes. As the leeks cook they begin to lose their form and will lie flat in the steamer. Remove them on the platform and set aside.

■ To Serve: Place a quarter of the steamed leeks on each dinner plate, arranging them in the shape of a raft, and cover with a piece of the smoked cod. Spoon 1 cup (236 ml) of the Marinated Vegetables on top and serve with ½ cup (118 ml) of the Barley Pilaf in a small side dish.

Helpful Hints and Observations

THE FOIL SAUCER. Early on in my experiments, I had some major problems with this smoking method. I recommend a large, thick-based pan (like our Scanpan Dutch oven), but unfortunately, not all pans are created equal. One of our viewers actually wrote to tell us that she destroyed an alloy-stainless pan. She sent an alloy ingot as proof! Thankfully the smoked chicken was still delicious.

I suggest that only cast aluminum or cast iron pans be used and that the foil saucer be made like a tambourine, with a good inch (2.5 cm) of crumpled foil lifting the saucer at least ½ inch (1.5 cm) above the base of the smoking pan. Following these instructions will make it work perfectly. (See page 73.)

About the Ingredients

EARL GREY TEA. To ensure the success of your tea smoke, I highly recommend the Earl Grey variety which is a blend of Chinese black teas flavored with the oil of bergamot, a Mediterranean citrus.

BLACK COD, OR SABLEFISH. Actually not a cod at all, sablefish is at home in the waters of the northern Pacific Ocean. What I like about this fish is its high oil content, which gives it a sweet, delicate flavor.

PAELLA

O*ne of the greatest contributions to "real food" comes from the Spanish coast around Valencia. This regional favorite combines rice, saffron and a wide variety of fish and shellfish, as well as chicken and ham.*

I set out to keep the essential flavor of paella but remove 39 grams of fat per serving. However, removing so much fat means that the rice will stick, unless it is cooked in another pot.

This reduced-fat version works because shrimp stock is used as the liquid, adding flavor, and the method is so much simpler than the traditional way that the threat of failure is removed.

Nutritional Profile

PER SERVING	CLASSIC	MINIMAX
Calories	1050	502
Fat (gm)	44	5
Saturated fat (gm)	12	1
Calories from fat	38%	10%
Cholesterol (mg)	351	269
Sodium (mg)	1746	480
Fiber (gm)	3	5

■ *Classic Compared: Paella Valencia*

Time Estimate: Hands on, 60 minutes

Cost Estimate: Celebrate

Serves 6
INGREDIENTS

SHRIMP STOCK:

4½ cups water (1.1 l)

2½ pounds raw jumbo shrimp (1.1 kg) (16 to 20 per pound)

PAELLA:

2 teaspoons extra-light olive oil, with a dash of sesame oil (10 ml)

½ onion, peeled and chopped

1 clove garlic, peeled, smashed and chopped

1 teaspoon fresh grated gingerroot (5 ml)

1 bay leaf

2 cups uncooked pearl rice (472 ml)

4 cups shrimp stock (944 ml)

½ cup de-alcoholized white wine (118 ml)

⅛ teaspoon saffron (0.6 ml)

¼ teaspoon freshly ground salt (1.25 ml)

¼ teaspoon freshly ground black peppercorns (1.25 ml)

SAUCE:

1 teaspoon extra-light olive oil, with a dash of sesame oil (5 ml)

½ onion, peeled and sliced

1 red bell pepper, seeded and cut into ½-inch (1.5-cm) slices

1 green bell pepper, seeded and cut into ½-inch (1.5-cm) slices

1 teaspoon fresh grated gingerroot (5 ml)

1 clove garlic, peeled, smashed and chopped

1 cup de-alcoholized white wine (236 ml)

1 cup tomato puree (236 ml)

1 cup fresh quartered mushrooms (236 ml)

3 tablespoons black olives (45 ml), chopped

2 teaspoons capers (10 ml)

1 cup frozen green peas (236 ml), thawed

3 tablespoons fresh chopped basil (45 ml)

GARNISH:

Freshly squeezed lemon juice

Fresh chopped mint leaves

NOW COOK

■ The Shrimp Stock: In a saucepan, bring the water to a boil, drop in the shrimp and cook for 3 minutes. Strain, reserving the liquid. Plunge the shrimp into ice water to prevent further cooking

and make them easy to handle. Peel and devein the shrimp, returning the shells to the reserved liquid. Set the shrimp aside.

■ Bring the reserved liquid and shrimp shells to a boil, reduce the heat and simmer 20 minutes. Strain —you should have 4 cups (944 ml) of shrimp stock.

■ The Paella: In a stewpot, heat the oil and cook the onion and garlic for 1 minute. Add the ginger, bay leaf and pearl rice, stirring until the rice is well coated. Add the shrimp stock, wine, saffron, salt and pepper, stirring until combined. Bring to a boil, reduce the heat and simmer over very low heat for 25 minutes, stirring every 3 minutes.

■ The Sauce: In another stewpot, heat the oil and sauté the onion, bell peppers, ginger and garlic for 3 minutes. Stir in the basil, the wine and tomato puree and bring to a boil; reduce the heat and simmer 10 minutes. Add the mushrooms, olives, capers, and peas.

■ To Assemble: Remove the bay leaf from the paella. Fold the sauce into the rice, then gently fold in the cooked shrimp. Remove the paella from the heat, cover and let stand for 10 minutes to allow the flavors to mingle.

■ To Serve: Spoon the paella into serving bowls. Sprinkle with fresh lemon juice and chopped mint.

Helpful Hints and Observations

RICE IN ANOTHER POT. Paella is *never* made in two pots! It is usually prepared in a well-seasoned paella pan, which is a large beaten-steel skillet with two loop handles that is kept well oiled and used often. When everything is perfect, the rice may resist sticking, but this isn't the rule when the pan is only used occasionally!

About the Ingredients

PEARL RICE. In traditional Valencian paella, one would use a Valencian rice. If you can find it, by all means use it. I've substituted pearl rice: a small, fat, white rice that is opaque with a creamy white center. Pearl rice gives very good results and has a texture very similar to the Valencian variety. Pearl rice is available at some local supermarkets and at specialty food stores. If you've run out of shops to try, substitute long grain white rice.

EASTERN-EXPOSURE SQUID

The future will undoubtedly see the squid become one of the world's most popular foods. There is only 28 percent preparation waste, the flesh is superlean and 18 percent protein. Already the quantity of squid eaten is staggering, with a catch of between one hundred and three hundred million tons a year. So why not start in on the future today and try this recipe?

Nutritional Profile

PER SERVING	CLASSIC	MINIMAX
Calories	1026	407
Fat (gm)	75	7
Saturated fat (gm)	10	1
Calories from fat	66%	16%
Cholesterol (mg)	560	203
Sodium (mg)	519	512
Fiber (gm)	6	4

■ *Classic Compared: Cajun Fried Calamari*

Time Estimate: Hands on, 35 minutes

Cost Estimate: Medium High

Serves 4
INGREDIENTS

8 ounces raw spaghetti (227 gm)

2 teaspoons extra-light olive oil, with a dash of sesame oil (10 ml)

12 ounces calamari-type squid (340 gm), cleaned and cut into ¼-inch (0.75-cm) rings

1 clove garlic, peeled and finely chopped

One 2-inch piece of gingerroot (5 cm), finely chopped

½ teaspoon red pepper flakes (2.5 ml)

One 5-ounce can sliced water chestnuts (142 gm), drained and rinsed

3 stalks bok choy, leaves separated, both thinly sliced

6 green onions, sliced diagonally

1 large red bell pepper, seeded and very finely sliced

1 tablespoon brown sugar (15 ml)

3 tablespoons low-sodium soy sauce (45 ml)

1 teaspoon toasted sesame oil (5 ml)

1 teaspoon arrowroot (5 ml), mixed with ¼ cup rice wine vinegar (59 ml)

1 tablespoon toasted sesame seeds (15 ml)

2 tablespoons fresh chopped cilantro (30 ml)

NOW COOK

■ Bring 6 quarts (5.7 l) of water to a boil and cook the pasta according to the package directions until just tender. Drain and set in a colander over a pot of hot water to keep warm.

■ Pour half of the oil into a wok or large skillet over medium heat and cook the squid ringlets, tossing continuously, for 2 minutes. You will notice the squid turning white and the edges curling gently. Remove and set aside.

■ Add the remaining oil to the same wok or skillet over medium-high heat and cook the garlic, ginger and red pepper flakes for 15 seconds. Add the water chestnuts, bok choy stalks and green onions and cook for 3 minutes, stirring frequently. Add the red bell pepper and cook for 1 minute. Add the brown sugar and soy sauce and cook just until the sugar is dissolved.

■ Add the reserved squid and heat through. Add the cooked pasta and the bok choy leaves, sprinkle in the sesame oil and toss lightly. Remove from the heat, stir in the arrowroot slurry, return to the heat and stir until the pasta is a glossy brown and all ingredients are well incorporated.

■ To Serve: Spoon onto dinner plates and sprinkle with the sesame seeds and chopped cilantro. This dish can be served as an elegant main course, or as an appetizer by cutting the portion size in half.

Helpful Hints and Observations

TENDERNESS. Be careful not to overcook squid, or its meat will turn rubbery.

OCTOPUS. You can also try this recipe with larger octopus. Literally dunk the whole piece in boiling water, count slowly to 5 and lift it out. Wait for two minutes, then plunge it back in. Let it cool completely and then return it to simmering water, stock or sauce to cook very gently until absolutely tender.

About the Ingredients

CALAMARI SQUID. The look of this sea creature might not be very appealing, but once it's dressed and cleaned I think you'll welcome it to many Minimax functions. Squid have ten tentacles, or arms, and a cylinder-shaped body, which pumps water in and out, driving the squid by jet propulsion. Calamari squid are smaller in size, with 4- to 5-inch (10- to 13-cm) tubes. At the market, it's important that the squid smell fresh, not fishy; see if you can get it already cleaned.

NOODLES IN ASIAN COOKING. Most of us associate pasta with Italian cuisine. However, Asian dishes include noodles of every description: wheat, rice, mung-bean flour and seaweed. If you want this recipe to be authentically Asian, try lo mein noodles instead of spaghetti.

THAI-STYLE SARDINES

*P*izza does not have to reign supreme—not when there is a stick of French bread and a can of water-packed sardines present. Here is a Thai twist to the European classic snack, sardines on toast—lots of aroma, color and texture replaces the oiliness of the classic. To my taste, the sardine salad puree in the crusty loaf is one of the great snacks of all time. I serve it with an herbed tossed salad on the side . . . delicious!

Nutritional Profile: Thai-style Sardines on Toast

PER SERVING	CLASSIC	MINIMAX
Calories	362	243
Fat (gm)	47	19
Saturated fat (gm)	7	1
Calories from fat	47%	27%
Cholesterol (mg)	120	37
Sodium (mg)	653	361
Fiber (gm)	1	2

■ *Classic Compared: Sardines on Toast*

Time Estimate: Hands on, 25 minutes

Cost Estimate: Medium

Nutritional Profile: Thai-style Sardine Salad

PER SERVING	CLASSIC	MINIMAX
Calories	240	199
Fat (gm)	17	7
Saturated fat (gm)	2	1
Calories from fat	63%	34%
Cholesterol (mg)	98	36
Sodium (mg)	473	230
Fiber (gm)	0	3

■ *Classic Compared: Thai Sardine Salad*

Time Estimate: Hands on, 25 minutes

Cost Estimate: Medium

Serves 4
INGREDIENTS

SARDINES:

¼ cup water (59 ml)

Peel of ¼ lemon, cut into matchsticks and bruised

1 teaspoon extra-light olive oil, with a dash of sesame oil (5 ml)

2 green onions, finely sliced diagonally

One 14½-ounce can peeled drained tomatoes (411 gm), chopped

2 dried red chili peppers, finely chopped

2 tablespoons fresh finely chopped mint (30 ml)

1 tablespoon fresh coarsely chopped cilantro (15 ml)

Juice of ½ lime

Three 3½-ounce cans water-packed sardines (99-gm each), drained

SALAD:

1 small head of butter lettuce, chopped into ¼-inch (0.75-cm) strips

1 plum tomato, cut into small dice

1 tablespoon fresh finely chopped cilantro (5 ml)

1 tablespoon fresh finely chopped mint (5 ml)

1 tablespoon freshly squeezed lime juice (15 ml)

¼ teaspoon freshly ground black pepper (1.25 ml)

OR

TOAST:

½ baguette (thin stick of French bread), hollowed out

NOW COOK

■ In a small saucepan, add the water to the lemon peel, bring to a boil for 1 minute. Strain and set the lemon peel aside.

■ In a large skillet, heat the oil and, over high heat, cook the lemon peel and green onions for 2 minutes. Add the tomatoes, chili peppers, mint, cilantro and lime juice and cook for 2 minutes. Remove from the heat, lay the sardines on top to warm through, then toss in the sauce until they break into pieces.

■ You can serve the sardines in 2 different ways:

THE SALAD: In a medium-sized bowl, toss the lettuce, tomato, cilantro, mint, lime juice and pepper. Make a ring around the edge of a serving plate with the lettuce salad and spoon the sardines and sauce into the center.

THE TOAST: Remove half of the sardines and sauce to a bowl and mash well, reserving the remaining sardines for another use. Fill the hollowed-out baguette with the sardine mash and place under the broiler until the bread is lightly toasted—about 2 to 3 minutes. Cut into slices and serve.

Helpful Hints and Observations

DON'T MASH THE "FUN FISH" FOR SALAD. Sardines make a great salad when broken into two or three pieces. They are not represented at their best when mashed like tinned tuna.

BUT DO MASH THEM FOR TOAST. There you have it: a personal recommendation.

About the Ingredients

RED CHILIES. Red chilies are an essential ingredient in Thai cooking. Have you ever eaten in a Thai restaurant where the menu asked how hot you want your dish—1, 2, 3 or 4 stars? These stars might as well be depicted as chili peppers. There are many varieties of hot peppers, but most common is the cayenne chili. Cayennes can be found ground or as whole red chilies in the spice section of the supermarket.

SARDINES. The name "sardine" is taken from the Island of Sardinia, where the canning of small herring began—sardines are actually small soft-boned herring. You can now find sardines packed in pure water rather than oil; this greatly reduces the fat and calories, while preserving the flavor of the fish.

RATNER'S GEFILTE FISH CREOLE

Eating at Ratner's Restaurant on Delancy Street in New York City is truly a wonderful experience. Everything that is warming and real about Jewish cookery can be found here. They serve excellent gefilte fish, both cold in its natural jellied stock and bubbling hot in a fragrant creole concoction that was introduced back in the 1940s—long before creole was "in"! I've made some Minimax changes and selected some fish that are more available than the whitefish, pike and carp that are normally used. But the tradition lives on! This is a great "food of the people" dish and should be eaten with gusto!

Nutritional Profile

PER SERVING	CLASSIC	MINIMAX
Calories	594	290
Fat (gm)	23	7
Saturated fat (gm)	5	1
Calories from fat	36%	21%
Cholesterol (mg)	293	101
Sodium (mg)	903	852
Fiber (gm)	1	2

■ *Classic Compared: Gefilte Fish*

Time Estimate: Hands on, 83 minutes; unsupervised, 3 hours, 10 minutes

Cost Estimate: Medium High

Serves 8
INGREDIENTS

FISH STOCK:

2 teaspoons extra-light olive oil, with a dash of sesame oil (10 ml)

1 large onion, peeled and sliced

½ cup chopped parsnips (118 ml)

1 cup sliced celery (236 ml)

4 carrots, peeled and sliced

2½ pounds whitefish bones (1.1 kg)

1 bruised bouquet garni (see page 36)

3 quarts water (2.8 l)

1 package agar-agar (10 gm) (an Asian gelatin substitute)

GEFILTE FISH:

1 pound halibut (454 gm)

1 pound sole (454 gm)

1 pound rockfish (454 gm)

6 slices challah bread (braided egg bread)

1 large onion, peeled

2 teaspoons freshly ground salt (10 ml)

1 teaspoon freshly ground white peppercorns (5 ml)

2 egg whites

8 cups fish stock (1.9 l)

CREOLE SAUCE:

12 black peppercorns

6 whole cloves

5 sun-dried tomatoes

2 heaping tablespoons fresh chopped thyme (30 ml)

¼ teaspoon cayenne pepper (1.25 ml)

1 tablespoon extra-light olive oil, with a dash of sesame oil (15 ml)

3 cloves garlic, peeled, smashed and chopped

1 medium green bell pepper, cored, seeded and finely sliced

1 large red bell pepper, cored, seeded and finely sliced

3 tablespoons arrowroot (45 ml), mixed with 4 tablespoons water (60 ml)

1 tablespoon fresh chopped cilantro (15 ml)

⅛ teaspoon freshly ground salt (0.6 ml)

NOW COOK

■ The Fish Stock: Heat the oil in a large Dutch oven and sauté the onion until translucent. Add the parsnips, celery, carrots, fish bones, bouquet garni and water. Bring to a boil, reduce heat and simmer for 30 minutes. Strain, reserving the bones and vegetables. Set aside 8 cups (1.9 l) of fish stock and freeze the rest for later use. With a pair of tweezers or tongs, remove the bones from the vegetables and set the vegetables aside.

■ The Gefilte Fish: Feed the halibut, sole, rockfish, challah bread and onion through a grinder, catching it in a large bowl. Sprinkle with the salt and pepper and stir to combine. Stir in the egg whites, mixing thoroughly. Turn the mixture out onto a cutting board and chop well, making sure the ingredients are thoroughly combined. Shape ½ cup (118 ml) of the fish mixture into an egg-shaped ball. Continue until all the mixture is gone. You should have 14 fish balls.

■ Put the fish stock in a large pot and bring to a boil. Drop in the fish balls and bring back to a boil. Place a piece of wax paper over the pot, pushing it down just to the top of the stock, lower the heat and simmer for 15 minutes. Transfer the fish balls to a shallow bowl. Strain the stock and set aside. You should have 8 cups (1.9 l) of strained stock. Reserve 4 cups (944 ml) for the sauce.

■ In a saucepan, bring 4 cups (944 ml) of the fish stock to a boil, add the agar-agar and stir until dissolved—about 15 minutes.

■ Spread the reserved vegetables across the bottom of a 9 x 13-inch (23 x 33-cm) casserole. Place the fish balls on top and pour in the agar-agar–thickened fish stock. Cover with a piece of wax paper and refrigerate until the stock is jellied —about 2 hours. Serve cold or hot, with the following Creole Sauce.

■ The Creole Sauce: In a small coffee grinder or blender, whiz together the peppercorns, cloves, tomatoes, thyme and cayenne pepper.

■ Heat the oil in a large saucepan and quickly sauté the garlic, peppers and "whizzed" mixture. Add the remaining 4 cups (944 ml) of reserved stock, bring to a boil, reduce the heat and simmer for 10 minutes. Remove the sauce from the heat, stir in the arrowroot slurry, and return to the heat, stirring until thickened. Season with the cilantro and salt.

MEAT LOAF WITH MUSHROOMS

It had to happen: the meat loaf meets Minimax! The result becomes a new standard recipe that challenges many of the old recipes that deliver great taste along with considerable health risk. This recipe reduces the risk without losing a scrap of flavor. In order to remove the eggs and extra meat fat that is added to the average meat loaf, I had to find another method of holding the loaf together, while still providing a smooth, moist texture. I achieved this by using a combination of pinto beans and egg whites.

One last note: a 7-ounce (198-gm) serving is a good deal more than is needed. I suggest a 5-ounce (142-gm) serving (ten slices from this meatloaf) would be a more reasonable size. This reduces the fat to 8 grams and the calories to 376 per portion.

Nutritional Profile

PER SERVING	CLASSIC	MINIMAX
Calories	565	376
Fat (gm)	34	8
Saturated fat (gm)	16	3
Calories from fat	54%	19%
Cholesterol (mg)	168	46
Sodium (mg)	890	589
Fiber (gm)	4	8

■ *Classic Compared: Market Street Meat Loaf*

Time Estimate: Hands on, 45 minutes; unsupervised, 60 minutes

Cost Estimate: Medium

Serves 10

INGREDIENTS

MEAT LOAF:

2 pounds lean ground beef bottom round (907 gm)

2 cups canned pinto beans (472 ml), drained and rinsed

4 slices whole wheat bread

¼ teaspoon freshly ground salt (1.25 ml)

¼ teaspoon freshly ground black peppercorns (1.25 ml)

1 teaspoon extra-light olive oil, with a dash of sesame oil (5 ml)

1 cup peeled and finely chopped onions (236 ml)

2 teaspoons peeled and minced garlic (10 ml)

½ cup finely chopped carrots (118 ml)

¼ cup finely chopped celery (59 ml)

½ cup finely minced red bell pepper (118 ml)

1 teaspoon fresh chopped thyme (5 ml)

6 ounces low-sodium tomato paste (170 gm)

½ cup canned low-sodium beef broth (118 ml)

¼ teaspoon ground allspice (1.25 ml)

¼ teaspoon ground cumin seed (1.25 ml)

¼ teaspoon cayenne pepper (1.25 ml)

2 egg whites

3 tablespoons fresh chopped parsley (45 ml)

SIDE DISHES: MASHED RED JACKETS AND STEAMED SWEET PEAS

3 pounds unpeeled red new potatoes (1.4 kg), quartered

¼ cup nonfat buttermilk (59 ml)

1 tablespoon fresh chopped parsley (15 ml)

2 cups green peas (472 ml)

1 tablespoon fresh chopped mint (15 ml)

2 tablespoons brown sugar (30 ml)

MUSHROOM SAUCE:

1 teaspoon extra-light olive oil, with a dash of sesame oil (5 ml)

3 tablespoons finely diced shallots (45 ml)

2 cups fresh sliced mushrooms (472 ml)

⅛ teaspoon cayenne pepper (0.6 ml)

1 tablespoon fresh chopped dill weed (15 ml)

1 tablespoon freshly squeezed lemon juice (15 ml)

2 cups low-sodium canned beef broth (472 ml)

2 tablespoons arrowroot (30 ml), mixed with ¼ cup de-alcoholized white wine (59 ml)

1 teaspoon fresh chopped parsley (5 ml)

NOW COOK

■ The Meat Loaf: Preheat the oven to 375°F. (190°C). Feed the beef, pinto beans and bread through a grinder and into a large bowl. Add the salt and pepper and stir thoroughly.

■ In a large skillet, heat the oil and sauté the onions until soft—about 2 minutes. Add the garlic and cook 1 minute. Stir in the carrots, celery, red bell pepper, thyme and tomato paste, mashing the sautéing vegetables into a flavor base. Cook over medium-high heat until there is a pronounced darkening in the tomato paste's color. After this occurs, add the beef broth, allspice, cumin and cayenne, scraping the sides and bottom of the skillet to incorporate any pan residues.

■ Spoon the cooked vegetables into the beef mixture and mix thoroughly. Mix in the egg whites and parsley. Spoon the meat loaf into a nonstick loaf pan, spreading it evenly. Bake in the preheated oven for 60 minutes. Remove, and let the meat loaf cool 10 minutes.

■ The Side Dishes: While the meat loaf is cooking, boil the potatoes in a medium-sized saucepan for 20 minutes. Drain, transfer to a large bowl and mash. Stir in the buttermilk and parsley. This is a rough mash—don't worry about the lumps, they provide a wonderfully rustic texture.

■ Steam the peas, covered, for 5 minutes. Remove to a bowl and combine with the mint and sugar.

■ The Mushroom Sauce: In a large skillet, heat the oil and sauté the shallots until translucent—about 5 minutes. Add the mushrooms, cayenne, dill, lemon juice and beef broth and stir well.

■ Remove the pan from the heat, add the arrowroot slurry, return to the heat and stir until thickened. Add the parsley and stir thoroughly.

■ To Serve: Pour a bed of the mushroom sauce onto a dinner plate and place a meat loaf slice on top. Serve with the mashed potatoes and green peas on the side. The extra sauce can be presented at the table in a sauceboat.

SAUERBRATEN

*O*ne of the world's greatest classics is the "sour meat" pot roast or "braise" that is about as German in style as a dish can get. Often very rich in saturated fats, it can pose a real health risk. I've made some minor changes and, for the identical-sized portion of meat, have substantially reduced the risk without changing the essential flavors.

This recipe uses the flavor injector. (See page 15.) If you do not have one, you can marinate the beef the traditional way. Wash the beef and place it in a small bowl. Pour in the marinade, including the spices and vegetables, making sure that the meat is completely immersed. Put the beef in the refrigerator and marinate for three to five days, turning the meat once every day. Remove from the marinade and dry completely with paper towels. It will only soften the outside and won't flavor the inside, but the sauce is delicious.

Nutritional Profile

PER SERVING	CLASSIC	MINIMAX
Calories	833	499
Fat (gm)	57	12
Saturated fat (gm)	25	5
Calories from fat	61%	22%
Cholesterol (mg)	154	86
Sodium (mg)	638	182
Fiber (gm)	5	6

■ *Classic Compared: Sauerbraten*

Time Estimate: Hands on, 1 hour 40 minutes; unsupervised, 90 minutes

Cost Estimate: Medium High

Serves 8

INGREDIENTS

MARINADE:

6 tablespoons raisins (90 ml)

¼ cup de-alcoholized red wine (59 ml)

2 tablespoons arrowroot (30 ml)

½ teaspoon extra-light olive oil, with a dash of sesame oil (5 ml)

1 onion, peeled and finely chopped

1 stalk celery, finely chopped

1 carrot, peeled and finely chopped

½ leek, finely chopped

2 whole cloves

1 bay leaf

6 black peppercorns

6 juniper berries

1½ cups de-alcoholized red wine (354 ml)

¼ cup red wine vinegar (59 ml)

BEEF:

3 pounds bottom round beef (1.4 kg)

1 teaspoon extra-light olive oil, with a dash of sesame oil (5 ml)

3 tablespoons low-sodium tomato paste (45 ml)

GARNISH:

1 tablespoon fresh chopped parsley

SIDE DISHES: MASHED POTATOES AND BROILED TOMATOES

3 pounds potatoes (1.4 kg), peeled and quartered

½ cup nonfat buttermilk (118 ml)

1 tablespoon chopped leeks (15 ml)

¼ teaspoon freshly grated nutmeg (1.25 ml)

¼ teaspoon caraway seed (1.25 ml)

⅛ teaspoon freshly ground salt (0.6 ml)

¼ teaspoon freshly ground black peppercorns (1.25 ml)

4 large tomatoes

8 teaspoons fresh chopped dill (40 ml)

8 teaspoons bread crumbs (40 ml)

NOW COOK

■ The Marinade: Soak the raisins in the ¼ cup (59 ml) wine until plump—approximately 1 hour. Drain through a sieve, reserving the wine. Set the raisins aside. Mix the reserved raisin-soaking wine with the arrowroot to form a paste and set aside.

■ In a medium-sized saucepan, heat the oil and sauté the onion, celery, carrot and leek until the onion is translucent—about 5 minutes. Add the cloves, bay leaf, peppercorns, juniper berries, 1½ cups (354 ml) red wine and vinegar. Bring to a boil, remove from the heat, cover and let sit for 30 minutes. Strain and set aside the marinade, reserving the vegetables and spices.

■ The Beef: Wash the beef, dry completely with paper towels and place on a cutting board. Pour 2 ounces (59 ml) of the strained marinade into a flavor injector. (See page 15.) Inject tiny amounts all over the beef's surface until the injector is empty. Fill the flavor injector with another 2 ounces (59 ml) of strained marinade and repeat the process. Reserve the leftover marinade.

■ In a large pressure cooker, heat the oil and brown the marinated beef and the tomato paste. Remove the beef and set aside.

■ Deglaze the pressure cooker with the reserved marinade and add the reserved spices and vegetables. Add the beef, secure the lid and cook for 25 minutes.

■ The Side Dishes: While the beef is cooking, boil the potatoes in a medium-sized saucepan for 20 minutes. Drain, transfer to a large bowl and mash. Add the buttermilk and whip thoroughly. Stir in the chopped leeks, nutmeg, caraway seeds and half of the salt and pepper. Cut the tomatoes in half and sprinkle with the dill, bread crumbs and remaining salt and pepper. Just before serving, put on a cookie sheet and pop under the broiler for 5 minutes.

■ Remove the cooked beef and place on a carving board. Strain the marinade from the pressure cooker through a sieve and into a saucepan. Add the plumped raisins and the arrowroot paste and stir until thickened.

■ To Serve: Carve the beef into ¼-inch (0.75-cm) slices. Place 2 slices on each dinner plate and serve with a broiled tomato half and 1 cup (236 ml) of the mashed potatoes. Drizzle with the marinade-gravy and dust with fresh chopped parsley.

STROGANOFF WITH BROWN RICE

"*Meat in the minor key.*" *This is one of the most useful techniques used in Minimax cooking (see "Meat in the Minor Key," page 51). I began, years ago now, with 2 pounds (907 gm) of meat for four people. It gradually inched back through 1½ pounds (680 gm) to 1 pound (454 gm) to even 12 ounces (340 gm). Now in this recipe I'm trying meat in the minor key: only 6 ounces (170 gm) to satisfy the same four people. Whenever meat moves from center stage,* something *must take its place! I've added an aromatic kick with the dill and the special quick herbed stock, but it's really the color and texture, from the added red peppers and snow peas, that does the trick. This is a definite upgrade on an old favorite.*

Nutritional Profile

PER SERVING	CLASSIC	MINIMAX
Calories	744	388
Fat (gm)	48	8
Saturated fat (gm)	24	2
Calories from fat	58%	19%
Cholesterol (mg)	231	25
Sodium (mg)	794	277
Fiber (gm)	2	6

■ *Classic Compared: Beef Stroganoff*

Time Estimate: Hands on, 45 minutes

Cost Estimate: Medium High

Serves 4
INGREDIENTS

STROGANOFF:

2 cups canned low-sodium beef broth (472 ml)

1 bouquet garni (see page 36)

6 ounces beef tenderloin (170 gm)

1 tablespoon extra-light olive oil, with a dash of sesame oil (15 ml)

2 medium onions, peeled and thinly sliced

1 medium red bell pepper, cut in thin strips

¼ teaspoon freshly ground black pepper (1.25 ml)

¼ cup low-sodium tomato paste (59 ml)

2 tablespoons fresh chopped parsley stalks (30 ml)

1 tablespoon Worcestershire sauce (15 ml)

2 cups loosely packed snow peas (472 ml), cut in thin strips

4 cups loosely packed fresh mushrooms (944 ml), stemmed and cut into ¼-inch (0.75-cm) slices

2 tablespoons cornstarch (30 ml), mixed with 4 tablespoons water (60 ml)

¾ cup strained yogurt (177 ml) (see page 85)

1 teaspoon fresh chopped dill (5 ml)

RICE:

3 cups water (708 ml)

1 cup uncooked brown rice (236 ml)

¼ teaspoon freshly ground salt (1.25 ml)

1 teaspoon fresh chopped dill (5 ml)

FIRST PREPARE

■ The Beef: When you don't have time to make a beef broth from scratch, you can use this method. In a medium-sized saucepan over high heat bring the canned beef broth to a boil. Add the trimmings from the vegetables being used in your recipe (in this case, small pieces of onion, red pepper, snow peas and mushroom stems) and a bouquet garni. Bring back to a boil and simmer for 5 minutes. A good flavor enhancement for all canned broths!

■ Pound the beef tenderloin until about ¼-inch (0.75-cm) thick. Slice into thin strips, 5 inches (13 cm) long and ¼ inch (0.75 cm) wide.

NOW COOK

■ The Rice: In a large saucepan, bring the water to a boil, then add the rice and salt. Bring back to a rolling boil and cook for 10 minutes. Strain through a sieve. Place sieve (full of rice) back over a saucepan a quarter filled with boiling water. Cover and steam for 15 minutes. Sprinkle rice with the dill.

■ The Beef: In a large skillet, heat the oil and quickly sauté the onions and red pepper, just to release their volatile oils—about 5 minutes. Remove and set aside.

■ In the same skillet, brown the beef slices *on one side,* for 1 minute. (See Helpful Hints and Observations.) Sprinkle with the black pepper. Flip the beef slices over and stir in the tomato paste, parsley stalks, Worcestershire sauce, cooked onions and red pepper, snow peas and mushrooms and cook for only 1 minute more, then remove from the heat.

■ Strain the beef stock, return to the saucepan and bring it to a boil. Remove from the heat and add the cornstarch slurry. Return to the heat and boil for 30 seconds, stirring constantly to thicken. After the stock thickens, remove the pan from the heat. The stock must cool slightly before you add the strained yogurt or it will "break," giving the appearance of curdling. Gently stir in the yogurt until just incorporated (see Basic White Sauce, page 31).

■ Pour the sauce over the beef and vegetables and reheat. Stir in the dill and taste for seasoning.

■ To Serve: Present this glossy, colorful Stroganoff with a mound of steamed rice on the side.

Helpful Hints and Observations

ONE-SIDE BROWNING. The meat is left to brown *well* on one side. This leaves the untouched sides open to absorb flavors and avoids the watery steaming that often happens when meats are shallow fried in very little fat.

About the Ingredients

BEEF TENDERLOIN. The classic cut for Stroganoff, tenderloin, is the most tender of all the beef cuts. The filet mignon, tournedo and beef Wellington are all derived from the tenderloin. When buying beef tenderloin, ask the butcher for a trimmed piece, without the chine muscle. Also ask him to remove the silverskin, the clear elasticlike casing that covers all muscles. If left on, it shrinks and is impossible to chew.

SNOW PEAS. Also called Chinese peas or sugar peas, snow peas are lovely, green crescents often gracing Oriental stir-fries. The peas are picked when very young, and the entire pod is edible. They cook quickly—heating them through for about 2 minutes is enough. Choose snow peas that are light green and not wilted or soft.

VEAL PIZZAIOLA WITH RISOTTO

"$\mathcal{N}$ow that'sa Italian!" We all know the taste, the heady aroma, the deep rich colors and . . . the cheese! I wrestled with the ingredients to create a reasonable nutritional level and yet not lose all that fabulous taste and texture. I used sun-dried tomatoes and sliced fennel to substitute for the flavor of the enormous amount of butter and cheese normally added to the classic risotto made in Milan. I do believe we did it . . . this one is a winner!

This dish is complete as is; the risotto is made with ingredients with entirely complementary flavors and gives the strong impression of a very rich dish, when in reality there is only 1 teaspoon (5 ml) of fat!

Spoon the sauce onto hot dinner plates, add the veal and more sauce and the risotto on the side. "Smashing!" as they sometimes say in Rome!

Nutritional Profile

PER SERVING	CLASSIC	MINIMAX
Calories	1248	640
Fat (gm)	72	20
Saturated fat (gm)	27	6
Calories from fat	52%	28%
Cholesterol (mg)	247	102
Sodium (mg)	2579	776
Fiber (gm)	7	12

■ *Classic Compared: Veal Pizzaiola*

Time Estimate: Hands on, 60 minutes

Cost Estimate: Celebrate

Serves 2
INGREDIENTS

RISOTTO:

¼ cup sun-dried tomatoes (59 ml)

1 teaspoon extra-light olive oil, with a dash of sesame oil (5 ml)

½ cup finely diced onion (118 ml)

½ cup fresh finely chopped fennel bulb (118 ml)

½ cup uncooked arborio rice (118 ml)

1½ cups homemade chicken stock (354 ml) (see page 34)

1 cup de-alcoholized white wine (236 ml)

¼ cup *very* finely chopped fennel bulb (59 ml)

1 tablespoon freshly grated Parmesan cheese (15 ml)

1 teaspoon fresh finely chopped fennel fronds (5 ml)

½ teaspoon fresh chopped parsley (2.5 ml)

VEAL:

6 ounces veal bottom round (170 gm) (have your butcher slice it very thin)

3 teaspoons extra-light olive oil, with a dash of sesame oil (15 ml)

⅛ teaspoon freshly ground salt (0.6 ml)

¼ teaspoon freshly ground black pepper (1.25 ml)

½ cup finely diced onion (118 ml)

3 cloves garlic, peeled, smashed and finely chopped

¼ cup finely chopped fennel bulb (59 ml)

1 fennel bulb, divided into quarter segments

3 cups peeled, seeded and chopped plum tomatoes (708 ml)

1 tablespoon fresh chopped oregano (15 ml)

1 tablespoon Worcestershire sauce (15 ml)

1 ounce mozzarella cheese (28 gm), julienned

1½ teaspoons fresh chopped parsley (8 ml)

1 teaspoon fresh chopped fennel fronds (5 ml)

GARNISH:

Fresh chopped parsley

FIRST PREPARE

■ The Risotto: To reconstitute the sun-dried tomatoes, put them in a small saucepan, cover with water, bring to a boil, then take off heat and let soak 30 minutes. Drain and chop.

■ The Veal: Pound the veal slices until very thin. Pour 1 teaspoon (5 ml) of the oil on a plate and sprinkle with the salt and pepper. Dredge each

slice through the seasoned oil on both sides and set aside.

NOW COOK

■ The Risotto: In a small Dutch oven, heat the oil and quickly sauté the onion and ½ cup (118 ml) finely chopped fennel bulb until translucent— about 5 minutes. Add the rice and stir until well coated.

■ In a small bowl, mix the chicken stock and wine and pour in enough to just cover the rice. Cook and stir over medium heat until the liquid is absorbed. Continue pouring and stirring until all of the stock and wine are absorbed. Stir in the sun-dried tomatoes and cook over medium heat for 35 minutes. Fold in the ¼ cup (59 ml) of very finely chopped fennel bulb, the Parmesan cheese, chopped fennel fronds and parsley.

■ The Veal: In a large saucepan over medium heat, lightly brown the veal slices on both sides. Remove to a plate.

■ Heat the remaining oil in a saucepan and cook the onion, garlic, the ¼ cup (59 ml) finely chopped fennel bulb and quartered fennel bulb segments, until translucent. Stir in the tomatoes and oregano and cook for 10 minutes. Add the Worcestershire sauce and cook 5 minutes more.

■ Stir the browned veal into the vegetable mixture. Lay the mozzarella strips on top and sprinkle with the chopped parsley and fennel fronds. Cover and heat through, letting the cheese melt.

■ To Serve: Place half the veal on each dinner plate, spoon half the vegetable mixture on top and serve with ¼ cup (59 ml) of the risotto. Garnish with an emerald dusting of chopped fresh parsley.

Helpful Hints and Observations

THE SECRET TO GLOSSY SAUCY RISOTTO. The important thing here is to cook the rice in a little oil and onion and then *gradually* add the wine and stock, a little at a time, stirring constantly as the rice softens. The final result will be a rich, glossy sauce from the starch released by the stirring.

THE TENDER VEAL TRICK. I use a quick sauté as a way to get four or more portions cooked in a regular-sized pan. When you reheat the veal, please just warm it through, never boil it; this only toughens the meat.

YANKEE POT ROAST

*H*ere *it is: instant nostalgia, the kind of food that fogs up the kitchen windows on a winter's day. The sort of food that Dad carves at one end of the table, while Mum sends the vegetables around from the other. I love low-risk nostalgia, so I've tweaked the classic, largely by reducing the meat and increasing the vegetables.*

I really do believe that some dishes should still be served family style. It seems so old-fashioned in our fast-paced lives, but surely one meal now and again could be enjoyed at length among both friends and family?

Nutritional Profile

PER SERVING	CLASSIC	MINIMAX
Calories	793	651
Fat (gm)	38	20
Saturated fat (gm)	13	8
Calories from fat	43%	28%
Cholesterol (mg)	230	144
Sodium (mg)	1060	330
Fiber (gm)	5	11

■ *Classic Compared: Pot Roast*

Time Estimate: Hands on, 45 minutes; unsupervised, 60 minutes

Cost Estimate: Medium High

Serves 8
INGREDIENTS

2½ pounds rump beef roast (1.1 kg)

3 tablespoons low-sodium tomato paste (45 ml)

1 teaspoon extra-light olive oil, with a dash of sesame oil (5 ml)

3 onions, peeled and finely chopped

6 carrots, finely chopped

8 stalks celery, finely chopped

1 bouquet garni (see page 36)

3½ cups beef stock (826 ml) (see page 35)

2 tablespoons cider vinegar (30 ml)

6 whole carrots, chopped into 2-inch (5-cm) pieces

1½ cups chopped turnips (354 ml), 2-inch (5-cm) cubes

1¼ pounds new red potatoes (567 gm)

10 small boiling onions, peeled

1½ cups fresh mushrooms (354 ml)

4 teaspoons horseradish (20 ml)

1 tablespoon fresh chopped parsley (15 ml)

4 tablespoons arrowroot (60 ml), mixed with
8 tablespoons de-alcoholized red wine (120 ml)

NOW COOK

■ Put a large pot or Dutch oven over high heat. When the pot is very hot, brown the beef and the tomato paste. Remove and set aside.

■ Heat the oil in the same pot and, over medium heat, sauté the finely chopped onions, carrots and celery for 10 minutes. This establishes a fragrant, aromatic base.

■ Return the browned roast to the bed of vegetables. Add the bouquet garni, beef stock and vinegar, bring to a boil, reduce the heat, cover and simmer gently for 30 minutes.

■ Remove the roast and set aside. Remove the vegetables and reserve, leaving the liquid in the pot.

■ Return the roast to the pot and add the carrots and turnips, the potatoes and the whole onions. Cover and cook over low heat for 20 minutes. Add the mushrooms and cook 10 minutes more.

■ While the roast continues cooking, puree the reserved cooked vegetables in a food processor. Stir in the horseradish and parsley. Set aside as a side dish for your roast.

■ Remove the roast to a carving board. Leave the vegetables and beef stock in the pot to keep warm. Carve the beef into thin slices.

■ Take the pot off the heat, remove the bouquet garni, stir in the arrowroot paste, return to the heat and stir until the stock thickens.

■ To Serve: Place 2 slices of roast on each dinner plate. Place cooked vegetables to the side and drizzle with the thickened beef juices. Serve the pureed vegetables at room temperature in a small side dish.

Helpful Hints and Observations

THE OLD VEGETABLES LIVE AGAIN! I've always thrown out the vegetables used as "pot seasoning" for pot roasts and braised meat. After an hour, the average carrot is tired and soggy. In the midst of this Minimax effort, I had the idea to remove the flavoring vegetables at halftime (after thirty minutes) and whiz them in a food processor (or blender) until they are a fine puree—still good vegetables cooked in great meat juices. I then added horseradish to this puree, and some parsley for color—*bingo!* Here was a cold vegetable dressing to go with the main dish! Our horseradish addition was designed to be family-strength—an added dollop for Uncle Fred might be needed!

About the Ingredients

HORSERADISH. Would you know a horseradish root if you saw it? Unfortunately most of us have only tasted prepared horseradish from a jar, which is really just a pale imitation of the zest-and-zing from the freshly grated root. Fresh horseradish is not common but can be found in specialty produce shops and can be special ordered by your supermarket's produce manager. But how will you recognize it? The root has a tan to brown skin that needs to be peeled away; it can then be grated, but only grate what you need as it discolors easily. If fresh horseradish cannot be found, use the prepared . . . reluctantly.

HAWKE'S BAY LAMB

Treena and I lived in New Zealand for over seven years. Our son, Andy, was born there and grew up with his sister Tessa. During their school years, we used to prepare a great dish of lamb leftovers that Treena invented (largely because she loved to serve a creamy onion sauce with roast lamb). We used to double the sauce and use it as a blanquette (white-wine stew with a creamy finish). The kids loved it. They still do, now that I've done a Minimax on it . . . so here goes . . .

Nutritional Profile

PER SERVING	CLASSIC	MINIMAX
Calories	720	510
Fat (gm)	44	14
Saturated fat (gm)	23	5
Calories from fat	55%	25%
Cholesterol (mg)	167	106
Sodium (mg)	316	387
Fiber (gm)	3	7

■ *Classic Compared: Hawke's Bay Lamb*

Time Estimate: Hands on, 45 minutes; unsupervised, 20 minutes

Cost Estimate: Medium High

Serves 4

INGREDIENTS

MASHED POTATOES:

1½ pounds potatoes (680 gm), boiled and mashed

1 cup nonfat buttermilk (236 ml)

⅛ teaspoon freshly ground nutmeg (0.6 ml)

¼ teaspoon freshly ground white peppercorns (1.25 ml)

⅛ teaspoon freshly ground salt (0.6 ml)

LAMB CASSEROLE:

2 teaspoons extra-light olive oil, with a dash of sesame oil (10 ml)

2 medium onions, peeled and sliced

¼ cup all-purpose flour (59 ml)

2½ cups nonfat milk (590 ml)

¼ teaspoon freshly ground white peppercorns (1.25 ml)

⅛ teaspoon freshly ground nutmeg (0.6 ml)

2 bay leaves

1 pound cooked roast lamb (454 gm), cubed (New Zealand spring lamb is preferable)

3 cups button mushrooms (708 ml)

½ cup de-alcoholized white wine (118 ml)

3 tablespoons fresh chopped parsley (45 ml)

¼ teaspoon paprika (1.25 ml)

SPINACH:

2 cups water (472 ml)

20 ounces spinach leaves (567 gm)

¼ teaspoon freshly ground nutmeg (1.25 ml)

⅛ teaspoon freshly ground salt (0.6 ml)

¼ teaspoon freshly ground white peppercorns (1.25 ml)

GARNISH:

Fresh parsley

Paprika

NOW COOK

■ The Mashed Potatoes: In a large saucepan over low heat, mix together the mashed potatoes, buttermilk, nutmeg, pepper and salt. Remove from the heat and cool just a bit. Spoon the cooled potatoes into a pastry bag.

■ The Lamb Casserole: In a large stewpot, heat the oil and sauté the onions, stirring to prevent any coloring, until soft—about 5 minutes. Remove from the heat, stir in the flour, return to the heat and gradually stir in the nonfat milk, pepper, nutmeg and bay leaves. Bring to a boil, reduce the heat and simmer 10 minutes.

■ Add the lamb and mushrooms and simmer for 30 minutes more. Stir in the wine, parsley and paprika.

■ The Spinach: In a large stewpot, bring the water to a boil and steam the spinach leaves, covered, for 4 minutes. Transfer the cooked spinach to a cutting board, sprinkle with the nutmeg, salt and pepper and chop it all together. The spinach should be in fine shreds.

■ To Serve: Pipe the potatoes out of the pastry bag and onto a plate, making a nest shape. Place the steaming hot spinach in the center of the potatoes and spoon the lamb casserole on top. Garnish with fresh parsley and paprika.

Helpful Hints and Observations

POTATO NESTS. The freshly cooked potatoes can be "too hot to handle" if you don't let them cool off a little before piping! When I have time, I pipe out the cooled potato and then pop it into a very hot oven or under the broiler. This reheats it and gives the top a light brown crust. If you are in a rush, simply mound the potato and make a well in the center; then fill it with the spinach and the lamb— and you're off and running!

NEW ZEALAND SPRING LAMB. New Zealand lamb is increasingly available around the world today. But unless you know someone flying on Air New Zealand, you are unlikely to get fresh New Zealand lamb outside the islands themselves. However, this great delicacy is available to us frozen. Because the lamb is killed, dressed and deep-frozen within an hour or two, it should be defrosted on a rack (for air circulation) over a plate to catch the drips, for three days in a normal refrigerator. When thawed, wipe the lamb all over thoroughly with a clean cloth soaked in vinegar.

New Zealand lamb is generally smaller than American or British lamb, 3½ to 4 pounds (1.6 kg to 1.8 kg) maximum, and is slaughtered between four and six months. The flavor is milder because of the smaller size, but also because of its natural feeding. New Zealand lamb is fed on mother's milk and grass, as opposed to the grain feeding of others.

LAMB THERESA

*L*amb *makes wonderful leftover dishes, but "leftovers" are not really cheap. They represent roasted meat, and in the case of a leg of lamb, you lose up to 50 percent in bone, fat and fluid loss. This means that lamb costing $4 a pound is actually $8 a pound, cooked. I took this to heart and used only 2 ounces (57 gm) per head (cost: $1) for the meat content. The result is colorful, aromatic, has good texture and is inexpensive. It is named after our eldest daughter, Tessa, who is also very colorful and a pure delight.*

Nutritional Profile

PER SERVING	CLASSIC	MINIMAX
Calories	702	584
Fat (gm)	28	8
Saturated fat (gm)	14	2
Calories from fat	36%	12%
Cholesterol (mg)	150	52
Sodium (mg)	773	79
Fiber (gm)	6	12

■ *Classic Compared: Lamb Theresa*

Time Estimate: Hands on, 30 minutes

Cost Estimate: Medium

Serves 4

INGREDIENTS

1 teaspoon extra-light olive oil, with a dash of sesame oil (5 ml)

2 cloves garlic, peeled, smashed and finely chopped

4 tablespoons low-sodium ketchup (60 ml)

1 tablespoon fresh finely chopped parsley stalks (15 ml)

1¼ cups tomato juice (295 ml)

8 ounces cooked roast lamb (227 gm), cut into ½-inch (1.5-cm) cubes

One 12-ounce can whole, peeled Italian plum tomatoes (340-gm), drained

One 15-ounce can kidney beans (425-gm), drained and rinsed

2 tablespoons arrowroot (30 ml), mixed with ¼ cup de-alcoholized white wine (59 ml)

1 cup chopped broccoli florets (236 ml)

¼ teaspoon freshly ground black pepper (1.25 ml)

RICE:

2 cups water (472 ml)

¼ teaspoon turmeric (1.25 ml)

1½ cups uncooked long grain white rice (354 ml)

NOW COOK

■ Heat the oil in a large skillet and sauté the garlic for 1 minute. Add the ketchup and cook until the color darkens. Add the parsley stalks and tomato juice and cook for 2 minutes. Add the lamb, tomatoes and beans, bring to a boil, reduce the heat and simmer for 5 minutes.

■ Remove from the heat, stir in the arrowroot paste. Return to the heat and stir until thickened. Stir in the broccoli florets, making sure they are submerged under the surface, bring to a boil, reduce the heat and simmer 5 minutes. Stir in the black pepper.

■ The Rice: In a medium saucepan, stir the water and the turmeric and bring to a boil. Add the rice and boil 10 minutes. Strain through a metal sieve, then place the rice-filled sieve over a pan of boiling water and steam, covered, for 5 minutes.

■ To Serve: This is very simple food and is served literally "as is," just a mound of yellow rice and a ladle of meat and vegetable sauce.

Helpful Hints and Observations

THE "TIME" FACTOR. Sometimes there is no time to breathe in this so-called "developed" world of ours. If we are to create food for our families quickly and avoid the high-fat, refined and oversalted "convenience" foods, we must resort to the can opener (at least in part). This recipe is almost aerobic in its use of the can opener. Please look for low-sodium labeling if you or any of your family is hypertensive.

About the Ingredients

PARSLEY. I'm such a fan of parsley that I once dedicated a book to this humble garnish! Of course, I'm not alone in the parsley fan club: its unique, fresh flavor and easy availability make it the most used of all the culinary herbs. There are two types: curly leaf and flat leaf, also known as Italian parsley. Did you know the stalks actually have more flavor than the leaves? This is why they are included in many of my recipes.

RED KIDNEY BEANS. Have you heard the old ditty, "Beans, beans, they're good for your heart"? Well, modern science is finding that there is some truth to this: evidence suggests that the soluble fiber in beans is capable of lowering blood cholesterol and the insoluble fiber is good for the digestive tract. The kidney bean is one of the most commonly used legumes. For convenience I use canned ones in this recipe rather than dried: research shows that you don't lose significant nutritional value in any of the canned varieties.

TOASTED SESAME OIL. This highly aromatic oil is used mainly for seasoning food after it has been cooked. I prefer the toasted variety over the regular: I think the flavor and amber color are enhanced by toasting the seeds before pressing them for the oil. I use just a smidgeon in my cooking oil to provide a nuance of flavor. (Smidgeon = 1/16 part to 1 part remaining olive oil; Nuance = a sigh!)

ROAST LAMB WITH ROMAN PLUM SAUCE

$\mathcal{R}$oast lamb is, for many millions around the world, about as good as food can be. In this recipe, I've taken a two-thousand-year-old Roman recipe for a plum sauce and married it to a small New Zealand leg of young lamb. With some new methods of handling, this turns out wonderfully. Once again, if it can possibly be done, please carve at the table. Some food traditions simply must not be lost. I believe that the dining table is truly our last remaining tribal meeting place, and the carving ceremony should be part of it!

It's a minimax recipe for Roman Plum sauce

Nutritional Profile

PER SERVING	CLASSIC	MINIMAX
Calories	726	635
Fat (gm)	50	22
Saturated fat (gm)	20	8
Calories from fat	62%	31%
Cholesterol (mg)	206	209
Sodium (mg)	164	248
Fiber (gm)	2	6

■ *Classic Compared: Roast Goat with Roman Plum Sauce*

Time Estimate: Hands on, 60 minutes; unsupervised, 2 hours

Cost Estimate: Celebrate

INGREDIENTS

MARINADE:

1 teaspoon extra-light olive oil, with a dash of sesame oil (5 ml)

1 large onion, peeled and finely chopped

1 cup de-alcoholized red wine (236 ml)

1 branch of rosemary

1 teaspoon fresh summer savory (5 ml)

ROAST LAMB:

One 4-pound (1.8-kg) leg of lamb

1 clove garlic, peeled

1 teaspoon fresh rosemary leaves (5 ml)

1 teaspoon fresh thyme leaves (5 ml)

⅛ teaspoon freshly ground salt (0.6 ml)

¼ teaspoon freshly ground black peppercorns (1.25 ml)

2 tablespoons all-purpose flour (30 ml)

PLUM SAUCE:

1½ cups canned low-sodium beef broth (354 ml)

2 cups diced plums (472 ml) (fresh are preferable, but you can use canned)

1 bouquet garni (see page 36)

1 tablespoon arrowroot (15 ml), mixed with 2 tablespoons water (30 ml)

SIDE DISHES: BAKED POTATOES AND STEAMED CARROTS AND GREEN BEANS

4 potatoes, baked

2½ cups carrots (590 ml), about 4 large, cut into matchsticks and steamed

2½ cups green beans (590 ml), steamed

GARNISH:

8 small fresh rosemary sprigs

FIRST PREPARE

■ The Marinade: In a medium-sized saucepan, heat the oil and cook the onion until translucent—about 5 minutes. Add the wine, rosemary and savory, bring to a boil, remove from the heat, cover and let stand for 30 minutes. Strain and set aside, reserving the onion.

■ Put the lamb on a cutting board and trim off all visible fat. Pour 2 ounces (59 ml) of the strained marinade into a flavor injector. Inject small amounts of the marinade all over the lamb's

surface. Refill the injector with 2 more ounces (59 ml) of marinade and repeat the process. Pour the leftover marinade into a measuring cup. If there isn't 1 cup (236 ml), pour in red wine until you reach that amount. Set aside.

■ Put the garlic, rosemary and thyme on a cutting board and chop together. Transfer to a small bowl and set aside.

■ Turn the lamb so the ball-and-socket joint is on your right and the inside of the leg is on top. Using a long knife, make an incision through the right end of the lamb, along the bone beyond the ball and socket. Push the knife in at least 4 inches (10 cm)—this creates a pocket for the seasonings. Stuff in the chopped garlic, rosemary and thyme. Score the meat in diagonal slashes, giving the lamb a crisscrossed appearance. Rub the salt and pepper into the slashes and dust lightly with the flour. Put the lamb on a rack in a roasting pan, outer side up. Preheat the oven to 350°F. (180°C).

NOW COOK

■ Roast the lamb in the preheated oven for 2 hours.

■ The Sauce: While the lamb is cooking, pour the beef broth and the reserved marinade into a medium-sized saucepan. Over medium heat, stir in the reserved marinated onion, diced plums and the bouquet garni. Bring to a boil, reduce heat, and simmer 30 minutes. Strain the sauce into another saucepan, pushing gently on the onion and plums to extract their juices, but not any of their solids. Set aside.

■ The Side Dishes: When the lamb has 50 minutes left to cook, put the potatoes in the oven. They will be cooked by the time you are finished carving the lamb. Steam the carrots and the green beans together for 10 minutes, just before you carve the lamb.

■ Remove the lamb from the oven, put it on a carving board and let it sit for 15 minutes to set its juices. Reserve the roasting juices in the pan.

■ Pour the pan juices into a fat strainer, let the fats rise to the top and pour them off. Pour the strained pan juices into the Plum Sauce. Add the arrowroot paste and return to low heat, stirring until thickened.

■ To Serve: Carve the lamb into thin slices and arrange two on each dinner plate, drizzled with a little sauce. Serve with half a baked potato, steamed carrots and green beans as side dishes. Garnish with a sprig of rosemary.

KARE POAKA

I created this dish in honor of the Queen Mother of England, who visited my National Food and Wine Center in New Zealand in 1963. The name is taken from the native Maori words for "curried pork." The dish is definitely Polynesian in style but has several international touches. Royalty do not taste things in passing, but she said she loved the aroma!

Nutritional Profile

PER SERVING	CLASSIC	MINIMAX
Calories	806	495
Fat (gm)	58	9
Saturated fat (gm)	43	3
Calories from fat	65%	17%
Cholesterol (mg)	182	47
Sodium (mg)	450	118
Fiber (gm)	10	4

■ *Classic Compared: Kare Poaka*

Time Estimate: Hands on, 40 minutes; unsupervised, 2 hours

Cost Estimate: Medium

Serves 4
INGREDIENTS

COCONUT CREAM:

1¼ cups boiling water (295 ml)
6 ounces unsweetened coconut flakes (170 gm)

COCONUT STOCK:

2 cups boiling water (472 ml)

KARE POAKA:

1 teaspoon extra-light olive oil, with a dash of sesame oil (5 ml)
12 ounces pork shoulder (340 gm), fat trimmed off, meat cut into 1-inch (2.5-cm) cubes
1½ cups Coconut Stock (354 ml) (see below)
1 medium onion, peeled and cut into very fine dice
2 green bell peppers, cored, seeded and cut into 1-inch (2.5-cm) dice
2 sweet potatoes, peeled and cut into 1-inch (2.5-cm) dice
1 clove garlic, peeled, smashed and chopped
1 tablespoon curry powder (15 ml)
¼ cup low-sodium tomato sauce (59 ml)
1 bay leaf
1 tablespoon arrowroot (15 ml), mixed with ⅔ cup Coconut Cream (156 ml) (see below)
1 teaspoon garam masala (5 ml) (an Indian curry spice mixture)
¼ teaspoon cayenne pepper (1.25 ml)
1 tablespoon freshly squeezed lemon juice (15 ml)
⅛ teaspoon freshly ground salt (0.6 ml)
Fresh chopped parsley

4 cups cooked long grain white rice (944 ml)

FIRST PREPARE

■ The Coconut Cream: In a medium bowl, pour the boiling water over the coconut, cover and let sit for 30 minutes. Line a sieve with a piece of cheesecloth (muslin) and place over a bowl. Strain the coconut cream through the cheesecloth, squeezing out all moisture. You should have ⅔ cup (156 ml). Reserve the coconut for use in making the Coconut Stock. Put the Coconut Cream into the refrigerator to let the fat rise to the surface —about 15 minutes. Skim off the fat and set aside.

■ The Coconut Stock: In a medium bowl, pour the water over the same coconut used to make the Coconut Cream, cover and let sit for 30 minutes.

Line a sieve with a piece of cheesecloth, (muslin) and place over a bowl. Strain the mixture through the cheesecloth, squeezing out every last flavorful drop, and set aside. You should have 1½ cups (354 ml). The difference between the cream and the stock is the cream will be slightly thicker and will have a higher fat content. In using the coconut twice, you can take full advantage of the remaining coconut flavor without the same level of fat.

NOW COOK

■ Preheat the oven to 350°F. (180°C). In a large ovenproof saucepan, heat half of the oil and brown the pork on one side—this will leave the other side "unsealed" to absorb sauce flavors. Remove the browned pork and set aside.

■ Deglaze the saucepan with the coconut stock, dredging up all pan residues, and pour over the browned pork.

■ In the same saucepan, heat the remaining oil and sauté the onion, half the green peppers, half the sweet potatoes, the garlic and the curry powder until the onion is translucent—about 5 minutes. Add the pork, tomato sauce and the bay leaf, bring to a boil, cover and remove from heat. Bake in the preheated oven for 30 minutes.

■ Remove from the oven, discard the bay leaf and stir in the remaining green peppers and sweet potatoes. Cover, return to the oven and bake for an additional 30 minutes.

■ Remove from the oven and stir in the arrowroot slurry until sauce thickens. Stir in the garam masala, cayenne pepper, lemon juice and salt.

■ To Serve: Since this is a curry, it can be served either in a deep bowl with steamed rice on the side or in a nest of rice with the Kare Poaka on top. In both cases, sprinkle with fresh chopped parsley.

Helpful Hints and Observations

COCONUT. Among the most highly saturated fats in the world, coconut has a wonderful aroma and it provides the incredibly smooth, luscious, mouthfeel of nearly solid fat.

Since fat is not soluble in water, the fat released when the coconut is boiled in water floats on the surface and can be easily skimmed off. By doing this, we remove over 36 grams of fat, which is 78 percent saturated, or 340 calories from each serving! The good news is that the remaining water retains the essential flavor, but is not as overpowering. So we get some of the aromatic benefit without the risk!

PORK TENDERLOIN IN RED WINE ONION SAUCE

Quick, juicy, tender, full of flavor, lots of great colors . . . frankly, it's hard to imagine a better plateful. Here is a complete dinner for guests or family, with under 550 calories per serving and less than 18 grams of fat.

Nutritional Profile

PER SERVING	CLASSIC	MINIMAX
Calories	1007	540
Fat (gm)	62	10
Saturated fat (gm)	19	3
Calories from fat	55%	17%
Cholesterol (mg)	211	105
Sodium (mg)	1683	194
Fiber (gm)	4	8

■ *Classic Compared: Braised Loin of Pork with Onions*

Time Estimate: Hands on, 80 minutes

Cost Estimate: Medium High

Serves 4
INGREDIENTS

POTATOES:

1 teaspoon extra-light olive oil, with a dash of sesame oil (5 ml)

1 large onion, peeled and sliced

1 clove garlic, peeled, smashed and chopped

1 tablespoon fresh finely chopped thyme (15 ml)

¼ teaspoon freshly ground black peppercorns (1.25 ml)

½ teaspoon freshly ground salt (2.5 ml)

4 large red new potatoes, thinly sliced

½ cup beef stock (118 ml) (see page 35)

ONION SAUCE:

1 teaspoon extra-light olive oil, with a dash of sesame oil (5 ml)

2 large onions, peeled and sliced

1 teaspoon caraway seed (5 ml)

1 teaspoon dill seed (5 ml)

¼ cup dark raisins (59 ml)

¾ cup de-alcoholized red wine (177 ml)

1 cup beef stock (236 ml) (see page 35)

PORK TENDERLOIN:

¼ teaspoon freshly ground black peppercorns (1.25 ml)

¼ teaspoon freshly ground salt (1.25 ml)

1 teaspoon extra-light olive oil, with a dash of sesame oil (5 ml)

Two ½-pound (227-gm each) pork tenderloins, fat and silverskin trimmed

¼ cup de-alcoholized red wine (59 ml)

2 tablespoons arrowroot (30 ml)

4 tablespoons de-alcoholized red wine (60 ml)

GARNISH:

1 tablespoon fresh chopped parsley (15 ml)

SIDE DISH: SPINACH-STUFFED RED PEPPER

1 large sweet red bell pepper, seeded and cut in half lengthwise

5 ounces spinach leaves, washed (142 gm)

1/16 teaspoon freshly ground salt (0.3 ml)

1/16 teaspoon freshly ground black pepper (0.3 ml)

⅛ teaspoon freshly ground nutmeg (0.6 ml)

NOW COOK

■ The Potatoes: Preheat the oven to 350°F. (180°C). In a large skillet, heat the oil and sauté the onion and garlic until the onion is slightly soft—about 3 minutes. Stir in the thyme, pepper and salt, heat through and set aside.

■ Layer the bottom of an 8 x 8-inch (20 x 20-cm) baking pan with a quarter of the potato slices. Spoon a third of the sautéed onion and garlic on top. Continue the layering process, finishing with a neat layer of potatoes on top. Pour the beef stock over the potatoes and bake in the preheated oven for 50 minutes.

■ The Onion Sauce: In a skillet, over medium heat, heat the oil and cook the onions, caraway and dill, without stirring, for 5 minutes. Stir once, then cover and cook for 5 minutes. Add the raisins, wine and stock and cook for 5 minutes more. Remove from the heat and set aside.

■ The Pork Tenderloin: Sprinkle the pepper and salt on a large plate. Drizzle the oil over the pepper and salt and stir together. Dredge the pork pieces through the seasoned oil.

■ Heat a large ovenproof skillet and quickly brown the pork on all sides to seal in the juices—about 5 minutes. Place the skillet in the preheated oven and bake for 15 minutes. (You can time this to bake with the potatoes for that dish's last 15 minutes.) Remove and carve each tenderloin into 6 even slices. Deglaze the skillet with the wine and add the liquid to the reserved onion sauce.

■ Return the onion sauce to the stove, and, over medium-high heat, bring to a simmer. Remove from the heat, add the arrowroot slurry and stir to thicken.

■ The Spinach-stuffed Pepper: In a stack and steam unit (see page 62), place red peppers on the lower platform and the spinach on the upper rack; or steam red peppers and spinach in two separate steamers. Cook each for 3 minutes or until spinach is slightly limp. Remove and chop the spinach coarsely, seasoning with the salt, pepper and nutmeg. Fill each pepper half with some of the spinach and cook for 2 more minutes. Remove and cut each pepper half in two.

■ To Serve: Spoon a quarter of the potatoes on each dinner plate. Make a bed of the onion sauce and place 3 pork slices on top. Garnish with a sprinkle of the chopped parsley. Serve with a stuffed pepper quarter on the side.

ROAST PORK AND PUERTO RICAN BEAN SALSA

$\mathcal{P}$uerto Rican people have a wonderful celebration every year around Christmas and New Year's Eve, when they barbecue whole suckling pigs. Here you'll find the fullness of aroma, color and texture—minus the whole pig. I've tried to capture the tastes in this new dish, dedicated to the vibrant Puerto Rican lifestyle and to Yvonne Ortiz, my culinary guide among her people.

Nutritional Profile

PER SERVING	CLASSIC	MINIMAX
Calories	1187	482
Fat (gm)	67	17
Saturated fat (gm)	27	6
Calories from fat	51%	32%
Cholesterol (mg)	277	98
Sodium (mg)	709	362
Fiber (gm)	8	3

■ *Classic Compared: Roast Pork and Beans*

Time Estimate: Hands on, 45 minutes; unsupervised, 90 minutes

Cost Estimate: Medium High

Serves 12
INGREDIENTS

PORK:

One 4-pound pork loin roast (1.8 kg)

1 banana, peeled

1 tablespoon fresh chopped cilantro (15 ml)

1 clove garlic, peeled, smashed and chopped

⅛ teaspoon freshly ground salt (0.6 ml)

¼ teaspoon freshly ground black pepper (1.25 ml)

SALSA:

1 teaspoon extra-light olive oil, with a dash of sesame oil (5 ml)

½ medium onion, peeled and finely diced

4 cloves garlic, peeled, smashed and chopped

2 jalapeño peppers, finely diced

Two 28-ounce cans peeled plum tomatoes (794 gm each), with their liquid

2 tablespoons fresh finely chopped oregano (30 ml)

1 cup uncooked long grain white rice (236 ml)

One 15-ounce can garbanzo beans (425 gm), drained and rinsed

¼ teaspoon freshly ground salt (1.25 ml)

¼ teaspoon freshly ground black pepper (1.25 ml)

1 red bell pepper, seeded and diced

One 16-ounce can black beans (454 gm), drained and rinsed

2 tablespoons fresh finely chopped cilantro (30 ml)

GARNISH:

1 banana, cut into 1-inch (2.5-cm) slices

Juice of ½ lime

1 tablespoon fresh chopped cilantro (15 ml)

4 sprigs fresh cilantro

FIRST PREPARE

■ Preheat the oven to 350°F. (180°C). Cut the pork in half and place the pieces side by side on a cutting board. Lay the banana lengthwise on top and down the center of one piece and mark its outline. Cut a shallow trench the length and width of the banana and half its depth. Repeat the process on the other piece of pork. Reserve the pork that is cut out and set aside.

■ Sprinkle the cilantro and garlic down the trenches, then season both pieces of pork with the salt and pepper. Put the banana in the trench in one of the pieces and cover with the other piece. Using string, tie the halves together.

NOW COOK

■ The Pork: Put the prepared pork on a rack in a roasting pan and cook in the preheated oven for 80 minutes or until a meat thermometer reads 160°F. (71°C). Remove and let rest for 10 minutes before carving.

■ The Salsa: Dice the reserved pork into ¼-inch (0.75-cm) cubes.

■ In a medium-sized stewpot, heat the oil and brown the diced pork on one side. Add the onion and garlic and cook until the onion is soft—about 5 minutes. Add the jalapeño peppers, tomatoes and their liquid and the oregano and simmer, uncovered, for 10 minutes. Add the rice, garbanzo beans, salt and pepper and bring to a boil. Decrease the heat, cover and simmer for 20 minutes.

■ Gently stir in the red pepper, black beans and cilantro and heat through.

■ The Garnish: Just before serving, mix the sliced banana with the lime juice and chopped cilantro.

■ To Serve: Carve the pork into ½-inch (1.5-cm) slices. Put 1 slice on each plate with some of the salsa and a spoonful of the banana garnish on the side. Top with a graceful green cilantro sprig. The bean salsa can also be served on its own as a vegetarian main dish, omitting the diced pork; there's enough for 6 hearty portions, with 415 calories, 6 grams of total fat and only 12 percent calories from fat per serving ... again these numbers are *without* the meat.

Helpful Hints and Observations

String knots used to securely tie together the two halves of the pork roast.

About the Ingredients

GARBANZO BEANS. Many recipes call for dried garbanzo beans, or chick-peas as they are more commonly known. I find the quality of canned beans to be exceptionally good—they also do not need to be cooked for three hours.

BLACK BEANS. *Frijoles negros,* as they are known in Spanish, are a great source of color and texture. When beans are eaten with grains, our bodies can fully utilize the combined proteins. Again, I've used a canned product to shorten the cooking time without taking away from the integrity of this festive dish.

STUFFED PORK CHOPS

$\mathcal{I}$ created the original dish, Pork Chops Ngauruhoe, for New Zealand Television in 1963 and over the years have had rave notices about it. The percentage of calories from fat for the Minimax version is really good for such a large meat serving. Oh yes, in case you're wondering, Ngauruhoe is one of New Zealand's largest mountains on the North Island.

Nutritional Profile

PER SERVING	CLASSIC	MINIMAX
Calories	1072	556
Fat (gm)	75	11
Saturated fat (gm)	42	3
Calories from fat	63%	17%
Cholesterol (mg)	250	57
Sodium (mg)	1184	221
Fiber (gm)	7	10

■ *Classic Compared: Pork Chops Ngauruhoe*

Time Estimate: Hands on, 60 minutes

Cost Estimate: Medium High

Serves 4

INGREDIENTS

SIDE DISHES: MASHED YAMS AND POTATOES:

1½ pounds yams (680 gm)

1½ pounds russet potatoes (680 gm)

¼ cup finely chopped green onions (59 ml), white bulb only

1 orange, peeled and chopped, peel reserved

⅛ teaspoon ground cloves (0.6 ml)

⅛ teaspoon freshly ground black pepper (0.6 ml)

½ pound steamed broccoli florets (227 gm)

STUFFING:

1 tablespoon very fine threads orange peel (15 ml)

1½ teaspoons very fine threads fresh gingerroot (7.5 ml)

¼ apple, peeled, cored and finely diced (Granny Smith is preferable)

2 tablespoons dark raisins (30 ml)

1⁄16 teaspoon ground cloves (0.3 ml)

⅛ teaspoon freshly ground salt (0.6 ml)

⅛ teaspoon freshly ground white peppercorns (0.6 ml)

3 fresh sage leaves, finely chopped

2 tablespoons finely chopped green onions (30 ml), green part only

PORK CHOPS:

4 pork rib chops, 1½ inches (4 cm) thick

1 teaspoon extra-light olive oil, with a dash of sesame oil (5 ml)

⅛ teaspoon freshly ground salt (0.6 ml)

¼ teaspoon freshly ground white peppercorns (1.25 ml)

SAUCE:

1 cup freshly squeezed orange juice (236 ml)

1 cup de-alcoholized white wine (236 ml)

2 tablespoons arrowroot (30 ml), mixed with 2 tablespoons de-alcoholized white wine (30 ml)

GARNISH:

Finely sliced green onion tops

FIRST PREPARE

■ The Mashed Yams and Potatoes: Preheat the oven to 350°F. (180°C). Wash the yams and potatoes well and prick each one several times with a fork. Bake in preheated oven for 1 hour. Remove from the oven and let cool.

■ When cool, peel off the skins and discard. In a large bowl, mash the yam and potato meat, then stir in the green onion bulbs, orange, cloves and the ⅛ teaspoon (0.6 ml) pepper, or more to taste.

■ The Stuffing: In a small bowl, combine the orange peel, ginger, apple, raisins, cloves, salt, pepper, sage and green onion tops.

■ The Pork Chops: Make a pocket for the stuffing by plunging a thin-bladed knife through the side of each pork chop, creating a horizontal incision through the fat to the bone. Without enlarging the initial cut, fan the knife blade back and forth along the bone side to create a large, triangle-shaped pocket. Stuff each prepared pork chop with 2 tablespoons (30 ml) of the stuffing. Fasten the opening shut with a toothpick.

NOW COOK

■ While the potatoes bake, cook the stuffed pork chops and the sauce.

■ The Pork Chops: Pour the oil on a plate and sprinkle with the salt and pepper. Using a pastry brush, brush the oil mixture around the plate, then moisten both sides of each pork chop by rubbing them on the plate. Place the pork chops in a large skillet over medium heat. Brown each side, then cook for 15 minutes, turning to prevent excessive browning. Remove and set aside.

■ The Sauce: In a small bowl, mix the orange juice and wine. Deglaze the pork-browning skillet with ½ cup (118 ml) of the orange-wine mixture. Strain the liquid back into the bowl with the rest of the orange-wine mixture. Pour into a small saucepan over medium heat and warm through. Remove from the heat, stir in the arrowroot slurry, return to the heat and stir until thickened.

■ Just before serving, put the mashed potatoes in a small saucepan over low heat and heat through. Briefly steam broccoli florets.

■ To Serve: Remove the toothpicks from the cooked pork chops. Place 1 chop on each dinner plate, accompanied by a heaping spoonful of Mashed Yams and Potatoes and a few bright green florets of steamed broccoli. Make a deep depression in the mashed potatoes and yams and fill it with sauce. Brush extra sauce over the pork chop to make it glisten and dust the whole dish with the sliced green onion tops.

RABBIT CASSEROLE

If you've never owned a pet rabbit, this dish could become one of your all-time favorites! The meat is as tender as chicken, but succulent and deeper in flavor. Rabbit has very little fat and adapts itself to many superb seasonings. This recipe is done very simply and tastes great. I always serve this dish with a puree of turnips, carrots and parsnips, seasoned with nutmeg and parsley—a wonderful vegetable dish for almost every meat or poultry, stew or casserole. Add your favorite bread and nobody will leave the table dissatisfied.

Nutritional Profile

PER SERVING	CLASSIC	MINIMAX
Calories	808	691
Fat (gm)	40	24
Saturated fat (gm)	14	7
Calories from fat	45%	32%
Cholesterol (mg)	285	198
Sodium (mg)	634	426
Fiber (gm)	1	7

■ *Classic Compared: Braised Rabbit with Onions*

Time Estimate: Hands on, 60 minutes; unsupervised, 30 minutes

Cost Estimate: Celebrate

Serves 4

INGREDIENTS

One 3-pound rabbit (1.4 kg)
1 tablespoon extra-light olive oil, with a dash of sesame oil (15 ml)
8 medium onions, peeled
8 fresh mushrooms
1 ounce ham (28 gm), trimmed from cooked ham hocks (see below)
3 tablespoons low-sodium tomato paste (45 ml)
2 cups de-alcoholized red wine (472 ml)
1 cup ham hock stock (236 ml) (see page 35)
1 bouquet garni (see page 36)
2 carrots, peeled and chopped into 1-inch (2.5-cm) pieces
2 turnips, peeled and chopped into 1-inch (2.5-cm) pieces
2 parsnips, peeled and chopped into 1-inch (2.5-cm) pieces
¼ teaspoon freshly ground nutmeg (1.25 ml)
3 tablespoons fresh chopped parsley (45 ml)
2 tablespoons arrowroot (30 ml), mixed with ¼ cup de-alcoholized red wine (59 ml)
⅛ teaspoon salt (0.6 ml)
¼ teaspoon freshly ground black pepper (1.25 ml)

FIRST PREPARE

■ Chop the rabbit into 8 pieces: hind legs, thighs, half saddles (the long strip from the shoulders to thighs) and shoulders. Cut the rib bones from the front legs and use the bones in making the ham hock stock.

NOW COOK

■ Preheat the oven to 350°F. (180°C). Pour the oil into a low-sided ovenproof casserole over high heat and brown the rabbit pieces, turning to expose all the sides—about 5 minutes. Remove and set aside.

■ In the same casserole, brown the onions and mushrooms. The mushrooms will brown in about 30 seconds; remove them and set aside, keeping the onions in the casserole until they're done— about 5 minutes. Add the ham hock meat and tomato paste and cook until the tomato paste darkens in color—about 5 minutes. Add the browned rabbit pieces, the 2 cups (472 ml) wine,

the ham hock stock and bouquet garni, bring to a boil and remove from the heat. Cover and put in the preheated oven to bake for 25 minutes. Uncover, stir in the mushrooms and bake 10 minutes.

■ While the rabbit casserole is baking, steam the carrots, turnips and parsnips until soft—about 12 minutes. Transfer to a food processor or blender, add the nutmeg and parsley, and puree until combined, but not smooth like a sauce. Spoon into a bowl and keep warm until ready to serve.

■ Remove the casserole from the oven. Transfer the rabbit pieces to a bowl, discard bouquet garni. Stir the arrowroot slurry into the liquid until thickened. Season with the salt and pepper.

■ To Serve: Place the rabbit pieces on a serving plate and drizzle with casserole liquid. Serve the pureed vegetables on the side.

Helpful Hints and Observations

ROYAL ASCOT ROOTS. My wife, Treena, and I used to manage the famous Royal Ascot Hotel near Windsor in England, where we introduced a soup of root vegetables that we called Farmhouse Vegetable Soup with Cream (it was rich!). Based upon that favorite, I developed the best vegetable side dish I know: the combination of carrot, turnip and parsnip. This really is a winner and comes off superbly when the vegetables are steamed until just tender—about twelve minutes—and then poured "dry" into a food processor. A few pulses should cut the vegetables together and distribute the nutmeg and parsley evenly. Don't whiz until it's as smooth as a sauce. It should retain some of its firm texture.

About the Ingredients

PARSNIPS. They look like a whiter version of the carrot, but they possess their own fresher taste. Parsnips are also a great source of fiber, making them a good substitute for bran in your diet. Look for smooth, firm, slender vegetables; the thicker ones have tough woody cores. The parsnips should not appear dry or shriveled.

RABBIT. Rabbits are now raised in captivity, like other livestock, and are a growing industry. Indeed, rabbit is becoming so popular that you will find it every day in most butcher shops.

■   *Rabbit Casserole*   185

COUSCOUS

In North Africa, there is a wealth of wonderful, colorful and aromatic dishes that don't have to swim in oil. I took a classic couscous, served with local Mediterranean tuna, and made it possible to fix this version after just one trip to a good supermarket. The result could be a breakthrough for both your family and your friends!

This Couscous is best served very hot from the steamer (or colander) and the fish in its broth ladled from a soup tureen (or bowl) at the table. The hot Harissa Sauce is added separately according to each individual's taste for self-inflicted wounds!

Nutritional Profile

PER SERVING	CLASSIC	MINIMAX
Calories	977	353
Fat (gm)	51	5
Saturated fat (gm)	10	1
Calories from fat	47%	14%
Cholesterol (mg)	117	35
Sodium (mg)	514	258
Fiber (gm)	21	14

■ *Classic Compared: Couscous and Fresh Tuna, Tunisian Style*

Time Estimate: Hands on, 60 minutes

Cost Estimate: Medium High

INGREDIENTS

HARISSA SEASONINGS:

6 dried red chili peppers
¼ teaspoon caraway seed (1.25 ml)
¼ teaspoon cumin seed (1.25 ml)
½ teaspoon coriander (2.5 ml)
1 clove garlic

COUSCOUS:

1 tablespoon extra-light olive oil, with a dash of sesame oil (15 ml)
2 medium onions, peeled and sliced thickly
2 cloves garlic, peeled, smashed and diced
1 medium green bell pepper, seeded and sliced thickly
1 medium red bell pepper, seeded and sliced thickly
1 medium yellow bell pepper, seeded and sliced thickly
1 fresh jalapeño pepper, seeded and chopped
½ teaspoon fresh chopped thyme (2.5 ml)
1 zucchini, cut into ½-inch (1.5-cm) cubes
2 cups instant couscous (472 ml)
6½ cups fish stock (1.5 ml) (see page 36)
3 large tomatoes, peeled, seeded and coarsely chopped
4 cups boiling water (944 ml)
¼ cup fresh chopped parsley (59 ml)
1 pound fresh sole fillets (454 gm), cut into 1-inch (2.5-cm) "diamond" slices
¼ teaspoon freshly ground salt (1.25 ml)

FIRST PREPARE

■ The Harissa Seasonings: In a small coffee grinder or food processor, whiz the dried red peppers, caraway seed, cumin seed, coriander and garlic. Spoon into a small bowl and set aside. If you have any difficulty finding these spices in their whole form, purchase them ground. The result will be a loss of some pungency, but not enough to discourage one from trying this recipe.

NOW COOK

■ The Couscous: Heat the oil in a large Dutch oven or pot and, over medium heat, fry the onions 1 minute. Add the garlic and cook 2 minutes longer. Stir in the bell peppers, the jalapeño, thyme and zucchini and cook 5 minutes. Add the instant couscous, 3½ cups (826 ml) of the fish stock and half of the tomatoes and stir well.

■ Spoon this couscous mixture into a steamer, cover and steam the couscous for 5 minutes. As an alternative, line a colander with cheesecloth; set in a Dutch oven over boiling water. Add couscous mixture, cover and steam for 5 minutes. Uncover and add the remaining tomatoes and the parsley. Stir lightly, cover and set aside.

■ The Fish: In a saucepan, bring the remaining fish stock to a boil and stir in 1 teaspoon (5 ml) of the Harissa seasonings and the sole slices. Cover, remove from the heat and let stand for 3 minutes; drain, reserving the stock.

■ Mix the remaining Harissa seasonings into the fish stock to make a sauce.

■ To Serve: Spoon the couscous into 6 individual soup bowls. Spoon a sixth of the sole on top of the couscous in each. Serve the Harissa Sauce on the side, allowing your guests to choose the amount of spice they would like to add to their life—or at least their Couscous.

Helpful Hints and Observations

PRECOOKED OR REGULAR COUSCOUS? I admit to being somewhat prejudiced about "instant-type" grains. To my taste they are watery and lack both flavor and texture—all for very little time saved.

On the other hand, I like precooked bulgur wheat. Couscous is hard durum wheat (semolina), either milled fresh or precooked and cracked like bulgur. I'm usually prone to get to my food *fast* before someone gets to it *first;* but in this case the convenience is really invaluable and makes sense—especially because it obviates the necessity to have a couscousiere (a special two-piece steamer). Our method uses either my own steamer design (see Stack and Steam, page 62) or a large colander: either way it's virtually a foolproof method.

About the Ingredients

COUSCOUS. Another versatile grain with endless springboarding opportunities! Couscous is simply ground durum wheat. Once cooked, its rather delicate taste is often heightened with spices, meat and vegetables. Couscous has been the basis for the classic main meal in North Africa for centuries.

HARISSA. In North Africa, this hot seasoning is not only used to spice up couscous, but many other dishes, including salads, soups and stews. Remember, a little goes a long way! You can store the leftovers in a covered container, refrigerated, for three to four days.

MASALA DOSA (INDIAN BEAN AND POTATO PANCAKES)

This is southern India's answer to the American hamburger, the British sausage roll, and the Australian floater and peas. An excellent restaurant, The Bite of India, in Bellevue, Washington, has sold over 32,000 in three years. I've made some slight changes, but owe the basic idea to Mrs. Usha Reddy and her great team. One special note on garam masala. I have used it as a generic description for all manner of creative combinations of warm aromatic spices. Other uses for warm spices are in POP. (See page 44.)

Nutritional Profile

PER SERVING	CLASSIC	MINIMAX
Calories	337	246
Fat (gm)	12	2
Saturated fat (gm)	5	0
Calories from fat	31%	8%
Cholesterol (mg)	0	0
Sodium (mg)	216	161
Fiber (gm)	7	4

■ *Classic Compared: Masala Dosa*

Time Estimate: Hands on, 60 minutes; unsupervised, 11 hours

Cost Estimate: Low

INGREDIENTS

DOSA (THE PANCAKE):

1¼ cups warm water (295 ml)

1¼ cups rice flour (295 ml)

½ cup split black lentils (118 ml), washed, soaked for 3 hours in 3 cups (708 ml) water and drained

½ cup water (118 ml)

⅛ teaspoon freshly ground salt (0.6 ml)

MASALA (THE FILLING):

½ teaspoon extra-light olive oil, with a dash of sesame oil (2.5 ml)

2 large onions, peeled and thinly sliced

1 teaspoon fresh finely chopped gingerroot (5 ml)

½ teaspoon whole cumin (2.5 ml)

½ teaspoon whole black or yellow mustard seeds (2.5 ml)

2 jalapeño peppers, finely chopped

½ teaspoon turmeric (2.5 ml)

1 cup water (236 ml)

3 large potatoes, peeled, cut into ¼-inch (0.75-cm) cubes, boiled and drained

¼ teaspoon freshly ground salt (1.25 ml)

½ teaspoon garam masala (2.5 ml)

Olive oil cooking spray

6 tablespoons mango chutney (90 ml)

GARNISH:

1 mango, sliced

1 lime, cut in wedges

FIRST PREPARE

■ Make the dosa batter the night before serving. In a medium-sized bowl, beat together the 1¼ cups (295 ml) warm water and the rice flour. In a food processor, puree the lentils, the ½ cup (118 ml) water and the salt. Add the rice flour mixture and puree again. Transfer the batter to a 6-quart (5.7 l) bowl, cover and put in a warm place, 80°F. (27°C), overnight.

NOW COOK

■ The Masala: In a 10-inch (25-cm) skillet, heat the oil and cook the onions until slightly translucent—about 2 minutes. Add the ginger, cumin and mustard seeds and cook 8 minutes, stirring frequently, to prevent scorching the mustard seeds. Stir in the jalapeño peppers and turmeric and cook 5 minutes. Add the water, stirring with a flat-ended

wooden spoon to deglaze the bottom of the pan. Add the boiled potatoes, stirring to combine, and cook 5 minutes. Season with the salt and garam masala and just heat through to allow the flavors to meld. Remove from the heat and set aside.

■ The Dosa: Spray the cooking surface of a medium-sized skillet with the oil. Whisk the batter until it's the consistency of a thin pancake batter, then spoon 1 cup (236 ml) into the center of the skillet and spread evenly in a spiral motion to the outside of the skillet. Cook for 3 minutes or until the dosa starts to turn brown underneath and the top surface is just set. Do not flip it over, just remove and set aside. Repeat this process until you have 6 dosas. Caution: Do not stack the dosas!

■ To Assemble: Spread each dosa with 1 tablespoon (15 ml) of the mango chutney and spoon one sixth of the masala down the center. Fold the sides over and roll tightly into a cylinder.

■ To Serve: Slice the Masala Dosa into 5 even pieces and fan the pieces out on a plate in the shape of a star. Garnish with the mango and lime on the side. You can also eat Masala Dosa whole . . . as a fast food. They are wonderfully delicious, full of flavor and very low in fat.

Helpful Hints and Observations

UNUSUAL FOODS. Please don't be put off by the unusual nature of some of these ingredients. They are readily available, if not in a supermarket, then in a specialty foods store.

Whole Cumin: In the spice section.
Mustard Seed: Yellow, in the spice section.
Fresh Jalapeño: In the produce department of some supermarkets.
Garam Masala: Specialty foods store, or make your own in an electric coffee mill (see page 44). Try a 2-inch (5-cm) piece of thin cinnamon stick—about ¼ inch (0.75 cm) diameter, 6 allspice berries, ¼ teaspoon (1.25 ml) freshly ground nutmeg and 4 whole cloves. Whiz them together and add to the dish as a last-minute seasoning—"Perfume of the Palate."
Black Lentils: Indian market or use regular brown lentils from the supermarket. The latter will change the color of the pancake but otherwise do the job. If you can't find black lentils, use a common crêpe batter for the dosa.
Rice Flour: Usually available at health food stores.
Major Grey's Mango Chutney: In the pickles and sauces section. If you cannot find Major Grey's, substitute any mango chutney.

HOPPIN' SKIPPIN' JOHN

This is classic "soul food," especially around Charleston, South Carolina, where it is eaten with either a turnip-top salad or collard greens on New Year's Day for good fortune. (The Italians do the same with lentils.) I've added some "bright notes," to keep the salt level low, and lessened the fat by removing the lard. This is not a colorful dish; it's not meant to be, and adding peppers, et al, would ruin it. The beans and rice complement each other's proteins and the collards add to super levels of nutrition—excellent food! I've heard many stories of how this dish gained its famed name. One is that children had to hop around the table on one leg before they ate it. Another implies that it was an invitation to come in and eat, as in "Hop in, John." No one is absolutely sure. If one of my readers has a clue, I'd love to hear from you.

Nutritional Profile

PER SERVING	CLASSIC	MINIMAX
Calories	571	368
Fat (gm)	26	10
Saturated fat (gm)	10	3
Calories from fat	42%	26%
Cholesterol (mg)	33	20
Sodium (mg)	1229	946
Fiber (gm)	9	5

■ *Classic Compared: Hoppin' John*

Time Estimate: Hands on, 45 minutes; unsupervised, 60 minutes

Cost Estimate: Medium

Serves 4

INGREDIENTS

1 cup dried black-eyed peas (236 ml)

One 2-pound ham hock (907-gm), trimmed of all visible fat

5 cups water (1.2 l)

2 teaspoons extra-light olive oil, with a dash of sesame oil (10 ml)

1 medium onion, peeled and finely chopped

1 stalk celery, finely chopped

1 tablespoon loosely packed fresh thyme leaves (15 ml)

4 whole cloves, freshly ground

2 bay leaves

1 cup uncooked long grain rice (236 ml)

¼ teaspoon freshly ground salt (1.25 ml)

¼ teaspoon cayenne pepper (1.25 ml)

⅛ teaspoon freshly ground black pepper (0.6 ml)

1 whole dried red chili pepper

½ lemon, seeds removed, thinly sliced

2 cups torn up collard greens (472 ml), 2-inch (5-cm) pieces

1 tablespoon freshly squeezed lemon juice (15 ml)

1 tablespoon fresh chopped parsley (15 ml)

1 teaspoon lemon zest (5 ml)

Fresh chopped parsley, to taste

FIRST PREPARE

■ In a medium-sized bowl, soak the black-eyed peas in 4 cups (944 ml) water overnight. To save time, an alternate method is to place the black-eyed peas in a stovetop casserole and cover with 4 cups (944 ml) of fresh water. Bring to a boil for 2 minutes, remove from the heat, cover tightly and let sit for 1 hour. Drain, discarding the water, and set aside.

■ Put the ham hock in a saucepan, with water to cover, bring to a boil for 2 minutes, then drain, discarding the water. Put the ham hock back into the saucepan, cover with the 5 cups (1.2 l) water and bring to a boil. Cover, reduce the heat and simmer for 1 hour. Strain through a sieve, reserving the ham hock stock—you should have 4 cups (944 ml). Cut the lean meat from the hock and set aside.

NOW COOK

■ In a large skillet, heat 1 teaspoon (5 ml) of the oil and cook the onion until soft—about 5 minutes. Add the celery, thyme, ground cloves, bay leaves, rice, ham and the soaked, drained peas and stir

well. Pour in 3 cups (708 ml) of the reserved ham hock stock, cover and simmer for 20 minutes over medium heat, until the rice is just tender. Discard the bay leaves; season with the salt, cayenne and black pepper.

■ In a low-sided stewpot, heat the remaining oil and cook the whole chili pepper and lemon slices, just to release their volatile oils—about 2 minutes. Remove the lemon slices and chili pepper and discard. To the same stewpot, add the collard greens and the remaining 1 cup (236 ml) of the reserved ham hock stock, cover and simmer gently for 5 minutes.

■ Fold the cooked collards and their pot juices into the peas and rice. Stir in the lemon juice, 1 tablespoon (15 ml) parsley and the lemon zest.

■ To Serve: Spoon into individual serving bowls and garnish with the fresh parsley to taste.

Helpful Hints and Observations

SALT OR BRIGHT NOTES? Rice and black-eyed peas beg for salt. I have held the line at a total of 227 mg per serving, which includes the added salt and the salt in the ham hocks, collards and celery. At this sodium level the dish tastes bland. I resisted the easy answer and looked for some "bright notes" to take the place of the missing salt. Lemon juice did well, but the real "skippin'" came with adding cayenne and lemon zest. There is no need to add more salt and the dish is wonderful.

About the Ingredients

COLLARD GREENS. Another sibling in the nutritionally famous cabbage family, these greens provide vitamins A and C and are essential for the good pot liquor that gives Hoppin' Skippin' John its extra character. Look for deep green leaves without blemishes or wilting. The tender, most succulent leaves are the ones that are 6 to 8 inches (15 to 20 cm) long.

BLACK-EYED PEAS. Also called cowpeas, or black-eyed beans, this dried legume is a favorite of cooks in the Southern U.S.A. No mystery where black-eyed peas got their name: they're tiny white fellows with a black speck in the middle. You can store all dried beans for a long time—up to a year! But they go bad eventually, so buy your beans at a store where they seem to sell well and fresh supplies are brought in often.

PUERTO RICAN RICE AND BEANS (ARROZ CON HABICHUELAS)

*O*ne *of the truly great dishes of the world, rice and beans is also one of those food combinations whose ingredients actually complement each other nutritionally. Beans and rice, when served together, provide more protein than when you eat them separately. Look at the numbers and you'll see the benefit. But the nutritional numbers are only half the battle! The real war is won with aroma, color and texture—and this dish takes the prize for all three! Served in a bowl it becomes a hearty meal with the addition of a colorful salad on the side (see page 80).*

Nutritional Profile

PER SERVING	CLASSIC	MINIMAX
Calories	474	311
Fat (gm)	29	4
Saturated fat (gm)	13	1
Calories from fat	55%	12%
Cholesterol (mg)	64	6
Sodium (mg)	651	110
Fiber (gm)	2	7

■ *Classic Compared: Arroz con Caldo de Frijoles*

Time Estimate: Hands on, 30 minutes

Cost Estimate: Medium

Serves 4

INGREDIENTS

4 cups water (944 ml)

8 ounces smoked ham hock (227 gm)

1 cup dried pinto beans (236 ml)

1 cup uncooked long grain white rice (236 ml)

1 teaspoon extra-light olive oil, with a dash of sesame oil (5 ml)

½ onion, peeled and diced

2 cloves garlic, peeled, smashed and chopped

1 large red bell pepper, cored, seeded and diced

2 jalapeño peppers, seeded and diced

1 tablespoon fresh chopped oregano (15 ml)

One 15-ounce can peeled plum tomatoes (425 gm), drained and juice reserved

½ teaspoon freshly ground salt (2.5 ml)

½ teaspoon freshly ground black peppercorns (2.5 ml)

3 tablespoons fresh chopped cilantro (45 ml)

2 tablespoons capers (30 ml)

NOW COOK

■ Place the water and ham hock in a pressure cooker, check to make sure the steam release holes are clear and cook for 5 minutes. Add the pinto beans and cook 20 minutes more. Add the rice, and when the pressure cooker "hisses," cook for another 5 minutes.

■ While the rice and beans cook, heat the oil in a large skillet and sauté the onion and garlic until the onion becomes translucent. Add the red pepper, jalapeño peppers, oregano and tomatoes, stirring and chopping as you go. Add ¼ cup (59 ml) of the reserved tomato juice, half of the salt and half of the pepper. Lower the heat and simmer 15 minutes.

■ After the rice and beans have cooked, remove the ham hock, slice off 2 ounces (57 gm) of lean meat and reserve. Add the cooked rice and beans to the pepper-tomato mixture in the skillet. Stir in the reserved ham hock meat, 2 tablespoons (30 ml) of the cilantro, the capers and the remaining salt and pepper.

■ To Serve: Spoon into bowls and garnish with the remaining cilantro.

Helpful Hints and Observations

THE PRESSURE COOKER WINS AGAIN. Nothing is faster (or better) at cooking beans (or rice) than a good pressure cooker. The microwave can't touch it! So if speed and quality are your bag it's time you took a deep swallow and purchased a pressure cooker, one that holds a minimum of 5 quarts (4.7 l). Then, use it to introduce rice, whole grains and legumes to *all* your meals. You'll get good plant protein, great textures and loads of fiber—with very little fat.

About the Ingredients

PINTO BEANS. These beans, called Mexican Strawberries by old Texas cowboys because of their strawberry seed–like speckles, are a favorite in Latin American cooking. Pintos are very nutritious and provide protein when complemented by grains, nuts or seeds or low-fat meats. Here I've combined them with rice to achieve just that.

SMOKED HAM HOCKS. It's not easy to achieve depth of flavor in a liquid without using fat. Here I use a smoked ham hock in the cooking liquid for the beans and rice. Using a flavored water provides a third dimension: ham, rice and beans instead of just rice and beans. Ham hocks come cured, smoked and fresh. The hock is the part of the front leg between the foot and the lower shoulder.

LENTIL, RICE AND PINTO BEAN CASSEROLE

$\mathscr{I}$ tested two methods for this simple and delicious recipe because I'd like you to consider the advantages of a pressure cooker. A pressure cooker will save you at least one hour and does a much better job than the standard oven bake.

This is an entire meal in one pot, featuring vegetables only—not even a meat stock! I thought that it lacked sufficient greenery and added a ½ cup (118 ml) of peas at the end of the cooking. The stored heat will warm them. As an alternative, you could add some finely sliced collard greens just before you serve it. The goat cheese–flavored bread is truly excellent as a side dish—please give it a go!

Nutritional Profile

PER SERVING	CLASSIC	MINIMAX
Calories	474	218
Fat (gm)	29	1
Saturated fat (gm)	13	0
Calories from fat	55%	4%
Cholesterol (mg)	64	0
Sodium (mg)	651	140
Fiber (gm)	2	7

■ *Classic Compared: Rice with Bean Broth*

Time Estimate: Hands on, 40 minutes

Cost Estimate: Medium

INGREDIENTS

BREAD SPREAD

4 tablespoons goat cheese (60 ml)

1 teaspoon fresh chopped basil (5 ml)

1 teaspoon fresh chopped thyme (5 ml)

1 teaspoon fresh chopped oregano (5 ml)

⅛ teaspoon freshly ground black peppercorns (0.6 ml)

½ green bell pepper, seeded and finely diced

½ red bell pepper, seeded and finely diced

1 teaspoon extra-light olive oil, with a dash of sesame oil (5 ml)

⅔ cup peeled and finely chopped onion (156 gm)

2 cloves garlic, peeled, smashed and finely diced

1 cup dried pinto beans (236 ml)

2 teaspoons fresh chopped basil (10 ml)

2 teaspoons fresh chopped thyme (10 ml)

2 teaspoons fresh chopped oregano (10 ml)

2 bay leaves

¼ teaspoon freshly ground salt (1.25 ml)

¼ teaspoon freshly ground black peppercorns (1.25 ml)

3 cups water (708 ml)

¾ cup dried lentils (177 ml)

½ cup uncooked brown rice (118 ml)

½ cup de-alcoholized white wine (118 ml)

¼ teaspoon ground cayenne pepper (1.25 ml)

1 tablespoon freshly squeezed lemon juice (15 ml)

GARNISH:

½ cup frozen green peas (118 ml), thawed, or 2 cups finely sliced collard greens (472 ml)

1 French baguette

FIRST PREPARE

■ In a small bowl, make the bread spread by combining the cheese, basil, thyme, oregano and pepper. Set aside. In another small bowl, mix the green and red peppers together. Set aside.

NOW COOK

■ In a pressure cooker, heat the oil and sauté the onion until translucent—about 3 minutes. Add the garlic and cook 2 minutes. Add half of the bell pepper mixture, the pinto beans, 1 teaspoon (5 ml) of the basil, 1 teaspoon (5 ml) of the thyme,

1 teaspoon (5 ml) of the oregano, the bay leaves, salt and pepper. Pour in the water, check to make sure the steam release holes are clear, put on the lid and cook for 10 minutes from when the cooker starts "hissing." Release the steam and uncover. Preheat the oven to 350°F. (180°C).

■ Add the lentils and brown rice to the pressure cooker. Cover and cook 15 minutes more from when the cooker starts "hissing."

■ Release the steam, uncover, remove the bay leaves and discard. Add the remaining 1 teaspoon (5 ml) each of basil, thyme and oregano. Pour in the wine and add the remaining bell pepper mixture, the cayenne pepper and lemon juice.

■ Cut the baguette in half and toast in the preheated oven until just brown around the edges —about 5 minutes. Spread with the Bread Spread and cut into "fingers."

■ To Serve: Spoon into individual serving bowls and sprinkle with the green peas or collard greens. Serve with a finger of toasted goat cheese bread.

Helpful Hints and Observations

WINE AND BEANS. Any fairly high-acid wine or fruit, like a tomato, added to beans and rice in the early stages of cooking, tends to toughen both the beans and the rice, especially in a pressure cooker. In this case, we held the wine to the end and let it provide its aromatic contribution as a flavor finisher.

PRESSURE-COOKED BEANS. As you know, one of my primary Minimax aims is to reintroduce dried legumes into the diet. Unfortunately, they do take time to cook, unless you have a good pressure cooker. I also find that pressure cooking does a better job of deepening the color and smoothing out the texture. But, as always, it's your choice.

About the Ingredients

LENTILS. This legume derives its name from the Latin word *lens,* which its physical shape closely resembles. Lentils can be brown, black, yellow, green or red in color and are readily available at your local supermarket. Because they need no presoaking before cooking and only take approximately thirty minutes to cook, lentils are surely "the convenience food" of the legume family.

GREEN RISOTTO

This has to be my favorite first course or the very best accompaniment you could serve with a plain, broiled chicken breast or fish steak. It can also become a "vegetables only" main dish—even if you double the serving size it still has less than 11 grams of fat and 470 calories per serving. I serve ⅔ cup (156 ml) per person on a warm plate, garnished with thin slices of fennel and a scattering of parsley, Parmesan cheese and black pepper—it looks wonderful and meets everyone's expectations!

Nutritional Profile

PER SERVING	CLASSIC	MINIMAX
Calories	550	232
Fat (gm)	25	5
Saturated fat (gm)	13	1
Calories from fat	40%	18%
Cholesterol (mg)	59	4
Sodium (mg)	1878	179
Fiber (gm)	2	4

■ *Classic Compared: Risotto ai Quattro Formaggi*

Time Estimate: Hands on, 45 minutes; unsupervised, 20 minutes

Cost Estimate: Medium

Serves 4

INGREDIENTS

RISOTTO:

2 teaspoons extra-light olive oil, with a dash of sesame oil (10 ml)

½ cup peeled, chopped onion (118 ml)

½ cup chopped fennel root (118 ml)

¾ cup uncooked arborio rice (177 ml)

3 cups strained vegetable stock (708 ml) (see page 36)

½ cup de-alcoholized white wine (118 ml)

¼ cup freshly grated Parmesan cheese (59 ml)

PEA MIXTURE:

1 cup frozen green peas (236 ml)

¼ cup strained vegetable stock (59 ml) (see above)

1 tablespoon fresh chopped basil (15 ml)

1 tablespoon fresh chopped parsley (15 ml)

7 large green butter lettuce leaves

¼ cup de-alcoholized white wine (59 ml)

GARNISH:

Freshly grated Parmesan cheese

Freshly ground black pepper

Sliced fennel bulb

Fresh chopped parsley

NOW COOK

■ The Risotto: In a large saucepan, heat the oil and sauté the onion for 3 minutes. Add the fennel root and rice and cook for 2 minutes, stirring until the rice is well coated. Add 1 cup (236 ml) of the vegetable stock and the wine and bring to a vigorous boil, stirring until the liquid is absorbed. Add another cup (236 ml) of the strained vegetable stock, bring back to a boil, and cook and stir until the stock is absorbed; repeat with the remaining cup (236 ml) of stock. This process should take about 25 minutes. Stir in the cheese and set aside.

■ The Pea Mixture: Pour the frozen peas into a large sauté pan over medium heat. Add the vegetable stock, basil, parsley and lettuce leaves, cover and cook 5 minutes. Turn the pea mixture into a food processor or blender, add the wine and puree until smooth.

■ Pour the pureed peas into the risotto and stir thoroughly.

■ To Serve: Garnish each serving with a sprinkle each of the Parmesan cheese, black pepper, fennel bulb slices and chopped parsley.

Helpful Hints and Observations

RICE AND PEAS. It's great to know how good this dish really is! Vegetables have plant proteins but these are not as complete as the proteins in meat. However, incomplete proteins can complement each other. The "N" symbol shows how. Wherever the N lines go, there is a completed protein. The line from rice (a grain) goes to peas (legumes) and cheese (milk product). Cheese and peas, or rice and corn (seeds) do not "complete" because the lines don't touch.

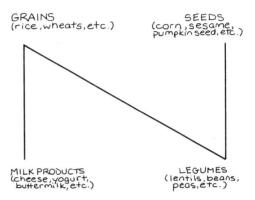

Where the straight lines connect, i.e., grains and legumes or grains and milk products, there is complete and/or enhanced protein.

About the Ingredients

ARBORIO RICE. If one could be passionate about a type of rice, the creamy mouthfeel, the exciting texture . . . All right, enough! The Italian short grain arborio is the king of rices when it comes to making a properly textured risotto, so by all means try to find it, if not in your supermarket then at an Italian foods shop. If you do substitute another rice, monitor the liquids closely—amounts will vary—in order to achieve the creamy texture.

BOSNBEANS PASTA SALAD

*O*ne of the most requested programs ever: "a pasta salad coated with cheese dressing . . . oh . . . and hold the fat, please." I've developed one with a solid cheesy taste and only 7.23 grams of fat per serving. The name comes from the pasta bows and the red kidney beans, hence, bos *(bows)* n *(and)* beans. *Well, at least it's a conversation point! I serve this salad on a bed of crisp, curly lettuce leaves. An ideal lunchtime energy dish that won't let you down in the midafternoon.*

Nutritional Profile

PER SERVING	CLASSIC	MINIMAX
Calories	1148	485
Fat (gm)	58	7
Saturated fat (gm)	9	4
Calories from fat	46%	12%
Cholesterol (mg)	4	17
Sodium (mg)	981	643
Fiber (gm)	21	10

■ *Classic Compared: Macaroni and Three Bean Salad*

Time Estimate: Hands on, 30 minutes

Cost Estimate: Medium

Serves 4

INGREDIENTS

7¼ cups of water (1.7 l)

8 ounces uncooked farfalle pasta bows (227 gm)

One 15-ounce can kidney beans (425 gm), drained and rinsed

8 green onions, sliced diagonally

1 cup 1% fat cottage cheese (236 ml)

2 ounces goat cheese (57 gm), chilled

1 tablespoon fresh chopped chives (15 ml)

1 teaspoon fresh chopped sage (5 ml)

¼ teaspoon cayenne pepper (1.25 ml)

¼ teaspoon ground cumin (1.25 ml)

¼ cup rice wine vinegar (59 ml)

1 tablespoon cornstarch (15 ml), mixed with 2 tablespoons water (30 ml)

⅛ teaspoon freshly ground salt (0.6 ml)

1 head green leaf lettuce washed and spun dry

NOW COOK

■ In a large pot or Dutch oven, bring 7 cups of the water (1.65 l) to a boil, add the pasta and cook for 11 minutes. Drain through a sieve and plunge into ice water to cool quickly. Drain and transfer the cooled pasta to a large bowl. Stir in the kidney beans and green onions.

■ Put the cottage cheese in a large bowl. Cut the goat cheese into thin disks, then chop it into the cottage cheese. Add the chives, sage, cayenne and cumin and mix thoroughly.

■ In a small saucepan, bring the remaining ¼ cup (59 ml) water and the vinegar to a simmer. Remove from the heat, add the cornstarch paste, return to the burner and bring to a boil.

■ Pour the vinegar sauce over the pasta. Lightly stir in the salt and the cottage cheese mixture until each bow is well coated.

■ To Serve: Pull off a few lettuce leaves and make a bed on each plate. Spoon the pasta on top and enjoy!

Helpful Hints and Observations

PASTA GLAZE. Oil is added to pasta to keep the pieces separate and to provide that glistening look that reflects a thousand points of light. However, the fat in oil is a high price to pay in the fight against sticky flatness. I turned to rice vinegar, water and cornstarch, and it does the trick perfectly. Be careful not to exceed the recipe quantity—too much and the glaze will cool to a thick jellied paste.

About the Ingredients

GOAT CHEESE. Goat cheese has an inherent tanginess that lends itself to the acid-base balance in this recipe. There are many goat cheeses on the market today—try a nibble and find the one that suits you. Remember, like all other cheese it is high in saturated fat and calories, so use judiciously.

FARFALLE PASTA. The names of different types of pasta refer to their shapes, in this case, a bow tie. I like the bow tie for salads because it provides a larger surface area to which the sauce can cling.

RICE WINE VINEGAR. Rice vinegar is milder and sweeter than traditional white vinegar. You can find it in the oriental foods section of your supermarket, or substitute white vinegar mixed with half the volume of water and sugar, to taste.

CANNELLONI

The classic cannelloni from Pappagallo in Bologna, Italy, has been my Number One Standard of eating pleasure for as many years as I can remember. I was reluctant to touch the recipe, since it had delivered so consistently! There are major changes, both in content and time in this version; but the result is truly edible, and enough of the unique flavors, textures and aromas are still there to make it a prized recipe.

An attractive way to serve this dish is to cook the manicotti in small, individual, oval ovenproof dishes and then serve it bubbling hot from the oven, setting the oval dish directly on a dinner plate. If the dish rattles on the large plate, simply slip a napkin underneath. I always serve a crisp green salad with lots of herbs and some good fresh crusty bread on the side. Sublime.

Nutritional Profile

PER SERVING	CLASSIC	MINIMAX
Calories	1105	430
Fat (gm)	49	10
Saturated fat (gm)	25	3
Calories from fat	40%	22%
Cholesterol (mg)	417	82
Sodium (mg)	793	415
Fiber (gm)	6	6

■ Classic Compared: Cannelloni

Time Estimate: Hands on, 60 minutes

Cost Estimate: Medium High

Serves 4

INGREDIENTS

BOLOGNESE SAUCE:

4 ounces lean pork (113 gm)

1 slice whole wheat bread

1 teaspoon extra-light olive oil, with a dash of sesame oil (5 ml)

2 cloves garlic, peeled, smashed and chopped

1 onion, peeled and finely diced

2 carrots, peeled and finely diced

¾ cup low-sodium tomato paste (177 ml)

1 cup de-alcoholized red wine (236 ml)

1 cup canned peeled and seeded plum tomatoes (236 ml)

1 tablespoon fresh chopped oregano (15 ml)

WHITE SAUCE:

1 bouquet garni (see page 36)

One 14-ounce can chicken broth (397 gm)

1½ tablespoons cornstarch (23 ml), mixed with 3 tablespoons water (45 ml)

½ cup strained yogurt (118 ml) (see page 85)

FILLING:

One 2-ounce piece mozzarella cheese (57 gm)

4 ounces pork (113 gm), cubed

10 ounces turkey thigh meat (280 gm), cubed

1 teaspoon extra-light olive oil, with a dash of sesame oil (5 ml)

½ green bell pepper, seeded and coarsely chopped

½ onion, peeled and coarsely chopped

2 cloves garlic, peeled, smashed and chopped

½ cup de-alcoholized white wine (118 ml)

1 slice whole wheat bread

2 egg whites

⅛ teaspoon freshly ground salt (0.6 ml)

¼ teaspoon freshly ground black peppercorns (1.25 ml)

¼ teaspoon freshly ground nutmeg (1.25 ml)

1 tablespoon fresh chopped oregano (15 ml)

PASTA:

4 quarts water (3.8 l)

10 large manicotti (Note: you will only need 8 manicotti for the final dish, but cook 2 extra in case of breakage during cooking.)

NOW COOK

■ The Bolognese Sauce: Feed the pork through a grinder, followed by the bread, to make sure all the meat has gone through.

■ Heat the oil in a large skillet and sauté the garlic and onion until the onion is translucent. Add the carrots and tomato paste and cook until the paste starts turning brown. Add the ground pork and cook for 10 minutes. Stir in the wine, tomatoes and oregano, bring to a boil; reduce heat and simmer for 20 minutes. Set aside.

■ The White Sauce: Put the bouquet garni in a medium-sized saucepan and pour in the chicken broth. Over medium heat, reduce to 1 cup (236 ml). Discard bouquet garni. Add the cornstarch slurry and bring to a boil, stirring until the broth thickens —about 30 seconds. Add 2 ice cubes to the broth to cool it rapidly (see page 30). Add the strained yogurt to the thickened broth, stirring until it is just incorporated. Set aside.

■ The Filling: Place the mozzarella cheese in the freezer for 10 minutes. Remove and finely grate.

■ Put the meats into a large bowl and pour in the oil, stirring to coat all the pieces.

■ Brown the oiled meat in a very hot large wok or skillet for 1 minute. Add the green pepper, onion and garlic and sauté for 3 minutes. Remove from the heat and stir in the wine. Put back over the heat, bring to a boil, cover and simmer for 10 minutes. Transfer the mixture to a large bowl and set aside. Reserve the pan juices.

■ Feed the cooked meat-vegetable mixture through a grinder, into a large bowl, followed by the slice of bread. Add the reserved pan juices, grated mozzarella cheese and egg whites. Season with the salt, pepper, nutmeg and fresh oregano and mix well.

■ The Pasta: In a large pot, bring the water to a boil, drop in the manicotti and boil 8 minutes. Drain, rinsing under cold water until cool and easy to handle.

■ To Assemble: Preheat the oven to 500°F. (260°C).

■ Carefully spoon the filling directly into the manicotti, or scoop it into a pastry bag and squeeze it inside. Place the filled manicotti in a large baking dish. Cover with the bolognese sauce, followed by the white sauce. Bake in the preheated oven for 15 minutes.

■ To Serve: Each of your fortunate dinner guests gets 2 of these delicious manicotti shells, smothered in the bolognese and white sauces.

ORZO PASTA WITH CHICKEN AND RED PEPPERS

𝒥 find myself inspired by a recipe for risotto to try cooking orzo, using the basic technique used in risotto. Orzo is pasta shaped into small ricelike pieces. (Orzo is actually Italian for barley.) I've added chicken for garnish, and a substantial amount of rosemary makes the dish really come alive. You could serve this as a main dish for supper with a garnish of freshly cooked peas or a mixed shredded salad on the side.

Nutritional Profile

PER SERVING	CLASSIC	MINIMAX
Calories	643	276
Fat (gm)	29	7
Saturated fat (gm)	9	2
Calories from fat	41%	24%
Cholesterol (mg)	87	54
Sodium (mg)	1134	192
Fiber (mg)	3	2

■ *Classic Compared: Orzo with Chicken*

Time Estimate: Hands on, 40 minutes

Cost Estimate: Medium High

Serves 4

INGREDIENTS

EASY CHICKEN STOCK:

Two 14-ounce cans chicken broth (397 gm each)

3 large stalks fresh parsley

3 stalks fresh rosemary

1 clove garlic, peeled and smashed

3 whole cloves

2 bay leaves

¾ cup water (177 ml)

1 cup de-alcoholized white wine (236 ml)

2 teaspoons extra-light olive oil, with a dash of sesame oil (10 ml)

½ yellow onion, peeled and sliced

2 cloves garlic, peeled and finely diced

1 tablespoon fresh finely chopped rosemary (15 ml)

1 tablespoon fresh finely chopped basil (15 ml)

2 tablespoons fresh finely chopped parsley (30 ml)

1½ cups raw orzo pasta (354 ml)

Three 5-ounce boneless chicken breasts, skin removed, cut into 2 x ½-inch (5 x 1.5-cm) strips

1 red bell pepper, seeded and thinly sliced

GARNISH:

4 tablespoons freshly grated Parmesan cheese (60 ml)

4 sprigs fresh basil

Parsley, to taste

Freshly ground black pepper, to taste

FIRST PREPARE

■ The Chicken Stock: In a saucepan, put the chicken broth, parsley, rosemary, garlic, cloves, bay leaves and water, bring to a boil, reduce the heat, cover and simmer 10 minutes. Remove from the heat and strain into a large bowl. Stir in the wine and set aside.

NOW COOK

■ In a large saucepan, heat 1 teaspoon (5 ml) of the oil and sauté the onion and garlic over high heat for 3 minutes. Stir in half of the herbs, the orzo and the chicken stock and cook over medium heat for 25 minutes, stirring from time to time.

■ While the orzo is cooking, heat the remaining oil in a large skillet and sauté the chicken pieces, red pepper and remaining herbs for 3 minutes. Stir into the cooked orzo.

■ To Serve: Spoon onto individual dinner plates and garnish each with a tablespoon (15 ml) of the Parmesan cheese, a sprig of basil, parsley and black pepper to taste.

Helpful Hints and Observations

KEEP STIRRING. Orzo loves to cling to the bottom of your saucepan. Do it and yourself a favor and keep stirring. This is where the flat-ended spurtle really comes into its own.

About the Ingredients

GARLIC. In the United States, until the early 1940s, garlic was considered a "food of the people," fit only for blue-collar immigrants. I'm glad culinary tastes have changed and garlic today is as common as its cousin the onion. When shopping for garlic, choose bulbs that are firm and free of green sprouting tops.

RED BELL PEPPERS. I'm also thrilled that this deliciously sweet vegetable is becoming so popular and easy to find. Select peppers that are firm and shiny; dullness is a sign of age and prolonged storage. You can easily freeze them: slice or chop the peppers into convenient-sized pieces, lay them on a tray and freeze until they are firm all the way through. Transfer into freezer storage bags and use them as needed for sauces, garnishes or salads.

PENNE PRIMAVERA

$\mathcal{I}$ *am delighted to introduce you to permissible lust (PL). This hot pasta with vegetables owes its reputation to fresh herbs, a superb vegetable broth and a colorful celebration of perfectly cooked vegetables.*

a colorful
celebration
of perfectly
cooked vegetables

Nutritional Profile

PER SERVING	CLASSIC	MINIMAX
Calories	1263	529
Fat (gm)	72	8
Saturated fat (gm)	44	2
Calories from fat	51%	13%
Cholesterol (mg)	224	8
Sodium (mg)	585	208
Fiber (gm)	14	15

■ *Classic Compared: Pasta Primavera*

Time Estimate: Hands on, 45 minutes

Cost Estimate: Medium High

Serves 4

INGREDIENTS

4 cups water (944 ml)

8 ounces penne pasta (227 gm)

1 teaspoon extra-light olive oil, with a dash of sesame oil (5 ml)

¼ red onion, peeled and finely sliced

12 spears of asparagus, cut into 2-inch (5-cm) pieces, separated into stalks and tips

7 green onions, cut into 2-inch (5-cm) pieces, separated into white and green parts

½ cup fresh shelled peas (118 ml)

2 cloves garlic, peeled and smashed

1 medium red bell pepper, seeded and chopped to the pasta's size

1 medium zucchini, chopped to the pasta's size

1 medium yellow squash, chopped to the pasta's size

2 cups cremini mushrooms (472 ml), quartered

1 cup sugar snap peas (236 ml)

3 cups vegetable stock (708 ml) (see page 36)

1 tablespoon fresh finely chopped chives (15 ml)

1 tablespoon fresh finely chopped thyme (15 ml)

¼ teaspoon freshly ground salt (1.25 ml)

¼ teaspoon freshly ground black pepper (1.25 ml)

12 cherry tomatoes

1 tablespoon fresh finely chopped basil (15 ml)

2 tablespoons arrowroot (30 ml), mixed with ¼ cup de-alcoholized white wine (59 ml)

GARNISH:

4 tablespoons freshly grated Parmesan cheese (60 ml)

NOW COOK

■ In a large Dutch oven, bring the water to a boil, add the pasta, cover and cook 8 minutes. Drain the pasta through a colander set over a large bowl. Discard the hot water and transfer the pasta to the warmed bowl.

■ Heat the oil in a large stewpot and fry the red onion, asparagus stalks, the white portions of the green onions, the peas and garlic for 1 minute. Add the red pepper, zucchini and squash and cook 1 minute.

■ Add the mushrooms, sugar snap peas, asparagus tips, ¾ cup (177 ml) of the vegetable stock and cook for 3 minutes. Add the chives, thyme, salt, pepper, green part of the green onions, tomatoes, basil and remaining vegetable stock. Bring to a vigorous boil. Remove from the heat, add the arrowroot slurry, return to the heat and stir until thickened.

■ Transfer the cooked vegetables to the pasta and stir until well combined.

■ To Serve: Spoon the Penne Primavera into individual bowls and garnish each with 1 tablespoon (15 ml) of the Parmesan cheese.

Helpful Hints and Observations

TIMING IS EVERYTHING! This is a wonderful dish, providing you cut and measure everything before you begin to cook. Once the cooking begins, it's virtually over within 10 minutes.

Please notice the order in which I add each item and line up your fully prepared ingredients in that same sequence. Heat the saucepan/stewpot for the vegetables and have the pasta water at the boil. Plunge the pasta into the water, and at the same time add the oil and hard vegetables to the saucepan. The vegetables cook in just 8 minutes— the exact time that it takes for the pasta.

VEGETABLE STOCK. Stock is *always* better than water. Please make at least a double batch and freeze the extra for the next time you want to make this magnificent dish—it won't be long.

About the Ingredients

PENNE PASTA. Penne is a tubular pasta, approximately 3 inches (8 cm) long. I've chosen to use penne because I wanted to incorporate that shape along with the vegetables to offer a dish that is pleasing not only to the palate, but also to the eye.

CREMINI MUSHROOMS. The cremini is a light brown version of the common button mushroom, but with more flavor. If you don't find them in your supermarket, ask the produce manager to order some; they are readily available.

VEGETABLE LASAGNE ROLL-UPS

$\mathcal{L}$asagne is definitely a comfort-food-of-the-people and has earned its place as a favorite of millions. This recipe drains the fat from the classic dish, adds a huge amount of fiber and allows for an unusual presentation that is much easier to serve. It becomes a complete meal when you serve it with a good crisp, colorful salad and lots of crusty bread.

Nutritional Profile

PER SERVING	CLASSIC	MINIMAX
Calories	403	324
Fat (gm)	23	7
Saturated fat (gm)	12	3
Calories from fat	52%	19%
Cholesterol (mg)	103	13
Sodium (mg)	1484	614
Fiber (gm)	2	7

■ *Classic Compared: Meat Lasagne*

Time Estimate: Hands on, 1 hour 30 minutes; unsupervised, 40 minutes

Cost Estimate: Medium High

Serves 8

INGREDIENTS

FILLING:

1 cup part-skim ricotta cheese (236 ml)

¼ cup part-skim mozzarella cheese (59 ml)

¼ cup freshly grated Parmesan cheese (59 ml)

8 ounces fresh spinach (227 gm), washed and coarsely chopped

One 15-ounce can white kidney beans (425-gm), drained and rinsed

2 tablespoons fresh chopped oregano (30 ml)

2 tablespoons fresh chopped basil (30 ml)

8 ounces raw lasagne noodles (227 gm)

SAUCE:

3 teaspoons extra-light olive oil, with a dash of sesame oil (15 ml)

2 cups chopped onions (472 gm)

2 cloves garlic, peeled and chopped

2 cups finely diced eggplant (472 gm)

1 large red bell pepper, seeded and finely diced

2 tablespoons low-sodium tomato paste (30 ml)

¼ teaspoon red pepper flakes (1.25 ml)

1 cup de-alcoholized red wine (236 ml)

One 16-ounce can whole tomatoes (454-gm), with liquid

1 tablespoon freshly squeezed lemon juice (15 ml)

½ teaspoon freshly ground salt (2.5 ml)

½ teaspoon freshly ground black pepper (2.5 ml)

2 tablespoons freshly grated Parmesan cheese (30 ml)

FIRST PREPARE

■ The Filling: In a large mixing bowl, combine the three cheeses, the spinach, half the beans, half the oregano and half the basil and set aside.

■ The Lasagne Noodles: Cook the pasta according to the package directions for just-tender (al dente) texture. Drain and run under cold water. Keep the cooled noodles in a bowl of cold water until ready to use.

NOW COOK

■ Preheat the oven to 350°F. (180°C). Pour 1 teaspoon (5 ml) of the oil into a large skillet over medium-high heat and fry the onions and the garlic for 5 minutes, stirring often. Transfer half to the spinach and cheese filling and set the other half aside. Wipe the pan clean.

■ Add 1 teaspoon (5 ml) of the oil to the same pan and, over medium heat, cook the eggplant for 8 minutes, stirring often. It's important that the bottom of the pan does not scorch. Spoon the cooked eggplant into the filling mixture and stir well. Wipe the pan clean.

■ Add the remaining oil to the same pan and, over medium heat, cook the red bell pepper for 3 minutes. Spoon the cooked pepper into the filling mixture. Wipe the pan clean.

■ The Sauce: Add the tomato paste to the same pan and, over medium heat, cook until it turns brown—about 5 minutes. It is very important it doesn't burn but just browns. Stir in the red pepper flakes and the wine, bring to a boil, lower the heat to a simmer and reduce the liquid by about one fourth—about 15 minutes. Add the canned tomatoes and their liquid, stirring until the tomatoes break into pieces.

■ Add the remaining beans, oregano, basil and reserved cooked onions and garlic and cook for 5 minutes at a very low simmer. Stir in the lemon juice, salt and black pepper and mix well.

■ Now Assemble: Lay a lasagne noodle flat on a cutting board. Form ½ cup (118 ml) of the filling into a rough ball, lay on one end of the lasagne and roll it up end to end. Repeat with the remaining noodles.

■ Pour the sauce into a 9 x 13-inch (23 x 33-cm) baking pan. Place the lasagne rolls on top, seam side down, and spoon some of the sauce over them. Cover with aluminum foil and bake for 40 minutes. Remove the foil, sprinkle with Parmesan cheese and bake for 5 minutes.

■ To Serve: Each dinner guest gets 1 roll-up. Ladle some of the sauce they were cooked in over each.

Helpful Hints and Observations

VEGETABLES, VEGETABLES, VEGETABLES! A recent survey revealed that the average adult in a Western industrialized nation eats only one third of the recommended amount of fresh vegetables and fruit (which should be at least 5 servings a day). By converting favorite meat-based dishes like this lasagne to a vegetable-legume base, you provide a vehicle to deliver exactly what you need nutritionally in a very attractive wrapping.

SUMMER SUCCOTASH

*U*nfortunately there are only a few accounts of the origin of this classic food of the North American Indian. We do know that the Zuni tribe loved to make a kind of hodgepodge, all-in-one stew that they called a "Summer Succotash." It was thickened with ground sunflower seeds and garnished with a variety of their summer vegetables.

I've changed the thickener to arrowroot to relieve the dish of the grittiness that comes with the ground sunflower seeds. This is a true Minimax food-of-the-people—enjoy celebrating its heritage.

Nutritional Profile

PER SERVING	CLASSIC	MINIMAX
Calories	371	303
Fat (gm)	19	9
Saturated fat (gm)	7	2
Calories from fat	48%	26%
Cholesterol (mg)	70	52
Sodium (mg)	567	465
Fiber (gm)	8	7

■ *Classic Compared: Zuni Summer Succotash*

Time Estimate: Hands on, 60 minutes; unsupervised, 45 minutes

Cost Estimate: Medium High

Serves 6
INGREDIENTS

2 teaspoons olive oil, with a dash of sesame oil
(10 ml)

1 yellow onion, peeled and finely chopped

1 clove garlic, peeled, smashed and chopped

1 jalapeño pepper, seeded and sliced into thin
matchsticks

3 red bell peppers, seeded and finely chopped

12 ounces lean lamb shoulder (340 gm), all visible
fat removed, chopped into ½-inch (1.5-cm) pieces

¼ teaspoon freshly ground salt (1.25 ml)

¼ teaspoon freshly ground black pepper (1.25 ml)

3 cups lamb stock (708 ml) (see page 35)

1 sprig fresh mint

3 cups freshly chopped summer squash (708 ml),
yellow crookneck if possible

3 cups corn kernels (708 ml)

2½ cups green beans, topped and tailed and finely
chopped (590 ml)

4 tablespoons arrowroot (60 ml), mixed with ½ cup
water (118 ml)

⅛ cup raw unsalted sunflower seeds (30 ml)

4 green onions, finely chopped

NOW COOK

■ Heat half of the oil in a large stewpot and brown
the onion and garlic for 2 minutes. Add the
jalapeño and red peppers and cook for 3 minutes.
Transfer the cooked vegetables to a bowl and set
aside.

■ Add the remaining oil to the same stewpot and
get the pan really hot. Add the lamb pieces, *one at
a time,* so that each piece will brown evenly and
provide depth of color to the dish. This will take
about 5 minutes. Add the cooked vegetables to the
meat, stirring to scrape up the residue from the
pan. Stir in the salt, black pepper, stock and mint,
cover and simmer for 45 minutes.

■ Remove the mint. Add the squash, corn and
beans and simmer, uncovered, for 15 minutes.

■ Remove the stewpot from the heat, mix in the
arrowroot slurry, return to the heat and stir until
thickened. Stir in the sunflower seeds.

■ To Serve: Ladle into individual soup bowls and
sprinkle with the chopped green onions.

Helpful Hints and Observations

TRIMMING THE FAT. You will have noticed that
this recipe calls for lean meat, "trimmed of all
visible fat." Some people object to the savage
cutting away of fat because it seems as though so
much winds up as garbage, which might be viewed
as wasteful, especially with an expensive meat like
lamb.

May I encourage you to be pleased about it.
You'll see from the nutritional analysis that there is
a 22 percent reduction in the amount of calories
from fat, but this is only possible by being really
serious in the fat-trimming stage,.

About the Ingredients

SUNFLOWER SEEDS. Nuts and seeds can provide
great texture and aroma in low-fat diets, but should
not be overused because of their high calorie and
fat content. Sunflower seeds are mild in flavor and
lower in fat than most others. I use raw, unsalted
sunflower seeds. They are available at the
supermarket or health food stores.

SQUASH. Squash comes in many shapes and
varieties, two basic types being summer squash,
which are soft skinned, and winter squash, which
are hard skinned. The most popular summer
squash is zucchini. It is a dark green or bright
yellow, and is perfect for eating at 6 inches (15 cm)
long. Choose zucchini that is firm, with a deep
color and a glossy skin. Zucchini cooks very
quickly, so add it toward the end of cooking.

FONDUE AND SALAD

I'm really very excited about this idea. I've now designed a Fondue and Salad with plenty to eat that contains less than 16 grams of fat per serving, including the fondue, croutons and the salad dressing. This concept of adding sweet potatoes could spark a renewed interest in this Swiss specialty. If you didn't sell the old fondue pot, it's time to dig it out of the attic! If it did go, then use a small casserole and some large forks—you really shouldn't miss the party! I suggest that you serve this Minimaxed salad because it, too, has been created in keeping with the low-fat content of the fondue.

Nutritional Profile

PER SERVING	CLASSIC	MINIMAX
Calories	737	483
Fat (gm)	37	13
Saturated fat (gm)	23	4
Calories from fat	45%	25%
Cholesterol (mg)	116	17
Sodium (mg)	746	663
Fiber (gm)	4	8

■ *Classic Compared: Fondue*

Time Estimate: Hands on, 40 minutes; unsupervised, 60 minutes

Cost Estimate: Medium High

Serves 4
INGREDIENTS

CROUTONS:

One 6-inch (15-cm) piece of a French baguette, about 2 ounces (57 gm) cut into ½-inch (1.5-cm) cubes

1 teaspoon dried sweet basil (5 ml)

¼ teaspoon dried tarragon (1.25 ml)

⅛ teaspoon freshly ground salt (0.6 ml)

⅛ teaspoon freshly ground black peppercorns (0.6 ml)

¼ cup clear chicken broth (59 ml) (see page 34)

4 teaspoons freshly grated Parmesan cheese (20 ml)

VINAIGRETTE:

¼ cup cider vinegar (59 ml)

2 tablespoons avocado oil (30 ml)

⅛ teaspoon freshly ground salt (0.6 ml)

⅛ teaspoon freshly ground black peppercorns (0.6 ml)

1 teaspoon fresh chopped basil (5 ml)

½ teaspoon dried tarragon (2.5 ml)

½ teaspoon Dijon mustard (2.5 ml)

1 teaspoon maple syrup (5 ml)

FONDUE:

1¾ pounds sweet potatoes (794 gm)

1 clove garlic, peeled

1 cup chicken broth (236 ml) (see page 34)

1 cup de-alcoholized dry white wine (236 ml)

1 tablespoon cornstarch (15 ml), mixed with 2 tablespoons chicken broth (30 ml)

2 ounces extra-sharp cheddar cheese (57 gm)

⅛ teaspoon freshly ground salt (0.6 ml)

¼ teaspoon freshly ground black peppercorns (1.25 ml)

1 tablespoon freshly squeezed lemon juice (15 ml)

1 loaf French bread, broken in small chunks

2 apples, peeled, cored and sliced, dipped in lemon juice

SALAD:

1 medium apple, peeled, cored and chopped

3 stalks celery, chopped

2 tablespoons fresh finely chopped basil (30 ml)

1 small head of tender butter lettuce

FIRST PREPARE

■ The Croutons: Preheat the oven to 350°F. (180°C). In a small bowl, combine the basil, tarragon, salt and pepper. Place the bread cubes in a pie pan, arranging them white side (not crust side) up. Using a pastry brush, coat the cubes with the chicken broth. Sprinkle with the mixed herbs and the Parmesan cheese. Bake on the middle rack of the preheated oven for 20 minutes.

■ The Vinaigrette: In a dressing jar or small bowl, mix the vinegar, oil, salt, pepper, basil and tarragon and shake or whisk to combine. Add the mustard and maple syrup and shake or whisk again.

NOW COOK

■ The Fondue: Bake the sweet potatoes at 350°F. (180°C) for 1 hour. Remove from the oven and cool. Cut the potatoes in half and gently scrape the inner meat away from the skin. Set the skins aside for another dish. In a large bowl, mash the potatoes.

■ Heat a nonstick wok or heavy saucepan and rub the clove of garlic around the inner surface. Pour in the chicken broth and the wine. Add the potatoes and whisk together. Cook the mixture until somewhat creamy. Add the cornstarch slurry and cheddar cheese and stir to thicken.

■ Strain the fondue by spooning it into a sieve over a large bowl. Rub the solid portions through with a wooden spoon. Return the fondue to the heated wok. Add the salt, pepper and lemon juice.

■ The Salad: Just before serving, combine the apple, celery and fresh basil in a large bowl. Drizzle the vinaigrette over the top and stir with a wooden spoon. Now add the lettuce leaves and croutons.

■ To Serve: Transfer the fondue to a fondue pot or serving bowl. Gather your friends and family around the pot, giving each a skewer to dip the bread chunks and apple slices into the fondue. Serve the salad on the side—a great time for all!

Helpful Hints and Observations

THE MOUTHFEEL FACTOR. One of the major pleasures to be experienced while eating is "mouthroundfullness." It usually comes from large concentrations of fat. However, in this dish, I managed to achieve an attractive smoothness with sweet potatoes, steamed and beaten to a creamlike consistency. I think you'll love it.

POPCORN

$\mathscr{I}$grew up in the European hotel business—a life utterly separated from popcorn. My first encounter with this ubiquitous American snack was developing these ideas for you.

　The question before us is, "How to enjoy serving popcorn without encouraging couch potato-itis in our family?" I know! Do the usual thing by putting your popcorn in a big bowl and bringing it out to the eager family sitting on the couch, but this time, don't turn on the television. Instead, try talking! It's tough at first, but wonderful when it catches on!

Nutritional Profile: Seasoned Popcorn

PER SERVING	CLASSIC	MINIMAX
Calories	168	61
Fat (gm)	14	2
Saturated fat (gm)	9	0
Calories from fat	77%	26%
Cholesterol (mg)	37	0
Sodium (mg)	284	3
Fiber (gm)	2	2

■　*Classic Compared: Home-Popped Corn with Butter and Salt*

Time Estimate for Both: 15 minutes

Cost Estimate for Both: Low

Nutritional Profile: Maple Popcorn

PER SERVING	CLASSIC	MINIMAX
Calories	375	149
Fat (gm)	16	4
Saturated fat (gm)	10	2
Calories from fat	39%	24%
Cholesterol (mg)	41	0
Sodium (mg)	335	7
Fiber (gm)	2	3

■ *Classic Compared: Baked Caramel Corn*

Serves 4
INGREDIENTS

SEASONED POPCORN

¼ cup popcorn kernels (59 ml)

1 teaspoon extra-light olive oil, with a dash of sesame oil (5 ml)

1 tablespoon freshly squeezed lime juice (15 ml)

⅛ teaspoon cayenne pepper (0.6 ml)

2 teaspoons brewer's yeast (10 ml)

MAPLE POPCORN

¼ cup popcorn kernels (59 ml)

¼ cup brown sugar (59 ml)

1 tablespoon pure maple syrup (15 ml)

¼ cup water (59 ml)

2 tablespoons grated coconut (30 ml)

4 tablespoons flaked almonds (60 ml)

1 teaspoon cinnamon (5 ml)

FIRST PREPARE

■ Pour the popcorn into an already heated hot-air popcorn popper (try saying that three times, fast!) and start popping, allowing the popped kernels to fall into a large bowl. Set aside.

NOW COOK

■ The Seasoned Popcorn: Pour the oil and the lime juice into a large-sized roasting bag and shake until evenly distributed. Add the popped kernels, trap air in the bag, twist closed and shake well!

■ Mix the cayenne pepper and brewer's yeast together. Sprinkle into the bag and shake again. Each piece of popcorn is now coated in a bright, spicy seasoning. A few pieces will be damp, but the flavor will compensate!

■ Maple Popcorn: In a large skillet, over medium heat, stir the brown sugar, maple syrup and water until it comes to a boil. Reduce to a thick syrup, 234° to 240°F. (112° to 115°C), the soft-ball stage on a candy thermometer. Test a drop of syrup in cold water. It should form a soft ball that flattens when removed and pressed between your fingers. Mix in the coconut and almonds.

■ Pour the topping over the popcorn, stirring gently to flavor each kernel. Sprinkle with the cinnamon. As it cools, the topping will harden. Before it cools completely, use your fingers to separate the popcorn kernels.

About the Ingredients

WHITE CAT CORN. I like this variety of corn because of its large-sized kernels and exceptionally "corn-y" taste. It's grown by Paul and Susie Atkins in Hamburg, Illinois. They named the corn after their white cat, who, instead of hunting mice around the farm, brought home weeds! The Williams-Sonoma catalog offers White Cat corn nationwide by mail order.

BREWER'S YEAST. Congratulations on being part of the great recycling process! After beer is brewed, the yeast is removed from the vats, debittered and dried into a powder. The result—nutritious brewer's yeast. You can find brewer's yeast in your local health food store.

FLAKED COCONUT. You don't have to get a whole fresh coconut; flaked coconut is available in supermarkets. Please try to find it unsweetened and without additives. Remember, in the Minimax kitchen coconut is always used in moderation. It's one of the few plant foods that contain a large quantity of saturated rather than unsaturated fat.

BROWNIES

*O*ne of the great rites of passage for young ladies in North American culture is to stay over at a girlfriend's home, make brownies, watch old science-fiction television movies, eat all *the brownies and sometimes get sick! It's all part of the* freedom to choose, I suppose. Is this somehow spoiled if the brownie is Minimaxed? We put it to the test with a new version of an old favorite. Frankly, as a self-confessed chocolate addict, with a sweet tooth, I feel that each brownie should be wrapped and labeled with its calories prominently displayed.

Nutritional Profile

PER SERVING	CLASSIC	MINIMAX
Calories	274	89
Fat (gm)	16	2
Saturated fat (gm)	7	0
Calories from fat	52%	18%
Cholesterol (mg)	69	0
Sodium (mg)	88	82
Fiber (gm)	2	2

■ *Classic Compared: Brownies*

Time Estimate: Hands on, 20 minutes; unsupervised, 25 minutes

Cost Estimate: Low

Serves 16

INGREDIENTS

1 cup all-purpose flour (236 ml)
⅓ cup dark brown sugar (78 ml)
½ cup unsweetened cocoa powder (118 ml)
2 teaspoons baking powder (10 ml)
½ teaspoon baking soda (2.5 ml)
½ teaspoon cinnamon (2.5 ml)
4 large egg whites
¼ cup granulated sugar (59 ml)
½ cup unsweetened applesauce (118 ml)
½ cup skim milk (118 ml)
1½ teaspoons vanilla (7.5 ml)
¼ cup flaked almonds (59 ml)
¼ teaspoon olive oil (1.25 ml)

NOW COOK

■ Preheat the oven to 375°F. (190°C).

■ In a large bowl, sift together the flour, brown sugar, cocoa powder, baking powder, baking soda and cinnamon. If you have tiny balls of brown sugar left over, just push them gently through the sifter into the bowl. Set aside.

■ In another bowl, whip the egg whites until they are frothy and about doubled in volume, then gradually whisk in the granulated sugar. Whisk in the applesauce, skim milk and vanilla.

■ Make a well in the center of the dry ingredients and gently fold in the wet ingredients.

■ Lightly grease a 9 × 9-inch (23 × 23-cm) baking dish with the olive oil. Spoon in the batter and spread evenly. Sprinkle with the almonds and bake in the preheated oven for 25 minutes.

■ To Serve: Let the brownies cool, then cut into 16 squares. Remember: only 1 square per serving (if you can!).

Helpful Hints and Observations

WATCH THE FOLDING! As with any incorporation of liquid into dry ingredients for cake (or other) batters, the liquid should be stirred in completely and gently—the fewer motions with the spoon, the more tender the result. The more you beat, the tougher the finished product becomes.

About the Ingredients

COCOA POWDER. Cocoa powders are not all created equal—there are many brands from different countries. I prefer cocoa that has gone through a process developed by a Dutchman named Conrad van Houten. In this process the cocoa becomes milder or less bitter, darker and easier to mix with a liquid. Droste is my brand of choice, but any brand, domestic or imported, will work.

CHOCOLATE AND STRAWBERRY ANGEL FOOD CAKE

𝓛ess well known than its almost white (more angelic?) cousin, this chocolate angel food cake is filled with a strained yogurt Papufa and fresh strawberries. Served chilled, this dessert delivers a delicious treat with only 0.3 grams of fat per serving.

The cake looks superb presented whole and sliced at the table, or presliced and served on individual plates. When the filling is added and the top and sides "frosted," it takes an hour in the refrigerator to completely set, although it can also be served moist immediately. Either way, have fun!

Nutritional Profile

PER SERVING	CLASSIC	MINIMAX
Calories	223	157
Fat (gm)	14	1
Saturated fat (gm)	7	0
Calories from fat	55%	4%
Cholesterol (mg)	33	1
Sodium (mg)	267	172
Fiber (gm)	3	1

■ *Classic Compared: Strawberry Shortcake*

Time Estimate: Hands on, 90 minutes; unsupervised, 80 minutes

Cost Estimate: Low

Serves 12
INGREDIENTS

CAKE:

¾ cup sifted cake flour (177 ml)

¼ teaspoon baking soda (1.25 ml)

¼ cup unsweetened cocoa powder (59 ml)

1 cup granulated sugar (236 ml)

11 egg whites, at room temperature

1 teaspoon water (5 ml)

1½ teaspoons cream of tartar (7.5 ml)

¼ teaspoon salt (1.25 ml)

1½ teaspoons vanilla (7.5 ml)

PAPUFA:

9 tablespoons nonfat dried milk powder (135 ml)

½ cup ice water (118 ml)

3 tablespoons superfine sugar (45 ml)

1 teaspoon safflower oil (5 ml)

¼ teaspoon vanilla (1.25 ml)

1 envelope unflavored gelatin

3 tablespoons cold water (45 ml)

3 tablespoons boiling water (45 ml)

1 cup strained yogurt (236 ml) (see page 85)

¾ pound strawberries (340 gm), stemmed and washed

GARNISH:

6 strawberries with leaves, cut in half

NOW COOK

■ The Cake: Preheat the oven to 350°F. (180°C). Sift the flour, baking soda, cocoa and ⅓ cup (78 ml) of the granulated sugar together 3 times, into a large bowl, and set aside.

■ In a very large bowl, beat the egg whites with an electric mixer at high speed until foamy. Add the water, cream of tartar, salt and vanilla and beat until soft peaks form. Gradually beat in the remaining sugar until stiff peaks form. Fold in the flour mixture ¼ cup (59 ml) at a time.

■ Pour the batter into an ungreased 10-inch (25-cm) angel food cake pan, spreading evenly. Bake for 35 to 40 minutes or until the cake springs back when lightly touched. Invert the pan and let the cake cool—about 40 minutes. Loosen the cake from the sides of the pan, using a narrow metal spatula, and remove from the pan.

■ Cut a 1-inch (2.5-cm) layer off the top of the cake. This can be done with a serrated knife or by the dental floss method. Here's how it goes: wrap 1 yard (91 cm) of dental floss around the circumference of the cake, 1 inch (2.5 cm) from the top. Cross the ends of the floss and pull, gently cutting the cake in two. Set the top layer aside.

■ Place the lower cake layer on a serving dish. Scoop out a 2-inch (5-cm) by 2-inch trench around the inside of this layer.

■ The Papufa: In a small metal bowl, beat the dried milk and ice water with a wire whisk for 6 to 7 minutes. Gradually beat in the sugar and oil. Add the vanilla and continue beating for 1 minute more.

■ In another small bowl, mix the gelatin with the cold water and let sit 3 minutes to soften. Stir in the boiling water to dissolve the gelatin.

■ In a large bowl, combine the milk mixture with the gelatin and strained yogurt.

■ To Assemble: Place the strawberries in the hollowed-out section of the cake. Spoon 1 cup (236 ml) of the Papufa mixture over the strawberries. Now place the top layer of the cake back in its original position, over the strawberries, and top with the remaining Papufa. As the Papufa drips down the sides of the cake, use a spatula to smooth and even the frosting, being sure to cover the entire cake. Garnish with the 12 strawberry halves, one for each slice, and serve immediately or refrigerate for 1 hour, to set.

Helpful Hints and Observations

PAPUFA. This is an acronym for "physiologically active polyunsaturated fatty acid"—one way of describing a totally *saturated*-fat-free, cholesterol-free topping for desserts.

About the Ingredients

CREAM OF TARTAR. Some people enjoy the science of cooking. In the case of angel food cake, this includes the way the cream of tartar reacts with the albumen, or egg white. Cream of tartar is solid salt or tartaric acid. By adding acidic cream of tartar, one lowers the pH value of the egg white, and that, in turn, stabilizes the foam to prevent it from overcoagulation.

CHOCOLATE CHERRY AND ALMOND CAKE

A friendly local restaurant recently announced in their dessert section that "the fat cake is back!!" They referred to a vast wedge of supermoist, midnight-brown chocolate cake—it didn't sell! "Did I know of a creative alternative?" they asked. We set to work and this came out well at 5 grams of fat per slice compared to 36 grams in the "fat cake."

Nutritional Profile

PER SERVING	CLASSIC	MINIMAX
Calories	536	185
Fat (gm)	36	5
Saturated fat (gm)	20	2
Calories from fat	60%	23%
Cholesterol (mg)	235	107
Sodium (mg)	204	92
Fiber (gm)	5	2

■ *Classic Compared: Chocolate Rum and Almond Cake*

Time Estimate: Hands on, 40 minutes; unsupervised, 20 minutes

Cost Estimate: Low

INGREDIENTS

SPONGE CAKE:

½ cup all-purpose flour (118 ml)

¼ cup unsweetened cocoa powder (59 ml)

1 teaspoon baking powder (5 ml)

4 eggs, separated

½ cup sugar (118 ml)

¼ cup skim milk (59 ml)

Olive oil cooking spray

FILLING:

1 tablespoon unsweetened cocoa powder (15 ml)

2 tablespoons cornstarch (30 ml)

1¼ cups skim milk (295 ml)

⅛ teaspoon almond extract (0.6 ml)

1 cup fresh or frozen, pitted dark sweet cherries (236 ml) (if unavailable, canned sweet cherries may be used)

1 packet NutraSweet

1 teaspoon pure maple syrup (5 ml)

2 tablespoons slivered almonds (30 ml)

GARNISH:

1 tablespoon confectioners' sugar

5 cherries, cut in half

NOW COOK

■ The Sponge Cake: Preheat the oven to 375°F. (190°C). Sift the flour, cocoa and baking powder into a medium-sized bowl, and set aside.

■ In a large bowl (preferably copper), over warm water, beat the egg yolks and sugar until the volume doubles—approximately 5 minutes. Add the milk and sifted flour mixture and mix at low speed with an electric mixer until well incorporated.

■ Clean and dry the mixer beaters. In a medium-sized bowl, beat the egg whites at high speed until stiff but not dry. Fold the egg whites into the batter mixture.

■ Pour the batter into a lightly greased 9-inch (23-cm) round cake pan. I like to use the spray-type olive oils, ensuring the minimum added fat. Tap the filled pan on the counter to release any trapped air bubbles. Bake the cake for 20 minutes and turn out to cool on a rack.

■ The Filling: Combine the cocoa, cornstarch and ¼ cup (59 ml) of the skim milk to make a paste.

■ In a medium-sized saucepan, bring the remaining milk just to a boil, stirring constantly to prevent scorching. Stir in the cocoa paste and remove from the heat. Stir in the almond extract, cherries, NutraSweet, maple syrup and almonds.

■ To Assemble: Slice the cake horizontally into 2 even layers. Place one layer on a serving plate and spread with the filling. Cover with the second cake layer. Garnish with a sprinkle of confectioners' sugar and the cherry halves.

■ To Serve: Cut into 8 wedges. No whipped or ice cream; the cherry custard should do the trick.

Helpful Hints and Observations

THE PIONEER PORTION PROBLEM. Nowhere is the risk of too much fat better illustrated than in the French influence on chocolate cake in the New World. Before La Cuisine Française, North Americans were quite happy using cocoa powder in their baking. Chocolate cakes were made and sliced in typical pioneer (large) portions. While across the Atlantic, the moist, buttery, smooth, chocolate French gâteau was sliced in delicate wisps.

In its transition, the French recipe was welcomed with open mouths, but the pioneer portions remained unchanged! A one-eighth slice of "fat cake" has 60 percent of its 714 calories from fat. A typical "French wisp slice" (one sixteenth) retains the same percentage of fat, but takes up only half the fat grams in the daily allowance.

The big issue is which wins out? Pioneer portions or Gallic restraint? Since the French recipe is so delicious, and our portions so traditional, the answer seems obvious—we want both, and what we now call devil's food cake becomes a real risk.

So I swerved away from dubious "restraint" on portion size and changed this recipe back to the cocoa powder days, when the good old one-eighth slice wasn't that risky. Of course it wouldn't hurt to serve a one-sixteenth slice . . . or perhaps a compromise at one-twelfth?

DOILY DALLIANCE. You can create a lovely design on the top of your cake with a paper lace doily. Just place it on top of the cake, fasten with toothpicks and sift confectioners' sugar evenly over the top. Remove the doily carefully and . . . voilà!

BUMBLEBERRY STRUDEL

One of our most favorite places to eat when we're in Victoria, British Columbia, is about seven miles from the city in a village called Oak Bay. There you will find the Blethering Place, an English tea shop owned by New Zealander Ken Agett, which serves a great "cuppa" (tea) and a wonderful mixed-fruit pie. I've kept the berries and changed the crust—grounds for diplomatic conflict?

Nutritional Profile

PER SERVING	CLASSIC	MINIMAX
Calories	440	485
Fat (gm)	26	6
Saturated fat (gm)	6	1
Calories from fat	54%	12%
Cholesterol (mg)	0	1
Sodium (mg)	46	459
Fiber (gm)	4	8

■ *Classic Compared: Bumbleberry Pie*

Time Estimate: Hands on, 50 minutes; unsupervised, 30 minutes

Cost Estimate: Low

Serves 6
INGREDIENTS

SAUCE:

1 tablespoon honey (15 ml) (fireweed is preferable)
1 cup strained yogurt (236 ml) (see page 85)

1 large Granny Smith apple, peeled, cored and chopped into ¼-inch dice (0.75-cm)
2 cups finely sliced rhubarb (472 ml)
1 cup frozen blackberries (236 ml)
1 cup frozen raspberries (236 ml)
½ cup brown sugar (118 ml)
2 tablespoons freshly grated lemon zest (30 ml)
½ teaspoon ground cloves (2.5 ml)
8 sheets phyllo dough
Olive oil cooking spray
½ cup dried bread crumbs (118 ml)
2 tablespoons honey (30 ml) (fireweed is preferable)

GARNISH:

6 fresh mint sprigs

FIRST PREPARE

■ The Sauce: Mix the honey and the strained yogurt until smooth and reserve.

■ In a large mixing bowl, combine the apple, rhubarb, blackberries, raspberries, brown sugar, lemon zest and cloves.

■ On a flat surface, stretch out a slightly damp dishtowel. Lay a sheet of phyllo dough on top of the towel running lengthwise. Spray lightly with olive oil and repeat with 3 more sheets of the pastry.

■ Sprinkle ¼ cup (59 ml) of the bread crumbs in a strip 3-inches (8-cm) wide down the length of the pastry, leaving 2 inches (5 cm) at either end. Now take half of the fruit mixture, and carefully spoon it along the bread crumb strip.

■ With the long side of the pastry and fruit filling in front of you, lift the edge of the damp cloth nearest you and roll the pastry slowly away from you as you would a jelly roll. Repeat for the remaining pastry and fruit mixture.

NOW COOK

■ Preheat the oven to 350°F. (180°C). Spray a cookie sheet lightly with oil, place the strudel seam side down. With a brush, lightly apply the honey to each roll. Bake for 30 minutes. When done, place the cookie sheet on a wire rack and let the strudel cool for 15 minutes before slicing. Slice each roll into thirds and serve with a dollop of honey-sweetened strained yogurt. Garnish with a sprig of mint.

Helpful Hints and Observations

KEEP IT DAMP AND WATCH YOUR NAILS. There are two basic problems when working with phyllo; first, you must keep the pastry covered with a damp cloth once it is removed from its wrapper; also keep it wrapped in wax paper and plastic wrap for storage in either the freezer or refrigerator. Secondly, do please, watch your nails (if you have long ones) as they so easily tear great holes in the phyllo.

About the Ingredients

RHUBARB. These tall red stalks might look exotic, but rhubarb is actually a cousin of a common weed called dock. Rhubarb is best from early spring to early summer, but is grown year-round in some of the more temperate areas of North America. Look for red or red-streaked, firm stalks. Keep rhubarb in the refrigerator, or dice it and freeze it for future use.

BERRIES. Blackberries and raspberries are close relatives, both the fruit of thorny bushes. Look for fresh berries that are firm and plump. Blackberries should be very black and raspberries very red. If you can't get them fresh, buy berries that have been frozen separately. Feel the package before you buy it to make sure they're not in a solid mass —this would indicate that they have been thawed, mushed together and then refrozen.

PEAR AND RASPBERRY COBBLER

This is COMFORT ZONE food, the stuff that brightens those dull, gray rainy days, and reminds you of the kind of home we see in black-and-white movies, but . . . in this case . . . it's colorized naturally. I have turned the cobbler upside down, in order to feature the fruit. The colors are great, and when served really hot from the skillet, the scent of wine and cinnamon fills the air.

the following dessert is brought to you in living color...

Nutritional Profile

PER SERVING	CLASSIC	MINIMAX
Calories	368	254
Fat (gm)	18	5
Saturated fat (gm)	7	0
Calories from fat	42%	16%
Cholesterol (mg)	23	0
Sodium (mg)	172	171
Fiber (gm)	3	4

■ *Classic Compared: Berry Cobbler*

Time Estimate: Hands on, 30 minutes; unsupervised, 30 minutes

Cost Estimate: Low

Serves 12
INGREDIENTS
RASPBERRY SYRUP:

½ cup de-alcoholized white wine (118 ml)

¼ cup brown sugar (59 ml)

One 12-ounce bag unsweetened frozen raspberries (340 gm)

2 tablespoons cornstarch (30 ml)

PEAR SYRUP:

¼ cup de-alcoholized dry white wine (59 ml)

2 tablespoons granulated sugar (30 ml)

3 large Bosc pears, peeled, cored and cut in half

BATTER:

2 cups all-purpose flour (472 ml)

2½ teaspoons baking powder (12.5 ml)

¼ teaspoon freshly ground salt (1.25 ml)

¾ cup brown sugar (177 ml)

½ cup regular rolled oats (118 ml)

¼ cup flaked almonds (59 ml)

2 teaspoons cinnamon (10 ml)

2 tablespoons extra-light olive oil, with a dash of sesame oil (30 ml)

1¾ cups skim milk (413 ml)

FIRST PREPARE

■ The Raspberry Syrup: In a small saucepan, combine the wine and brown sugar and heat and stir until the sugar dissolves. Pour over the raspberries in a medium bowl and let sit for 10 minutes.

■ Remove ¼ cup (59 ml) of the raspberry syrup and place in a small bowl. Stir in the cornstarch to form a paste and then stir it into the raspberries.

■ The Pear Syrup: Pour the wine into a 10-inch (25-cm) ovenproof skillet. Over low heat, stir in the sugar until dissolved. Bring just to a boil.

■ Put the pear halves into the syrup, alternating, round side down, round side up, and with the stem ends pointing toward the center. The position is important because this determines how the finished cobbler will look. Let the pear halves steam in the syrup for 5 minutes, then turn them over and steam 5 minutes more. Watch the syrup carefully for close to 10 minutes: don't let it turn brown.

■ The Batter: Sift the flour, baking powder, salt and sugar together into a large bowl. Add the oats, almonds and cinnamon. Pour in the oil and milk and stir until smooth.

NOW COOK

■ Preheat the oven to 375°F. (190°C). Note: if you don't have a large ovenproof skillet, you can transfer the pears and their syrup to a 10-inch (25-cm) round, straight-sided, baking pan at this point. Pour the raspberries in the thickened raspberry syrup over the pears in the skillet, making sure that the raspberries get into the spaces between the pears and cover the bottom of the skillet.

■ Pour the batter slowly and carefully to cover the pears and raspberries completely. Don't worry if the batter is thinner in some places than others.

■ Put a baking sheet on a lower rack in the oven to catch the drips. Place the skillet on the middle rack of the preheated oven and bake the cobbler for 45 minutes.

■ To Serve: Don't leave the cobbler in its baking pan too long or it will overcook. To remove it from the skillet, put a serving plate on top and flip the skillet over. Voilà! Gorgeous plump pears, nestled in pink raspberries. Slice the cobbler so each person gets a quarter of a pear.

Helpful Hints and Observations

THE WINE SYRUP. In the early stages of this recipe, I put sugar and wine in the pan to begin to soften the pears. This syrup mingles with the fruit juices and creates a glaze that will help the final presentation. Please watch it carefully. We used medium heat, and cooked the pears until there was a hint of amber color in the syrup. This is the time to add the raspberries, and this prevents a heavy caramel from forming.

THE CRUST. I added the almonds and the oats to give a special texture that is ordinarily missing. It is this coarse quality, coupled with the raspberries, that gives a country feel to the cobbler, as well as a very healthy dose of dietary fiber (4 grams per serving!).

About the Ingredients

ORGANIC ROLLED OATS. In this recipe the oats provide texture as well as fiber and carbohydrates. I always prefer to use organic products over nonorganic, as long as there is no difference in the quality. Using nonorganic oats will not make a difference in the cobbler's outcome.

SPICED APPLE PIE

$\mathcal{W}$*herever there are apples you'll find a variation of the apple pie, but nowhere in the world has it been enshrined as part of the national identity as in the United States. I set out to bake a big one with top and bottom crust and to try and keep it to our Minimax standards—it worked! I let the pie cool before cutting; this keeps the slices intact and makes it easily reheatable in a microwave or toaster oven. A ½ cup (118 ml) scoop of nonfat frozen yogurt adds 68 calories and no fat, compared to ice cream at 175 calories and 12 grams of fat per serving.*

Nutritional Profile

PER SERVING	CLASSIC	MINIMAX
Calories	650	474
Fat (gm)	36	11
Saturated fat (gm)	19	2
Calories from fat	50%	21%
Cholesterol (mg)	90	2
Sodium (mg)	142	316
Fiber (gm)	3	5

■ *Classic Compared: Apple Pie*

Time Estimate: Hands on, 75 minutes; unsupervised, 2 hours

Cost Estimate: Low

Serves 10

INGREDIENTS

CRUST:

3 cups all-purpose flour (708 ml)

½ cup wheat germ (118 ml)

½ cup rolled oats (118 ml)

⅛ teaspoon freshly ground salt (0.6 ml)

12 tablespoons margarine (180 ml) (Promise is preferable)

10 tablespoons ice water (150 ml)

2 tablespoons granulated sugar (30 ml), mixed with 1 teaspoon cinnamon (5 ml)

1 tablespoon 2% fat milk (15 ml)

FILLING:

8 tart apples, (such as Granny Smith) peeled, cored and thinly sliced

½ cup dark brown sugar (118 ml)

2 tablespoons cornstarch (30 ml)

½ teaspoon cinnamon (2.5 ml)

⅛ teaspoon ground cloves (0.6 ml)

1 tablespoon grated lemon zest (15 ml)

1 cup dark seedless raisins (236 ml) (flame raisins are preferable)

5 cups nonfat frozen yogurt (1.2 l) flavor of your choice

FIRST PREPARE

■ The Crust: Sift the flour into a bowl and stir in the wheat germ, oats and salt.

■ Cut the margarine into 12 pieces and lightly work it into the flour mixture with the tips of your fingers until it has the texture of cornmeal. This will give you lovely flecks of margarine throughout the crust.

■ Stir in the ice water until the dough forms a stiff mass that binds together when pressed. Separate into 2 equal parts. Roll each part into a long rectangle.

■ Fold the bottom third of the rectangle toward the center and the top third on top of that. Give the dough a quarter turn, roll the dough into a long rectangle again and fold as before. Repeat this process once more, then repeat with the other dough rectangle. Wrap the rectangles in plastic and refrigerate for 1 hour or overnight.

■ Roll out the chilled dough into two 12-inch (30-cm) circles. Sprinkle 1 circle with half the cinnamon-sugar mixture and reserve the remainder for the top of the top crust.

■ Transfer the other circle of dough into a 10-inch (25-cm) pie plate and press it into the bottom and sides of the plate. Trim the edges, leaving a ¼-inch (1-cm) overhang.

■ Preheat the oven to 350°F. (180°C).

NOW COOK

■ The Filling: Put the apple slices into a strainer and gently shake over the sink to remove any excess moisture. Turn into a large bowl.

■ Pass the brown sugar, cornstarch, cinnamon and cloves through a sieve, into a bowl. Pour the sieved mixture into a plastic bag and add the lemon zest and raisins. Seal the top of the bag and shake for 30 seconds. Open and add the drained apple slices. Close and shake 30 more seconds.

■ Scoop the apple mixture out of the bag and into the pie crust. Pack it in, shaping it to rise to an even dome. Brush the edge of the crust with water.

■ Place the top crust over the apples with the cinnamon-sugared side facing the apples. Trim off any excess crust, allowing a ¼-inch (0.75-cm) overhang. Seal the edges of the crusts together by crimping with your fingertips. Cut a few small vents in the top crust and brush lightly with the milk. Sprinkle the remainder of the cinnamon-sugar mixture over the top.

■ Bake in the preheated oven for 1 hour or until the filling is bubbling and the top is golden brown.

■ To Serve: Cut the pie into 10 wedges and present each slice with ½ cup (118 ml) of nonfat frozen yogurt on top or on the side.

Helpful Hints and Observations

BOTTOM CRUST. Have you noticed how often the bottom crust is doughy, white—almost raw? If you leave out the bottom crust, the calories fall by 112 per serving and the fat is reduced to 6 grams—15 percent. Can you settle for a bottomless pie? Or would this undermine the very foundation of American culture? As always, the choice is yours!

BAG-TOSSED SEASONING. It isn't easy to evenly coat this many apple slices with the spice mixture. It helps to use a turkey-sized roasting bag.

TRIM COMES OFF THE NUMBERS. I've given you enough pastry to line and cover a 10-inch (25-cm) pie dish. This is a large pie, but you will have about 7 ounces (198 gm) of dough left over—perfect for an apple turnover? In any event, it isn't added into the nutritional numbers since you won't be eating it—at least not yet!

LEMON KIWI CUSTARD PIE

A light fruit tart with a strongly astringent lemony bitter-sour taste is the perfect ending to a good meal. I wanted to go for a deep-dish appearance, giving the pie some height, so we really had to work at keeping the numbers down. This one has but 1 gram of fat in its 282 calories, and it looks and tastes terrific.

Nutritional Profile

PER SERVING	CLASSIC	MINIMAX
Calories	499	282
Fat (gm)	21	1
Saturated fat (gm)	12	0
Calories from fat	37%	2%
Cholesterol (mg)	179	1
Sodium (mg)	257	204
Fiber (gm)	0	6

■ *Classic Compared: Lemon Tart*

Time Estimate: Hands on, 25 minutes; unsupervised, 3 hours

Cost Estimate: Medium

Serves 8

INGREDIENTS

CRUST:

1¼ cups whole pitted dried dates (295 ml)

1¾ cups Grape-Nuts cereal (or granola) (413 ml)

½ teaspoon freshly grated nutmeg (2.5 ml)

Zest of ½ lemon, grated

LEMON CUSTARD:

1 envelope unflavored gelatin

3 tablespoons cold water

¼ cup hot water (59 ml)

¼ cup freshly squeezed lemon juice (59 ml)

Zest of 1 lemon, grated

6 tablespoons sugar (90 ml)

2¼ cups strained yogurt (531 ml) (see page 85)

6 kiwi fruit, peeled and cut into ¼-inch slices (0.75-cm)

GARNISH:

1 kiwi fruit, peeled and thinly sliced

FIRST PREPARE

■ The Crust: In a food processor or blender, process the dates, cereal and nutmeg for 2 minutes or until thoroughly combined. Add the lemon zest and process for another 3 minutes. The crust should have a moist, crumbly texture and stick together easily when pressed.

■ Transfer the crust into a 9-inch (23-cm) high-sided springform pan, pressing it into the bottom and all the way up the sides. (Dip your fingers in a small bowl of water if they start to get sticky.) Set aside.

NOW COOK

■ The Lemon Custard: In a small bowl, mix the gelatin first with the cold water to soften and then add the hot water and let sit until the gelatin is clear—about 1 minute.

■ In a medium-sized bowl, combine the softened gelatin, lemon juice, lemon zest, sugar and strained yogurt and whisk together until smooth.

■ Place the kiwi fruit in the crust-lined springform pan. Pour the custard over the fruit and refrigerate until firm—about 3 to 4 hours.

■ To Serve: Remove from springform pan. Cut the pie into 8 wedges and garnish with the kiwi slices. For a dinner party I'd slice it into 12, for about 150 calories each serving. It has a wonderful palate-cleansing property.

Helpful Hints and Observations

WATER FOR THE FINGERS. When pressing the crust into the dish, dab your fingers in cold water. It helps to make an even job without getting into a sticky mess!

About the Ingredients

GRAPE-NUTS. Although it was one of the first commercial breakfast cereals developed more than a hundred years ago, Grape-Nuts has remained very close to its original recipe. A carefully chosen cereal is a good breakfast choice because of its ease of preparation and contribution of fiber to the diet. The use of Grape-Nuts in this recipe helps lower fat and still provides wonderful texture in solving what is ordinarily a real problem: what to substitute for high-fat pastry crusts.

DATES. For thousands of years, dates have supplied desert dwellers in the Middle East with one of nature's highest energy foods. Iraq grows over four hundred types, but most of the world knows of two: the Deglet Noor and the Medjool. Unless you live in a date-producing area, you will probably find only dried dates. Choose ones that are plump and well shaped. They will last for six months to a year in a tightly sealed container.

LEMON ZEST. Have you ever made a recipe and thought, "This needs some perking up, some zest"? That's it—lemon zest! Lemon zest is just grated lemon peel. It can be added at the last minute instead of salt to enhance flavor. Use it in fruit pies, salads, soups or fish dishes.

TUROS PALASCINTA

Turos are Hungarian sweet pancakes, smothered in cottage cheese and sugar. After being reheated in the oven, they are topped with fruit jam and dollops of sour cream. My Minimax turos recipe uses red raspberries, blueberries and white cottage cheese for a remarkably patriotic dessert—depending, of course, on your nationality! Turos can be served hot on a cold winter's night by baking the filled pancake at 325°F. (165°C) for 10 minutes, then coating with the sauce and adding the garnish. We also like them cold on a warm summer's night—your choice!

Nutritional Profile

PER SERVING	CLASSIC	MINIMAX
Calories	943	280
Fat (gm)	61	4
Saturated fat (gm)	37	1
Calories from fat	58%	13%
Cholesterol (mg)	316	75
Sodium (mg)	575	59
Fiber (gm)	3	7

■ *Classic Compared: Crêpes Snow White*

Time Estimate: Hands on, 30 minutes; unsupervised, 30 minutes

Cost Estimate: Low

Serves 4

INGREDIENTS

CRÊPE BATTER:

1 whole egg

1 egg yolk

1 teaspoon grated lemon zest (5 ml)

1¼ cups nonfat milk (295 ml)

1 cup all-purpose flour (236 ml)

1 teaspoon extra-light olive oil, with a dash of sesame oil (5 ml)

FILLING:

½ cup 1% fat cottage cheese (118 ml)

½ cup fresh or frozen blueberries (118 ml)

1 tablespoon honey (15 ml) (fireweed is preferable)

½ teaspoon vanilla (2.5 ml)

SAUCE:

3 cups raspberries (708 ml)

¼ cup de-alcoholized white wine (59 ml)

1 tablespoon cornstarch (15 ml), mixed with 2 tablespoons water (30 ml)

¼ cup strained yogurt (59 ml) (see page 85)

½ teaspoon vanilla (2.5 ml)

2 tablespoons honey (30 ml) (fireweed is preferable)

GARNISH:

A jar of honey (fireweed is preferable), kept warm in a saucepan of hot water

¼ cup raspberries (59 ml)

¼ cup blueberries (59 ml)

1 teaspoon confectioners' sugar (5 ml)

FIRST PREPARE

■ The Crêpe Batter: In a medium-sized bowl, beat the whole egg, egg yolk, lemon zest and milk. Sift the flour into another bowl, make a well in the center of the flour and stir in the liquid. Cover and let rest for 30 minutes. Strain and set aside.

■ The Filling: In a medium-sized bowl, mix the cottage cheese, blueberries, honey and vanilla. Set aside.

NOW COOK

■ The Sauce: Push the raspberries through a sieve into a medium-sized bowl. You should have approximately ⅔ cup (156 ml) of raspberry puree.

Transfer the puree to a saucepan, stir in the wine and bring to a boil. Remove from the heat and add the cornstarch slurry. Bring back to a boil for 30 seconds to thicken the puree, stirring constantly. Remove from the heat and let cool.

■ Smooth out any small lumps in the strained yogurt and stir it gently into the sauce until it is just incorporated. Add the vanilla and honey. Return to a low heat to keep warm until serving.

■ The Crêpes: In a crêpe pan, heat the oil, then tip it into the batter and stir thoroughly to create a self-releasing batter. Pour ¼ cup (59 ml) of the batter into the pan and swirl to make a round crêpe. Cook until slightly brown, then flip and brown the other side—approximately 1 minute on each side. Set aside, then cook the other 3 crêpes.

■ To Serve: Spread each crêpe with 2 tablespoons (30 ml) of filling, roll into a cylinder and place on a serving plate. Brush the crêpes with warm honey to make them glisten. Spoon the raspberry sauce delicately over the top. Garnish with a few raspberries and blueberries on each side and dust lightly with confectioners' sugar.

Helpful Hints and Observations

PREVENTING YOGURT MELTDOWN. Because strained yogurt (see page 85) is fat free, its rich, smooth "feel" will not hold up if beaten hard or heated beyond a simmer. Any hot sauce to which it is added must first be well thickened—usually with cornstarch because arrowroot and potato starch become slippery when used with the yogurt. Remove the hot sauce from the heat and cool it down with a couple of ice cubes. Add the yogurt all at once and stir gently until just combined. The gentle stirring will not "break" the smooth texture. Serve immediately because, if left on its own, it will quickly lose its feel.

About the Ingredients

COTTAGE CHEESE. Cottage cheese is a fresh curd cheese that also can be low in fat if you choose carefully. In supermarket dairy cases, you can find 1%, 2% or 4% fat varieties. I recommend the lowest percentage fat you can find for this recipe.

CONFECTIONERS' SUGAR. Confectioners', or powdered, sugar is simply granulated sugar that has been ground into a fine powder. It's a common ingredient in cake icings. Because it absorbs moisture easily and has a tendency to clump, anticaking agents such as cornstarch are added.

MAPLE MERINGUE

This is an old favorite revisited. It's hard to imagine a more dramatic dessert. It also has a sweetness that only pure maple syrup can achieve . . . lots of flavor without a cloying aftertaste.

Nutritional Profile

PER SERVING	CLASSIC	MINIMAX
Calories	543	197
Fat (gm)	9	0.5
Saturated fat (gm)	5	0.06
Calories from fat	14%	2%
Cholesterol (mg)	23	0
Sodium (mg)	263	135
Fiber (gm)	0	3

■ *Classic Compared: Baked Maple Meringue*

Time Estimate: Hands on, 50 minutes; unsupervised, 30 minutes

Cost Estimate: Low

Serves 4

INGREDIENTS

2 medium Granny Smith apples, peeled and cored

4 egg whites

⅛ cup cold water (30 ml)

⅛ teaspoon salt (0.6 ml)

½ cup confectioners' sugar (118 ml)

¼ cup pure maple syrup (59 ml)

6 ounces frozen unsweetened raspberries, thawed, no syrup (170 gm)

¼ cup strained yogurt (59 ml) (see page 85)

FIRST PREPARE

■ Cut pieces of parchment paper, brown paper or aluminum foil long enough to tie around small individual soufflé dishes and high enough to come 1 inch (2.5 cm) above the rim. Wrap the paper around each soufflé dish and secure in place with a rubber band. This creates a collar that prevents the meringue from puffing over the sides while baking.

■ Cut the apples in half. You will now have 4 halves, each with a flat side and a rounded side. Cut enough off the rounded side to leave a 1-inch (2.5-cm) thick slice of apple.

NOW COOK

■ Preheat the oven to 350°F. (180°C). In a 9-inch (23-cm) skillet, add enough water to fill to ¼ inch (0.75 cm) in depth. Over medium-high heat, bring the water to a simmer and poach the apple slices 5 minutes on each side. The apple should not be mushy, but just cooked through.

■ In a large bowl, with an electric mixer at medium speed, beat the egg whites with the cold water and the salt, gradually increasing the speed to high, until the mixture forms soft peaks (see Helpful Hints). Beat in the confectioners' sugar until a spoonful of meringue held upside down holds a 3-inch (8-cm) drip.

■ In a small saucepan, heat the maple syrup. Then very gradually, drizzle the heated syrup into the meringue, stirring to incorporate. The meringue will be ready when a spoonful turned upside down holds a 1-inch (2.5-cm) drip. It will be a glossy, creamy-beige color.

■ Place the apple slices in the soufflé dishes. Add 1 tablespoon (15 ml) of the raspberries to each dish. Spoon about 5 tablespoons (75 ml) of the meringue on top of the raspberries in each dish. Just drop in the spoonfuls. Do not stir them! Try not to get the meringue on the parchment paper.

■ Put the filled soufflé dishes into a baking pan, place in the preheated oven and pour boiling water into the pan to about ½ inch (1.5 cm) up the sides of the soufflé dishes. Bake for 30 minutes or until the meringue has puffed up and looks a toasty light brown.

■ While the meringues bake, make a raspberry-yogurt sauce. Over a small bowl, push the remaining raspberries into a sieve. Don't push too hard—you just want the juice, not the fiber. You should have ¼ cup (59 ml) of the sieved raspberry juice. Stir in the strained yogurt and put in the refrigerator to set.

■ To Serve: The meringues should be served as soon as possible after baking or they will start deflating. Remove the parchment paper and put each soufflé dish on an individual serving plate. Serve the raspberry-yogurt sauce on the side and offer a spoonful to each guest at the table. This sauce offsets the sweetness of the meringue and provides multiple counterpoints—cold to hot; sour to sweet; red to fawn.

Helpful Hints and Observations

MORE MARVELOUS MERINGUE. The cold water and salt will enhance the thickening process. Gradually increasing the beating speed to high allows more air to remain in the meringue and gives you a fluffier end product.

About the Ingredients

SUGAR. The small white granules kept in the nicely crafted bowl are common to almost every table in the world. Sugarcane and its products, refined sugar, brown sugar, molasses and raw sugar sweeten our cakes, cookies, breakfast cereals and coffee. Sugar provides carbohydrates which the body can use as fuel, but otherwise offers little nutritional value.

APPLES. Apples are a wonderful fruit when cooked. Baked whole and made into apple butter, are just two of my favorite ways of serving them. For this dish, Granny Smiths, Rome Beauties, or Jonathans are best suited.

HONEY AND APPLE FLAN SOUFFLÉ

The Spanish people have a wonderful way with flan, their word for an egg custard. This is real comfort food: very sweet and unfortunately often made with countless egg yolks and heavy cream. I've taken their soufflé flan and used egg substitute to replace the eggs. This is a radical departure, but it really does work!

Nutritional Profile

PER SERVING	CLASSIC	MINIMAX
Calories	476	182
Fat (gm)	31	2
Saturated fat (gm)	15	0
Calories from fat	59%	10%
Cholesterol (mg)	497	2
Sodium (mg)	92	106
Fiber (gm)	1	1

■ *Classic Compared: Flan-Soufflé al Miel*

Time Estimate: Hands on, 20 minutes

Cost Estimate: Low

Serves 6
INGREDIENTS

FLAN:

1 cup water (236 ml)

1 cup liquid egg substitute (236 ml) (Fleischmann's Egg Beaters is preferable)

½ cup superfine sugar (118 ml)

1½ cups de-alcoholized white wine (354 ml)

3 tablespoons honey (45 ml) (fireweed is preferable)

¼ teaspoon almond extract (1.25 ml)

¼ teaspoon vanilla (1.25 ml)

2 tablespoons cornstarch (30 ml), mixed with ¼ cup de-alcoholized white wine (59 ml)

1 cup cored and finely diced Granny Smith apple (236 ml)

3 tablespoons sliced almonds (45 ml)

PAPUFA TOPPING:

9 tablespoons nonfat dried milk powder (135 ml)

½ cup ice water (118 ml)

3 tablespoons superfine sugar (45 ml)

⅛ teaspoon orange flower water (0.6 ml)

¼ teaspoon vanilla (1.25 ml)

1 tablespoon safflower oil (5 ml)

GARNISH:

12 thin apple slices

2 tablespoons fresh lemon juice (30 ml)

NOW COOK

■ Flan: In a medium-sized saucepan, bring the water to a boil. Set a copper bowl into the saucepan, creating a double-boiler effect. Beat the egg substitute and sugar in the bowl until creamy.

■ In a small saucepan, bring the wine to a boil. Remove from the heat and add the honey, almond extract, vanilla and cornstarch paste, return to a boil and stir until thickened . . . about 30 seconds.

■ Slowly whisk the wine-syrup mixture into the egg substitute and sugar. Stir in the apple and almonds and set aside.

■ Papufa Topping: In a small metal bowl, beat the dried milk and ice water with a wire whisk for 6 to 7 minutes, then gradually beat in the sugar, orange flower water and vanilla. Be sure to chill the water until nearly iced and do not give up beating too early. The whole adventure is great aerobic exercise when you do it by hand.

■ To Serve: Spoon the flan into wineglasses and dollop with 2 spoonfuls of the topping. Garnish with lemon juice dipped apple slices, overlapping them to form a heart shape. This dessert can be served hot or cold.

About the Ingredients

NONFAT DRIED MILK POWDER. Did you know that this milk product is actually spray dried? Nonfat milk is sprayed as a fine mist into a dryer at 350°F. (180°C). When the spray is heated in this way, it is instantly dehydrated. Steam is then added to the milk-flake product, causing it to stick together, and it is dried again. After that it's boxed to be ready for the consumer.

ORANGE FLOWER WATER. One of the sweetest perfumes of cooking, this fragrant liquid is used mainly in pastries and desserts. Use it in very small quantities and it will provide intrigue, complexity and excitement for your dishes. Imagine all that going on in the kitchen! I can find orange flower water at my local supermarket in the spice section; if you can't find it there, try a specialty foods shop or a Middle Eastern foods shop.

CRÈME CARAMEL

Crème caramel is a great favorite in many restaurants. It is basically a superrich baked egg custard made with added heavy cream. It looks small and innocent, but packs a devastating amount of "shadow energy" (many calories with few nutrients). Our substitutions are indeed radical . . . but they are delicious, and reduce the fat significantly.

Nutritional Profile

PER SERVING	CLASSIC	MINIMAX
Calories	759	220
Fat (gm)	63	5
Saturated fat (gm)	37	3
Calories from fat	74%	19%
Cholesterol (mg)	523	18
Sodium (mg)	67	232
Fiber (gm)	0	0

■ *Classic Compared: Crème Caramel*

Time Estimate: Hands on, 30 minutes; unsupervised, 2 hours

Cost Estimate: Low

Serves 4

INGREDIENTS

4 cups 2% fat milk (944 ml)

Two 4-inch (10-cm) sprigs of rosemary

1 orange, zested in strips

1 tablespoon vanilla (15 ml)

1 cup liquid egg substitute (236 ml)

4 tablespoons superfine sugar (60 ml)

3 cups hot water (708 ml)

4 teaspoons pure maple syrup (20 ml)

GARNISH:

4 sprigs of rosemary

NOW COOK

■ Preheat the oven to 300°F. (150°C). In a large saucepan, heat the milk, rosemary and orange zest until just about to boil. Strain into a large bowl and stir in the vanilla, egg substitute and sugar. Pour the custard into 4 individual soufflé dishes.

■ Place a 9 x 9-inch (23 x 23-cm) baking dish on the oven rack. Place the filled soufflé dishes in the dish and pour in the hot water—the soufflé dishes should be about three-quarters submerged. Cover the baking dish loosely with foil and bake for 1 hour—the custard should be well set. Take the soufflé dishes out of the water and let them cool a bit—about 1 hour.

■ To Serve: Loosen the custard from the soufflé dish with a knife. Invert the dish over an individual serving plate and shake the custard out. Spoon 1 teaspoon (5 ml) of the maple syrup over the top, garnish with a sprig of fresh rosemary on the side and . . . voilà! You can serve Crème Caramel at room temperature or cold.

Helpful Hints and Observations

VANILLA POD VS. VANILLA ESSENCE. Clearly the economic answer to vanilla flavor is to buy a good vanilla essence (extract) from natural sources. There is a wonderful alternative that you may want to try for very special occasions: a whole vanilla pod! A good-quality pod is flexible (not dried out) and has a warm, obvious aroma. In this recipe, you soak it in the milk and simmer it with the rosemary and orange zest. It is then extracted and split open lengthwise to scrape out the fine seeds and pulp, all of which provide an incredible depth of flavor.

About the Ingredients

VANILLA EXTRACT. True vanilla extract, which is sometimes referred to as vanilla essence, must say that it is "pure" on the label. The synthetic product must say "artificial," but it could be in small print —let the buyer beware. Another important point: not all pure extracts are the same. Usually the higher the price, the higher the quality of beans used to make it, resulting in a better finished product.

ROSEMARY. The Latin name for rosemary is *rosmarinus,* "dew of the sea," a beautiful and fitting name for this silvery green native to the Mediterranean coastline. Rosemary is a hardy perennial in temperate climates, and I grow some on my patio, bringing it indoors during the colder winter months. Try growing it yourself and experience a hint of the sunny Mediterranean in your kitchen! Otherwise, look for fresh rosemary in the produce section of your supermarket.

SUMMER PUDDING

*I*t's a summer rite of passage in Britain—When the berries are ready, the summer puddings begin. Huge bowls full of mixed berries and sliced bread are set firm with gelatin or in pectin and served in glistening wedges amid clouds of whipped cream. With this Minimax version, I hope you'll start a tradition for your family, too. I've removed the bread and added rhubarb for the same soft texture and used our Papufa Yogurt Cream as the topping. I also used frozen berries so one can make it year-round.

Nutritional Profile

PER SERVING	CLASSIC	MINIMAX
Calories	717	160
Fat (gm)	17	1
Saturated fat (gm)	10	0
Calories from fat	21%	4%
Cholesterol (mg)	56	1
Sodium (mg)	253	32
Fiber (gm)	10	7

■ *Classic Compared: Summer Pudding*

Time Estimate: Hands on, 70 minutes; unsupervised, 8 hours

Cost Estimate: Low

Serves 16
INGREDIENTS

5 stalks rhubarb, cut diagonally into 2-inch (5-cm) pieces

4 cups water (944 ml)

1 cup sugar (236 ml)

3 cups frozen strawberries (708 ml)

3 envelopes of unflavored gelatin, dissolved in ½ cup of warm water (118 ml)

3 cups frozen raspberries (708 gm)

3 cups frozen blueberries (708 gm)

3 cups frozen blackberries (708 gm)

6 envelopes of unflavored gelatin, dissolved in ½ cup of warm water (118 ml)

PAPUFA YOGURT CREAM:

9 tablespoons nonfat instant dried milk (135 ml)

½ cup ice water (118 ml)

¼ teaspoon vanilla (1.25 ml)

3 tablespoons superfine sugar (45 ml)

1 teaspoon safflower oil (5 ml) (optional, but use it if you miss the fatty mouthfeel of whipped cream)

1 cup strained yogurt (236 ml) (see page 85)

NOW COOK

■ In a large Dutch oven, place the rhubarb, the water, ¾ cup (177 ml) of the sugar and the strawberries, bring to a boil, cover and boil vigorously for 10 minutes. Strain, separating the rhubarb and strawberries from their juice, and reserve both.

■ In a 12-inch (30-cm) bowl, place the rhubarb and strawberries and stir in the 3 envelopes of dissolved gelatin—it will be really thick. Set aside.

■ Mix the remaining berries into the rhubarb and strawberries.

■ Place a 9-inch bowl (23-cm) on top of the rhubarb-strawberries mixture, center and submerge until the tops of the two bowls are even —one inside the other. Pour 1 cup of cold water (236 ml) and 1 tray of ice cubes into the inner bowl. Place in the refrigerator for 2 to 3 hours or until completely set.

■ Spoon the ice water out of the inner bowl and pour in 1 cup of hot water (236 ml). Twist the inner bowl slightly to loosen and very gently release it from the suction of the gelatin in the outer bowl.

■ In a large bowl, put 2¾ cups (649 ml) each of the raspberries, blueberries and blackberries. Add 3 cups of the reserved rhubarb-strawberry juice, the remaining sugar and the 6 envelopes of dissolved gelatin and stir well.

■ Now pour the warm berry gelatin into the crater left behind by the small inner bowl. Return pudding to the refrigerator to set overnight.

■ For the Papufa Yogurt Cream: In a large bowl, beat the milk and water at high speed for 6 minutes until light and frothy. Add the vanilla, sugar and oil and beat at low speed until stiff and glossy. Gently stir in strained yogurt until there are no lumps. Refrigerate until ready to use.

■ To Serve: Cut the Summer Pudding into wedges and serve with a dollop of the Papufa Yogurt Cream.

Helpful Hints and Observations

GELATIN. It's a good idea when using plain gelatin granules, to soak them first in a small amount of cold water before adding the warmed liquid. I always soften gelatin in this way, and then by using a clear glass measuring cup and stirring in the warm liquid with a metal spoon, I can check a spoonful to see that not a single gelatin fleck remains.

About the Ingredients

RHUBARB. See page 221.

BERRIES. See page 221.

SORBETS

I cannot even begin to understand why restaurants fail to offer genuine low-fat, low-calorie desserts on their menus. For instance, why not offer sorbets? Both of these examples make a wonderful end to any meal. So drop off this recipe at your favorite eatery and, who knows?

If you have some really fine glasses, especially some of the old green-stemmed "hock" glasses, the berry sorbet looks great garnished with a fresh mint leaf. The tropical sorbet speaks for itself. You could carve it at the table for an extra flourish.

Nutritional Profiles

PER SERVING	CLASSIC	MINIMAX STRAWBERRY	MINIMAX BANANA/ PINEAPPLE
Calories	349	98	120
Fat (gm)	24	1	1
Saturated fat (gm)	15	0	0
Calories from fat	61%	6%	5%
Cholesterol (mg)	88	1	1
Sodium (mg)	108	49	33
Fiber (gm)	0	4	2

■ *Classic Compared: Ice Cream*

Time Estimate: Hands on, 40 minutes; unsupervised, 60 minutes

Cost Estimate: Medium

Banana/Pineapple Tropical Sorbet

Serves 6

INGREDIENTS

1 pineapple
2 cups chopped bananas (472 ml)
3 tablespoons sugar (45 ml)
1 cup plain nonfat yogurt (236 ml)
1 tablespoon honey (15 ml) (fireweed is preferable)

FIRST PREPARE

■ Because this sorbet is frozen in the pineapple shell, you must cut out the flesh according to the following special method. First, slice off the top, just at the point where the edges begin to straighten. Now stand the pineapple up on its bottom end. Insert a long, thin-bladed knife into the exposed flesh, next to the pineapple's tough outer skin. Push the knife in the entire length of the pineapple, stopping just above the bottom—careful, you don't want to penetrate *through* the bottom. Cut in a circle around the edge just inside the skin. You've now created a long cylinder of pineapple flesh that's connected to the shell only at the bottom.

To separate the bottom of this fruit cylinder, insert the knife into the side of the pineapple, about 1 inch (2.5 cm) from the bottom. Without enlarging the hole that is the knife's entry point into the pineapple, fan the blade back and forth, cutting through the inside fruit cylinder in a large V. Repeat this procedure on the opposite side. Now the long, central pineapple cylinder is free.

Invert the pineapple over a bowl to catch the juice. Plunge a fork into the pineapple cylinder's exposed top end and (with firm determination) pull it out into the bowl.

Now you must remove the pineapple's tough central core. To do this, put the cylinder on a cutting board, reserving the juice in the bowl. Slice the cylinder into quarters lengthwise. You can see the tough core as a thin, lighter colored section running the length of each wedge. Just slice this off and discard. Remove any "eyes." Roughly chop the remaining pineapple flesh and put it in the bowl with the reserved juice.

And don't worry: the rest of the recipe is considerably easier!

NOW COOK

■ In a blender or food processor, puree the pineapple, pineapple juice and bananas, gradually adding the sugar, yogurt and honey.

■ Transfer the fruit mixture to an ice cream maker and process according to the manufacturer's directions.

■ Scoop the sorbet into the hollowed-out pineapple shell, cover with plastic wrap and put in the freezer for at least 1 hour.

■ To Serve: Just before serving, remove the pineapple from the freezer. Slice it from top to bottom, into 6 even wedges. Put one on each plate and celebrate a taste of the tropics.

About the Ingredients

PINEAPPLES. Most of the world's supply of this popular fruit comes from Hawaii, where they have been cultivating pineapples since the late 1800s. Choose fruit that feels "heavy." To ensure juiciness, the skin should have an orange tint, which tells you that the pineapple was ripened on the plant.

Peppered Strawberries with Mint Sorbet

Serves 4
INGREDIENTS

4 cups fresh strawberries (944 ml), tops trimmed

3 tablespoons sugar (45 ml)

1 cup plain nonfat yogurt (236 ml)

1 tablespoon honey (15 ml) (fireweed is preferable)

1 tablespoon fresh chopped mint leaves (15 ml)

¼ teaspoon freshly ground black peppercorns
(1.25 ml)

GARNISH:

4 fresh sprigs of mint

4 to 8 fresh strawberries (optional)

NOW COOK

■ Puree the berries in a blender or food processor, gradually adding the sugar, yogurt, honey, chopped mint and pepper.

■ Scoop the mixture into an ice cream maker and process according to the manufacturer's directions.

■ Transfer the sorbet to a bowl with a tight-fitting lid and put in the freezer for at least 1 hour.

■ To Serve: An ice cream scoop will help serve the sorbet in glistening globes. Garnish with fresh mint and perhaps a whole strawberry or two.

Index

Let's Stay In Touch!

u.s. mail

Dear Reader,

Now that you've had a chance to explore my new Minimax way of cooking, I'm hoping you'll want to join me in learning more about this exciting and healthy way of making food both delicious and good for you.

I believe we've only scratched the surface and there is so much new work to be done which can always be more fun (and rewarding) if I can count on the encouragement and personal input of people like YOU.

I need your feedback, ideas, suggestions and comments. Give me your "springboard" recipes. Tell me how you'd change mine ... what works for you. Start by filling out the "Stay in Touch" coupon below. In return I'll send you — every few months — a free copy of my news-you-can-use catalog. It's got lots of minimum risk maximum flavor ideas, recipes, new products — lots of good stuff!

I look forward to hearing from you!

Yours aromatically,

Graham Kerr

P.S. I also promise to keep you posted on future TV shows, too. There are lots of plans in the works and you can be among the first to know.

Detach and mail to: Graham Kerr, P.O. Box 9700, Seattle, WA 98109

- -

™ Graham KERR

"I want to stay in touch!"

YES! I want to stay in touch and discover more new ideas about the Graham Kerr Minimax Foodstyle. *Thankyou!*

Please check: ☐ Under 40
☐ 40-59
☐ Over 60

My Name _____

Address _____

City _____ State/Zip _____

Phone Number (Optional): (___) _____
Area Code

MAIL TO: GRAHAM KERR, P.O. BOX 9700, SEATTLE, WA 98109